Erased

Erased

THE UNTOLD STORY OF THE PANAMA CANAL

Marixa Lasso

Harvard University Press

CAMBRIDGE, MASSACHUSETTS

LONDON, ENGLAND

2019

First printing

Library of Congress Cataloging-in-Publication Data

Names: Lasso, Marixa, author.
Title: Erased : the untold story of the Panama Canal / Marixa Lasso.
Description: Cambridge, Massachusetts : Harvard University Press, 2019. |
Includes bibliographical references and index.
Identifiers: LCCN 2018030885 | ISBN 9780674984448 (alk. paper)
Subjects: LCSH: Panama Canal (Panama)—History. | Cities and Towns—
Panama—Canal Zone—History. | Canal Zone. | Land Use—Panama—
Panama Canal—Planning.
Classification: LCC F1569.C2 L27 2019 | DDC 972.87/5—dc23
LC record available at https://lccn.loc.gov/2018030885

Contents

Erased

Introduction

The Panama Canal Zone

My earliest memories of the Zone are as a child looking out the window of my father's car. It was the 1970s, and the Zone—a ten-mile strip of land, five miles on either side of the canal—belonged to the United States, which had acquired it through the Hay-Bunau-Varilla Treaty of 1903. The treaty gave the United States the right to build and control the canal and to rule over the Zone as if it were a sovereign. Running down the middle of the Republic of Panama, the Zone bordered Panama City and divided the country in two, making it impossible to travel to Panama's western countryside without crossing through it. My family had to drive through the Zone every time we left Panama City to spend a Sunday at the beach or a week in the small town where my grandmother grew up. I remember looking forward to the moment when we crossed its border. For a child like me, the Zone was exotic. Inside the Zone the highway passed through jungle instead of the arid cattle ranches that bordered other stretches of Panama's Pan-American Highway. From the car I looked with fascination at the big oropendola nests hanging from the trees. In the Zone of my childhood, the jungle served as background to military bases and a few suburban-style American towns. There was something magical about the contrast between the jungle and the towns with their impeccable lawns, swimming pools, and air-conditioned houses.

I remember how as a child living in Panama I saw the Zone as a place of desire and denial. Its many swimming pools, tennis courts, movie theaters, and restaurants were closed to Panamanians, unless invited by a Zone resident. In all of Panama only beaches in the Zone had iron mesh fences, in order to protect swimmers from sharks. Being invited to its parks, swimming pools, and beaches was considered a privilege. At the same time, the chain-link fences with "Do Not Trespass" signs and checkpoints at the gates of the twelve military bases were a constant reminder of the Zone's many restrictions. I remember being told that throwing a candy wrapper on a sidewalk in the Zone would bring punishment. But what I most vividly remember is the luxuriant green of the Zone's tropical jungle.

Little could I have imagined that there was nothing virgin about the jungle landscape typical of the Zone, that it was a twentieth-century creation that had erased 400 years of local urban and agricultural history. By the 1970s, most Panamanians had forgotten that in 1912 the Zone was one of the most densely populated areas of Panama, that it was filled with towns that were smaller versions of Panama City and Colón, and that these towns included tenements, saloons, and public markets. It seemed like the Zone and its jungle had always been there. President William Howard Taft's 1912 executive order to depopulate the Zone had become a vague memory, its details forgotten. Yet the depopulation of the Zone was one of the most traumatic events in early twentieth-century Panama, perhaps even more traumatic than its secession from Colombia in 1903. It was an enormous transformation of the landscape that was as impressive as the construction of the canal.

Between 1913 and 1916, the Panamanian towns of the Zone were dismantled one by one; approximately 40,000 people were expelled from what until then had been one of the country's most important regions (see Map I.1). To put this figure in context, according to the 1912 Canal Zone census the Zone had a population of 62,810, while the population of Panama City was 24,159 in 1896 and 66,851 in 1920.[1] For comparison, in 1911, 63,364 people lived in Chiriquí, Panama's most populous province, while in Coclé, an average-sized province, there were 35,011 people. Panama's population in 1911 was 427,176, and people living in the Zone represented roughly 14 percent of that total.[2]

Contrary to what is commonly believed, the depopulation of the Zone was not due to the technical requirements of canal construction. While Lake Gatún, at the time the world's largest artificial lake, partly flooded some towns like Gorgona, other towns, like Emperador and Chagres, never flooded.[3] Moreover, town dwellers who were relocated because of canal construction could have stayed within the Zone's limits. Indeed, that is what happened initially. When the Panamanian river town of Gatún was relocated in 1908 to create space for the Gatún locks, its inhabitants were not expelled from the Zone but instead relocated nearby. They would not be expelled until 1915, one year after the canal's inauguration. The story of the depopulation of the Zone is the history of political—rather than technical—decisions. And the decisions that led to this enormous transformation happened slowly and were not predictable. During most of the canal's construction, US officials did not try to dismantle Panamanian towns but instead sought to regulate, civilize, and tax them.

To understand the depopulation of the Zone, it is important to remember the symbolic importance of the Panama Canal at the turn of the twentieth century, as well as US ideas about Latin America, particularly tropical Latin America. The United States that began the

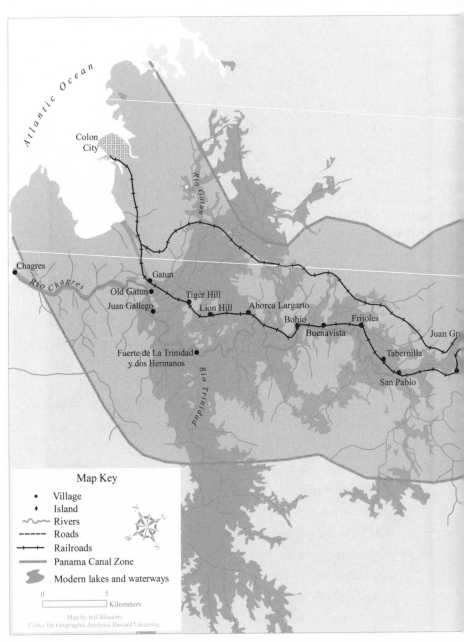

MAP I.I The historic towns of the Panama Canal Zone
Credit: Jeff Blossom, Center for Geographic Analysis, Harvard University.

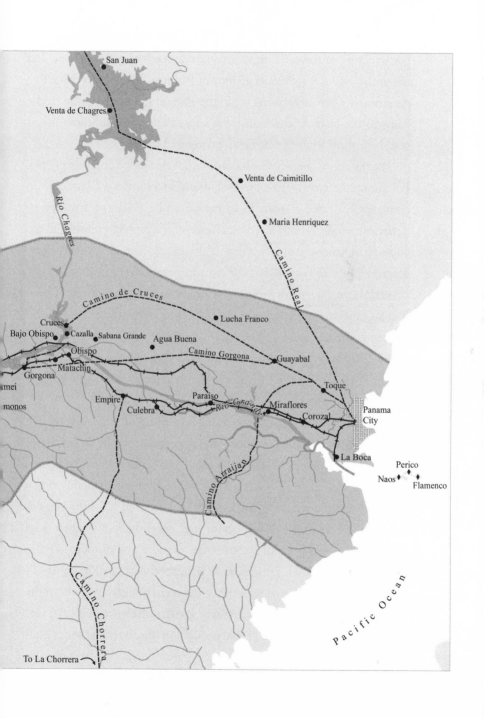

San Juan

Venta de Chagres

Rio Chagres

Venta de Caimitillo

Maria Henriquez

Camino de Cruces

Lucha Franco

Camino Real

Cruces
Bajo Obispo • Cazalla Sabana Grande   Agua Buena
Obispo   Camino Gorgona   Guayabal
mei   Gorgona   Matachin
monos   Toque
              Empire   Paraiso   Rio Grande
                   Culebra   Miraflores
                                         Corozal   Panama
                                                          City
                                               La Boca
                                                         Perico
Camino Atraijan   Naos ◆   ◆
                                                         Flamenco

Pacific Ocean

Camino Chorrera

To La Chorrera

construction of the canal in 1904 was an ascendant global power, and the entire world watched its actions in Panama, for good reason. The Americans were attempting what the French had failed to do in the Zone in the 1880s. If successful, the United States would show that it could triumph where a European power had failed.

The Panama Canal symbolized different things for different people. For some, the canal—like the 1893 World's Columbian Exposition in Chicago—became a space to showcase and glorify the triumph of American modernity.[4] The colossal scale of the project symbolized the triumph of American engineering.[5] The successful eradication of yellow fever in Panama symbolized the triumph of modern medicine in the United States. For many Progressive Era reformers, the Panama Canal was an experiment that would test the ability of the state to intervene for the common good and to succeed where private enterprise had failed. Progressives—and their opponents—visited the canal to publicize or criticize how the US government was handling the project and treating its workers.[6]

For Latin Americans, the canal was important for other reasons. In their eyes, Panama was a symbol of the disrespect that the United States had for their republics. To build the canal, the United States had helped Panama gain independence from Colombia, thereby dismembering a sister republic to secure a canal treaty that secured US interests. For all of these reasons the canal became highly symbolic. Even before its completion it was a popular tourist destination, and numerous pamphlets, books, and news stories were published about it. The construction of the Panama Canal was one of the most popular subjects in the early twentieth-century United States.[7] Picture after picture showcased for Americans the technology that brought to life one of the seven marvels of the modern world, with its gigantic locks, enormous dam, modern steam cranes, and the world's largest artificial lake.

In this context, what happened in the towns of the Zone had enormous significance. Some canal officials believed that if the canal was an example of US technological might, then the transformation of Panamanian towns in the Zone into perfect modern municipalities would be an example of US political and sanitary prowess. Theodore P. Shonts, the second chairman of the Isthmian Canal Commission (ICC), believed that the United States could create "a modern state in a ten by fifty mile stretch of tropical wilderness, scourged by deadly fevers and pestilence, and practically uninhabitable by natives of other climes."[8]

Despite the stated aims of the United States to bring modernity to the wilderness, the opposite happened. The American occupation and eventual depopulation of Zone towns eliminated the nineteenth-century political and economic modernity of the isthmus's corridor.[9] When canal construction started in 1904, the Zone was nothing like the imagined "jungle" of nineteenth-century travel books, which portrayed naïve "natives" easily surprised by the wonders of Western civilization and technology. Global trade and global labor had been at the center of Panama's economy since the sixteenth century. Spanish ships and galleons brought European merchandise and Andean silver to its ports, and African slaves transported them across the isthmus. In the 1850s, American capital and West Indian and Chinese labor built the first transcontinental railroad in the Americas, and Panama's ports were serviced by steamships, railroad, and telegraph lines—the latest in nineteenth-century transport technology. And although the French failed to build a canal in the 1880s, their presence enhanced the cosmopolitan character of Panama's towns and brought greater access to modern technology. By 1904 the population of the isthmian route was composed of the descendants of the various waves of peoples who had worked in Panama's transport economy since the sixteenth century.

Far from being disconnected from the latest political developments of the nineteenth century, the Panamanian towns of the Zone had played a role in one of the first global experiments in constitutional representative politics. As citizens of the Republic of Colombia since 1821, Panamanians had participated in republican electoral politics when most of the world was still ruled by monarchies. Panamanian citizens had also enjoyed legal equality, regardless of their color. Indeed, nineteenth-century travelers often commented on—and lamented—the region's "black republicanism." In short, when the United States began canal construction in 1904, the area around the canal was densely populated, immersed in republican politics, and deeply marked by railroad tracks, railroad towns, river towns, agricultural plots, and French canal machinery.

The story of the lost towns of the Panama Canal is the history of a forgotten and failed experiment to create perfect towns and municipalities in the middle of the "Central American Jungle." The United States would show the world that it had conquered the most "difficult" of natures: tropical nature. This conquistador would not bring Christianity but instead health, paving, and sewage treatment. Its glory would be represented not with cathedrals but with clean sidewalks and running water. Yet governing and housing a population of 60,000 people of multiple nationalities and multiple political allegiances, while maintaining order and keeping labor costs down, was not a simple task.[10] It was further complicated by the assumption that new housing conditions would represent the triumph of American Progressive ideals against slums and tenements, and showcase an ideal vision of urban modernity, one where every worker had access to a clean house, a public school, paved streets and sidewalks, and a park.[11] Slowly the idea that "native" towns did not belong in the Canal Zone began to circulate among Zone authorities.

This is not a history of American technological triumph but rather one of doubt and failure that ended with the depopulation of the Zone. It resulted from the complex question of how to organize the native towns and people in the Zone. Would Americans govern and "civilize" native towns, or would they dismantle them and send their inhabitants to the cities of Panama and Colón? The answer was not immediate; it was the product of careful debates among American officials in the Zone. Thus, this history is also the story of a failed experiment in exporting Progressive Era policies to the tropics. Its failure cannot be explained by any personal failing of the protagonists, but instead should be understood as a project doomed from the start by its racial ideology and the contradictions inherent in attempting to bring progress and development to others.[12] Although Zone towns would eventually boast clean sidewalks and running water, these urban improvements neither happened on the scale American officials had originally imagined nor benefited all the inhabitants of the Zone. The pristine urban landscape of manicured lawns and impeccable houses that would eventually be associated with the Zone became a reality only after the 1913–1916 depopulation of the Zone and the elimination of private businesses, houses, and farms had turned it into a sparsely populated area without politics or private property.

To understand the history of this experiment, it is important to return to the first years of canal construction and retrace the steps that led to the decision to depopulate. Only in this way can we recreate the history of these towns, recover their lost landscapes, and question the inevitability of their depopulation. In his classic *Path between the Seas*, David McCullough portrays the initial years of canal construction as ones of chaos and inefficiency; that would change when George W. Goethals became the chairman of the ICC in 1907 and reorganized the Zone government and canal construction in a way that led to the successful completion of the canal.[13] Most canal stories have followed McCullough's narrative and given little attention to the first three years of construction. Yet these years are crucial for understanding the transition of Zone towns from Panama's jurisdiction to that of the United States. Although much has been written about the transfer of the Canal Zone back to Panama, next to nothing has been written about the Zone's complex processes of transition from Panamanian authorities to American authorities. This moment of transition was important for the future of the Zone, because during the initial years of US control there were important debates between Panamanians and Americans over the future of the Panamanian towns in the Zone. Initially, both Panamanians and Americans imagined a very different Zone, one that would remain fully populated and retain its previous Panamanian municipalities and mayors, along with its private businesses and private houses.

The 1912 depopulation order eliminated a rich political and urban history from the Zone's landscape. When Panamanian towns disappeared so too did their municipal traditions, their republican electoral politics, and their nineteenth-century histories of global commerce. What had been a complex space subjected to the vagaries of nineteenth-century political, economic, and technological changes became a simple space in which progress focused only on engineering and sanitation. In this process, US policy and rhetoric recharacterized both Panamanian—mostly black—citizens into "natives" and the Zone's intricate commercial landscape into a wilderness in need of intervention. The fact that canal officials portrayed and imagined the Zone as a tropical wilderness and its inhabitants as "natives" made it politically and ideologically easier for the Zone to be depopulated once its Panamanian municipalities had been transformed into "native towns," its citizens into "natives," and its landscape into the jungle. If it appeared

INTRODUCTION

that the canal had been built in a jungle, then no previous urban land-scape had been erased. There was nothing to miss or remember.[14]

Contemporary ideas about the tropics and tropical peoples influenced how US officials made decisions about Panama. US officers often differed with each other about the appropriate course of action to be taken in Panama. This book pays attention to their disagreements. Not every US officer was in favor of depopulating the Zone. As we will see, one of the most famous and powerful officers, Colonel William Gorgas, was against depopulation. His story shows that depopulation was neither inevitable nor the only option for governing the Zone. In spite of their differences, however, US officers shared a particular view of the United States as a harbinger of progress and of Panama as a backward tropical place. This overarching ideology shaped their actions and ultimately affected the lives of the Zone's inhabitants. Without it, the depopulation of the Zone would not have been possible. While this ideology didn't cause the depopulation of the Zone, it certainly made it possible.

From Tropical to Underdeveloped: Forgetting Spanish America's Nineteenth-Century Modernity

What happened in the small and highly symbolic space of the Zone is illustrative of a larger transformation that affected Spanish America as a region. For most of the nineteenth century, Spanish America had been at the vanguard of political modernity as one of the few regions in the world where republicanism was the dominant form of government.[15] In the words of a Mexican orator in 1868, "The Eagles of American democracy, crossing the Atlantic, will import into the Old World the modern doctrines of political association, thereby emancipating those peoples."[16] For this Mexican, democracy was something that Mexicans, and other Americans, exported to Europe, not the other way around. Yet, by the early twentieth century, the notion that Spanish America could have played a role in the creation of modern republican and democratic politics was fast disappearing from local political discourse.[17] One century later, in 2008, it was possible for a historian of Latin America to state confidently that "the new republican constitutions of América seemed a bit like exotic plants on Colombian or Chilean soil—remote indeed from the historical experience of the people."[18] The pioneering role of Spanish America in the history of republicanism had been forgotten and erased from "the historical experience" of the people of Spanish America. It had become commonplace for scholars and observers to portray Latin America as a region that was always behind, trying to catch up with European and US political modernity. To adapt a formulation of Meltem Ahiska, Spanish America was now "always already late . . . to the destination of history."[19]

We still need to understand how a region that became the workshop of democracy was transformed into a region that merely copied the political innovations of other peoples. Historians of Latin America have only begun to ask this question.[20] We don't yet have a clear picture of how this transformation happened. Nevertheless, what is clear is that the idea of Latin America as a region of elite imitators and traditional peasants is a caricature that obscures the region's complex history. We need, instead, to understand how we learned to think of regions like Panama as backward and traditional places. Even more, we need to become aware of the long-term consequences of this ideological transformation.

The historical erasure of Latin American modernity was part of a larger cultural transformation that positioned different world regions in very different relations to historical time, nature, and technology. A crucial aspect of this change was the conversion of entire regions of the world into tropical regions in the eighteenth and nineteenth centuries.[21] Places as far away from each other as India and Latin America, which had very different histories, languages, and cultures, became part of one geographical area—the tropics. This was a crucial change because for the people of the nineteenth century, the tropics were more than an area between the tropics of Cancer and Capricorn with particular types of animals and plants. The tropics were everything that Europe and the United States were not. If the latter were regions of progress of technological innovation, of civilization, the tropics were not. Nineteenth-century travelers popularized images of the tropics that depicted them as savage places, the antithesis to civilized modernity. Their descriptions of tropical regions emphasized their luxuriant vegetation and wild animals. These descriptions made people into part of the landscape. They were primitive; they were "natives" who shared in the wilderness of their jungle surroundings. They did not alter or "civilize" their landscape; that was left to European and American colonizers.[22] Travelers' descriptions of Latin America ridiculed any aspects of Latin American modernity. They taught their readers to laugh at the contrast between modern technology and jungle landscapes and "natives" and at the oddity of modern technology in the tropics. Political modernity in the tropics was also ridiculed. Non-white republican politicians were often mocked as imitators who performed ill-fitting roles. The mocking of republican institutions in tropical spaces culminated with the coining of the term "banana republic" in O. Henry's novel *Cabbages and Kings;* this was a powerful and enduring term that, more than any other, has influenced how we continue to view tropical republics.[23]

The idea that modernity did not belong in the tropics had enormous implications for the understanding of technology and historical time in the tropics. By the end of the nineteenth century, railroads, steam power, and steamships were common in many parts of the tropics, often arriving at the same time, or not much later than, they did in Europe and the United States. As in other parts of the world, the arrival of these technologies to Panama and Latin America profoundly shaped people's lives. However, when modern technology arrived in the tropics, it was not associated with the landscape it altered, the peoples whose lives it changed, or the people who worked with it. It was only linked to the investors who had imported it. Even if located in the tropics, these technologies did not belong there. Tropical peoples and landscapes remained frozen in a natural, "primitive," "native" time.[24] By their mere location in the tropics they were incapable of being modern.

For example, the harsh conditions that characterized the lives of workers in both Manchester's textile mills and on Central American banana plantations were the product of industrialization. Both endured the new working rhythms of mass production and both suffered the effects of new technology—in Britain textile machines and in Central America dangerous agricultural chemicals. Yet only the Manchester workers were considered modern protagonists of a new industrial era. If located in the tropics, the victims of industrial modernity are somehow unable to be modern.[25] This is why, even today, some Europeans and Americans are surprised to find highways and skyscrapers in the capitals of the underdeveloped world.

At the same time that travelers and novelists were popularizing an image of the tropics as the antithesis of civilization, historians were developing a new idea of history that would also contribute to the erasure of Spanish-American contributions to nineteenth-century politics. This new concept was Western Civilization. It is no accident that the building of the Panama Canal coincided with the consolidation of this concept. During the same years that workers were busy digging the Panama Canal, historians in the United States and Europe were busy creating a new cultural concept, the West, and writing and teaching its history. Although the idea of Western Civilization is based on the notion that the origins of the West can be traced back to the times of ancient Greece, it is important to remember that this was a new idea that was popularized and developed by historians of the early twentieth century like Oswald Spengler and Arnold Toynbee. But what was the West and who belonged in Western Civilization? Not Europe, as neither Spain nor Eastern Europe was included. Not the Americas, as the United States was the only part of the Americas that was incorporated. The West was composed of the political and economic powers of the time—the United States and Western Europe—and Western Civilization was the culmination of a forward movement in human progress that began with the agricultural developments of the ancient Near East, moved west, and continued its development with subsequent contributions from classical Greece, Renaissance Italy, and Enlightenment France. In this version of history, the torch of humanity's genius was passed from one place to the other and now rested in the hands of the West. Other cultures might have contributed to humanity's early progress, but now they were only the passive recipients of Western progress. England and the United States, not contemporary Greece, were the rightful heirs to the genius of Pericles or Aristotle. According to one academic account of the development of Western Civilization published in 1907, "Modern Civilization is the result of the appropriation by Teutonic peoples . . . of the outcomes of the Israelitish, the Greek and Roman social life."[26] In this and other historical accounts of the period, action and forward movement during the modern era resided solely in the West. And it was now in the hands of the West to further humanity's progress.[27]

Just as the tropics were everything that Europe was not, the West was everything that the tropics were not. If the West was action, the tropics were indolence. If the West was civilization and progress, the tropics were backwardness and savagery. If the West represented the future of humanity, the tropics represented the origins of humanity. The history of Western Civilization worked hand in hand with the scientific racism of the early twentieth century. While scientific racism promoted the biological superiority of the white race, helping to justify its control over other peoples, Western Civilization claimed the cultural superiority of the United States and Western Europe, helping to justify their power over other regions. And just as scientific racism was not science, Western Civilization was not history. The first relied on faulty cranial measurements to claim that the brains of Caucasians were larger than and superior to the brains of people from other races; the second relied on faulty history to claim its superiority. The trick of Western Civilization was to erase humanity's common heritage and common contribution to historical change. For example, the fact that the Muslim Mediterranean world was as much an heir to classical Greece as Western Europe and the United States was not part of the history of Western Civilization. Nor were the contributions of free and enslaved black Haitians to our ideas of freedom and equality, or the contributions of Spanish-American lawyers to constitutional history or to the modern concept of international law.[28] Contemporary action and innovation rested solely in the West.

Early histories of the Panama Canal reflected and confirmed the Western Civilization saga. The construction of the canal was a clear example of Western Civilization's progress, innovation, and action. Just as the West was the rightful heir to the genius of classical Greece and Renaissance Italy, US engineers were the rightful heirs of the Spaniards who first conceived the idea of a canal across the Panamanian isthmus. What the genius of the conquistadors had dreamed, the genius of US doctors and engineers had accomplished![29] Yet early histories of the Panama Canal also featured the silences of histories of Western Civilization. Absent from these canal histories was Panama's management of the isthmian route from the sixteenth century to the early twentieth century. They ignored the Panamanian muleteers, boatmen, lawyers, engineers, and peasants who had lived and worked on the isthmian route for 400 years as equal partners of, or predecessors to, US canal construction.

This book is about these lost histories and the processes through which they were ignored. Each one of the initial chapters tells the story of one aspect of Panama's nineteenth-century modernity that was silenced. They also tell the story of the many Panamanians who sought to challenge these silences. The last chapters tell the story of the very real consequences that the silencing of their history had on the inhabitants of the Zone, how it affected their lives, and how, ultimately, it contributed to the depopulation of the Zone.

The history of the depopulation of the Panama Canal Zone speaks to the question of the long-term consequences of the silencing of Spanish-American nineteenth-century modernity. It suggests that the silencing of Spanish-American nineteenth-century modernity opened the possibility of imagining the region as a backward space in need of foreign aid and intervention. That is, it established the foundation for thinking of the region as underdeveloped. How does a region become underdeveloped? We have learned to think of underdeveloped regions as places where things like poverty, inferior health care, imperfect democracy, or low or inadequate technology are common. Yet as historians of the concept of development have shown, the notion of a world divided into developed and underdeveloped regions was the result of powerful cultural and political constructs. The concepts of development and underdevelopment emerged after World War II when Europe had to restructure its relationship with its colonies in Africa and Asia, which were in the process of gaining independence. The ideas of development and underdevelopment helped maintain hierarchical relationships between ex-colonies and ex-colonial powers, which were now framed as mutually beneficial relationships. Ex-colonies became the recipients of European and American technological aid to improve their standards of living.[30]

Although we have learned much about the history of the idea of development, we still need to examine in greater depth how we came to think of regions of the world with very different histories, cultures, languages, and societies as sharing one characteristic: underdevelopment. This transformation required the identification of regions based exclusively on certain health and economic indicators, which allowed them to be characterized as deficient and in need of help and intervention. Most important, and unacknowledged by the scholarship on the subject, for a region to become underdeveloped, it had to forget its nineteenth-century modernity and its participation in the creation of the modern world. Underdeveloped regions, by definition, never were—or are never—truly modern. Modernity is always presented as an aspiration, not as a reality. Even if the meaning of modernity is constantly redefined, underdeveloped nations are always conceived as not quite having it.

To be seen as underdeveloped, a region first had to be conceived of as traditional. This transformation happened in Spanish America before World War II and before the crisis of European empires in Africa and Asia. In Spanish America, countries that had been modern according to the political and technological standards of the nineteenth century became "traditional." It was also in Spanish America that one of the characteristics of the language of underdevelopment first took hold—the characterization of the relations between developed and underdeveloped nations as relations of nominal equality between independent nations with equal status under international law. This restructuring of international power relations happened in the early twentieth century in tropical republics like Panama. Unlike the relationship between Europe and its colonies in Asia and Africa of this period, the relationship between the United States and Panama was that of sister republics governed according to the same rules of international law.[31] Because of its importance as a place of US intervention at the turn of the twentieth century, Panama is crucial for understanding the transition between the nineteenth-century languages of tropicalization and the languages of underdevelopment that flourished after World War II. Panama's place at the forefront of nineteenth-century political and technological innovations makes it an ideal case for understanding how a country at the center of technological and political changes was transformed into a backward tropical space.

Of course, this is not to argue that the ideas that shaped the relationship between the United Sates and Panama in the early twentieth century were identical to future ideas about development and underdevelopment. I am only arguing that some of the roots that led to this particular way of understanding and dividing the world existed in the early twentieth century.[32]

As historians have long known, our version of history shapes how we view ourselves and how we see and treat others.[33] It also shapes the type of space in which we live, as every worldview produces a particular type of urban geography.[34] The transformation of the Panama Canal Zone during the first two decades of the twentieth century is a dramatic example of a particular historical period during which the United States looked at the world in terms of tropicality,

Western Civilization, and Progressive Era ideas of social improvement. The legacies of this way of looking at the world are still with us today. This book is about these legacies. The history of the lost towns of the Panama Canal is a story about the effects of forgetting our common contribution and participation in the construction of the world in which we live. It is a story about how the people of regions known as the third world, the underdeveloped world, or the global south came to live in a political and technological world that is part of their daily lives, but that is constantly thought of as originating somewhere else and belonging to other peoples.

I

The Port and the City

The Port of Panama

THE PORT OF Panama is the oldest Pacific port built by Europeans in the Americas. It has never been quaint or traditional. From the galleon fleets and mule trains of the sixteenth century to the steamships, railroads, and telegraph lines of the nineteenth, the port has always been at the forefront of global transportation technology. Since its beginnings it has been an international port from which important global commodities have departed or arrived. In the sixteenth and seventeenth centuries, it was silver, slaves, and textiles; today, it is oil, cars, and other industrial products.

When canal construction started in 1904, the ports of Panama and Colón already had a very active trade with merchandise arriving from Europe, China, and the United States.[1] The Pacific telegraph line arrived in the Port of Panama and the West Indian line in the Port of Colón, and from both ports telegraph companies transmitted to North and South America and to Europe.[2] The Port of Panama also received small steamers and sailboats that connected the city with Panama's countryside. Continuous international trade, constant contact with foreigners, and the frequent arrival of immigrants had shaped the habits of the people of Panama City. In 1823, the French explorer Gaspard Mollien observed that the people of Panama were very different from the people of the Colombian Andes and more similar to people of other Pacific ports, like Manila and Lima. Like them, they sold everything at very expensive prices; and, like them, they preferred coffee to chocolate. He noted the good organization and abundant supply of Panama City stores, which offered a large variety of items imported from the United States, as well as wines and liquors of all types.[3] In 1904, the Valdés geography—the first of Panama—commented proudly that Panamanians were noted for "their great aptitude to speak foreign languages," and that many spoke "with enough fluency English and French."[4]

Although the shape, location, and relationship of the Port of Panama to its environment changed over time, some things remained constant: its marshes, its global trade, and the islands of Naos, Perico, and Flamenco, which are located 2.5 miles away from the port. From the sixteenth to the late nineteenth century, marshes near the port forced large ships engaged in long-distance trade to anchor in the deep waters off Naos, Perico, and Flamenco. There, passengers and merchandise were transferred to smaller boats that carried them to the city's port during high tide. This method of loading and unloading continued even after the arrival of steamboats and the inauguration of the Panama Railroad in 1855. Like their wind-powered predecessors, steamboats continued to anchor near Naos and Perico. Tenders belonging to the Panama Railroad and the Pacific Steam Navigation Company carried passengers and cargo to their wharves in Panama City.[5]

Each subsequent incarnation of the port—the colonial Spanish, the nineteenth-century republican, and the American—reflected a different urban understanding of the relationship between port, city, and power. Of particular relevance are the changes that took place during the construction of the Panama Canal. During this period the relationship between Panama City and its port underwent a dramatic transformation when for the first time the city was separated from its international port.

Until the end of the nineteenth century, the relationship between the port and the city was intimate. From the walls of the city, onlookers could watch the arrival of ships to Naos and Perico. Government officials, merchants, sailors, and stevedores all lived in the city and walked its streets. The institutions that organized and regulated the port's trade were located in the city, the urban layout of which reflected the close relationship between civic power and trade. During colonial times, the customs house was near the sea door *(puerta de mar)* of the walled city that opened to the port. The city's political and religious center—the cathedral, the main square, and the town council—was located two blocks away. New economic actors continued to follow urban patterns established when the Spanish Empire controlled Panama. The offices of the French canal company and the British telegraph agency were located in Panama City near the municipal building and the governor's house.

In the late nineteenth century, there was still a close spatial connection between local and international trade. The wharves of the Panama Railroad and the Pacific Steam Navigation Company were built farther east, not too far from the old sea door. International and local trade shared the port. Tenders with international passengers and merchandise landed next to local boats trafficking in native products. The four large wharves (the American wharf, the English wharf, the coal wharf, and the market wharf) that connected Panama City to the world were located close to each other and close to Panama City's public market.[6] The spatial use of the port reflected dominant liberal ideologies of free trade. Different companies from different countries mixed together. In the Bay of Panama, small boats like *cayucos* mingled with scows, sloops, and schooners. Carriages and wagons constantly traveled between the center of the city and market and the wharves. A new coaling station was established on Taboga Island nearby, and steamers were also repaired on a sand bank of the same island during low tide.[7] The words *quaint* or *primitive* could hardly have described a city where "the noise caused by the railroad and by the carriages and wagons . . . lend this place the lively aspect and air of greatness peculiar to all busy ports."[8]

The French attempt to construct a canal in the 1880s brought the first disruption to the close spatial connection between Panama City and its port. When the French canal company built a wharf at the town of La Boca at the entrance of the Río Grande, about three miles away, it relocated an important part of international trade from the wharves near the public market in Panama City to the mouth of the Río Grande, which was connected to Panama City by a branch of the railroad. This location would be the one eventually selected for the construction of the American port of Ancón (later named Balboa) when the mouth of the Río Grande became the Pacific terminus of the Panama Canal. Changes in railroad and port technology had allowed the French to overcome the old problem of tidal marshes that rose and fell more than twenty feet. Thanks to continuous dredging, steamers did not have to stop at Naos anymore, and could dock at La Boca regardless of the tide. By the beginning of the twentieth century, vessels docked at a wharf that was "constructed wholly of steel, with a roof and sides of corrugated iron." La Boca harbor had a large pier that "contained facilities for docking three large ships at the same time." It had sixteen steam cranes and four electric cranes on the dock. On the end of the pier there was a "large 20-ton crane."[9] The landscape of large steam cranes that would symbolize American modernity and innovation at the Panama Canal was already in place as a result of the French canal construction.

In spite of these changes, Panama City remained the spatial center of power of the isthmian route. The headquarters of the French canal company were located in the traditional center of political and economic power: the main square of Panama City. Political control of the new Port of La Boca continued to be in the hands of Colombia's government and located in Panama City. La Boca was only a new location within the historic range of the international Port of Panama, which went from Panama City to Naos, Perico, and Flamenco. With the creation of the Republic of Panama and the signing of the Hay-Bunau-Varilla Treaty in 1903, the relationship between the city and the port would change dramatically. This change was not immediate, and during the year after the treaty came into force the port's future became one of the most important subjects of negotiations between the governments of the United States and Panama.

Losing the Port of Panama

The first major controversy between Panama and the United States arose over the question of which country would control the canal's port. In the 1903 treaty, Panama had given in perpetuity to the United States a five-mile zone on either side of the canal, with one exception: "the cities of Panamá and Colón and the ports adjacent to these cities would not be included . . . in this concession." However, not two months had passed since Panama had officially handed the Zone to the US government before great differences over the meaning and definition of "ports adjacent to the city" arose. The United States interpreted that phrase in the narrowest sense. The Port of Panama included the docks next to Panama City and a small part of the Bay of Panama, between Punta de Chiriquí and Punta Paitilla. According to Panama's secretary of foreign relations, Tomás Arias, this interpretation was absurd. Exasperated, he stated that this area "was not properly a port, but barely an inlet."[10] For the government of Panama, "the ports of Panamá and Colón are, because of the characteristics of the land, the very entrances of the Canal."[11]

Arias was only repeating what was common knowledge among his contemporaries. Just a few years earlier, in 1890, a Colombian traveler and politician had written that "the islands of Perico and Flamenco . . . were the city's true port."[12] The Zone's governor, General George W. Davis, had a very different interpretation of the canal treaty. He considered the port at the mouth of the canal to be different from the Port of Panama and gave it a new name: the Port of Ancón. On June 25, 1904, US Secretary of War William Howard Taft ordered the renaming of La Boca as the Port of Ancón, designated it as one of the ports of the Zone, opened it to international commerce, and established a customs house that would charge the same import duties as other US ports.[13] The dispute over the Port of Panama and the diplomatic correspondence between Panama and the United States reveal their contrasting views about Panama's history and identity. Was Panama a modern city that could continue to control its international port as it had done during the past four centuries? Or was it backward, incapable of managing the ports of one of the greatest engineering feats of the twentieth century? In 1904, the answer was not obvious.

To understand Panama's position about the ports we need to appreciate how Panamanians at the turn of the twentieth century viewed themselves and their history and how this view contrasted with US ideas about the tropics and tropical peoples. The legal mind behind Panama's defense of its right to control the canal's ports was the brilliant lawyer and politician Eusebio A. Morales (see Figure 1.1). To

FIGURE 1.1 Eusebio A. Morales
Credit: Photo by Carlos Endara. Courtesy of the Ricardo López Arias / Ana
Sánchez collection.

understand him and other Panamanians of his generation and to appreciate how they saw their nation's place in the world, we need to
understand the years and events that preceded the signing of the 1903
treaty, when Panamanians suddenly found themselves negotiating
alone with one of the most powerful nations on earth.

Morales was born in 1864 in Sincelejo, in what was then the Colombian department of Bolivar, and belonged to a generation of politicians who came of age at a time when Colombia and Panama were part of the same republic. He grew up during a crucial period in Colombian history, when the Liberal Party, his party, had led Colombia to a series of political changes, placing it at the vanguard of global democratic politics.[14] In 1851, the Colombian Congress declared the abolition of slavery, more than ten years before the United States did. Two years later, it enacted laws that granted freedom of the press, the separation between church and state, and universal manhood suffrage. These reforms were of particular importance in a place like Panama, where the majority of the population was black and the climate tropical, two traits that since the eighteenth century the scientific community—including Francisco José de Caldas, Bogota's foremost scientist in the eighteenth century—had considered incompatible with civilization.[15]

Panamanians found themselves in the unlikely situation of being at the center of political innovations in a world that increasingly considered them incapable of civilization. Educated black Panamanians like Jose Domingo Espinar and Carlos A. Mendoza challenged these views with their words and actions (see Figure 1.2). They became staunch advocates of democracy and universal manhood suffrage. Espinar wrote in 1851 that the nineteenth century was the "century of the majorities" and asked "whoever does not abide by its sovereign decisions, to leave the country forever." He was fully aware of the ramifications of such statements in places like Panama, where these majorities were not white. He also challenged the idea that skin color had any influence on human nature, as everyone had "their own skin tone," one "that nature and happenstance had bestowed [upon] them at birth."[16] A member of the Liberal Party, Mendoza also emphasized in his writings

FIGURE 1.2 Carlos A. Mendoza
Credit: Photo by Carlos Endara. Courtesy of the Ricardo López Arias / Ana Sánchez collection.

and actions his belief in Panama's right and ability to progress and modernize according to the democratic ideals of the nineteenth century.[17]

Another Panamanian, the famous politician and diplomat Justo Arosemena, also confronted the geographic and racial determinism of his time. Unlike Mendoza and Espinar, he was a member of Panama's traditional white elite, but like them he was a strong supporter of democracy. Although earlier in his life he had shared the negative opinion of black, indigenous, and Spanish people typical among white scientists and politicians of his time, he would later change his view. In 1856, he argued that democracy was the salvation of the "Latin race," which "had only begun its civilization with democracy." Far from being alien or disconnected from Latin culture, democracy provided "the source of its strength, of its progress and of its glory." Like other Colombians of his time, he saw his country as a bastion of republican and democratic values in a world dominated by monarchies and in which the most powerful republic in the Americas, the United States, continued to allow slavery.

In 1878, Arosemena timidly confronted the geographic determinism of his fellow Colombians. Since the eighteenth century, Colombian scientists and intellectuals had divided their country's geography between the Andean heights, which had the temperate climate of Europe and thus were capable of civilization, and the tropical lowlands with a hot climate that made them unsuitable for civilization. Arosemena argued the opposite. Paying no attention to climate, he focused on history. Civilization depended on movement, trade, and cultural interactions; and it was in the hot coastal lowlands, not the Andean highlands, where this happened. This contact led to a racial mixture that he now judged positively as the "intelligent and hybrid race of *zambos* and *mulatos* that constitute the majority of the population in the hot lands of the new world."[18]

Mid-nineteenth-century Colombian liberals were also the driving force behind a federal constitutional reform that gave autonomy to the regional governments of states like Panama. This autonomy was particularly dear to a Panamanian merchant and political elite that had developed its own sense of global relevance and felt that Bogotá, its capital, was too distant and too different to understand Panama's peculiar needs as a maritime region.[19] As citizens of Colombia, Panamanian intellectuals cultivated a regionalist ideology informed by current notions of free trade, federalism, and the impact of geography on politics and society. They were keenly aware of Panama's strategic importance and believed that Panama's history and geographic location made it a natural commercial emporium. Panama only needed enough autonomy from Bogota's political influence to fulfill its economic destiny. Panamanians were staunch federalists who used their special geographic importance to wrestle political concessions and special autonomy from Colombia's central government. Some members of Panama's merchant elite had even imagined Panama as a modern replica of small, commercial medieval city-states. One of Panama's leading nineteenth-century intellectuals saw in the medieval merchant cities of the Hanseatic League a good model on which to base Panama's republic.[20]

Eusebio A. Morales, and other liberals like him, also witnessed how the aforementioned wave of reforms came to a halt with the Colombian constitution of 1886, which began what in Colombian history is known as "the Regeneration." With the 1886 constitution Colombia became a centralist government and states like Panama lost their autonomy; the new constitution also curtailed freedom of the press and ended universal manhood suffrage by imposing a literacy requirement for voting in national elections.[21] Eusebio A. Morales was one of many Colombian liberals who chose exile in Panama to escape conservative control.[22] Throughout these years Morales continued to be involved in liberal politics and was an active writer who published in Colombian and Panamanian newspapers, as well as in US journals like the *North American Review*. In 1902, he wrote a scathing critique of Colombia's conservative government in which he asked how it was possible to have so many years of conservative rule in a country where the majority sympathized with the Liberal Party.[23] In 1899, conflicts between liberals and conservatives escalated into a bloody civil war—the War of the Thousand Days—that ended in 1902 with the victory of the Conservative Party. The war was heavily fought in Panama, the only region of Colombia where liberals had triumphed. Panamanian liberals signed a peace treaty on November 21, 1902, on the American gunboat *Wisconsin*. Morales was one of the signatories of the treaty.

It was in this context, and in a country ravaged by war, that the question of a canal treaty with the United States arose. After three years of war, some Panamanians saw in a new canal their only hope for economic recovery. On January 22, 1903, the United States and Colombia signed the Herran-Hay Treaty, which granted the United States the right to build the Panama Canal. But Colombia's Congress rejected the treaty on August 12, 1903, because, among other things, it considered harmful to Colombia's sovereignty a clause that gave the United States control over a six-mile-wide zone for 100 years. Some Panamanians shared Colombia's view. Others interpreted Bogota's rejection of the treaty as yet another sign of its disregard for Panama's welfare.

A group of Panamanians began to organize a separatist movement, which after receiving the support of the US government, declared Panama's independence from Colombia on November 3, 1903.[24] Eusebio A. Morales played an important role in this movement. He and his close friend, the Panamanian black politician Carlos A. Mendoza, authored some of the most important documents of Panama's separation from Colombia. Mendoza wrote its declaration of independence and Morales the "manifest" of Panama's separation, as well as the provisional government's message to Panama's 1904 Constitutional Convention.[25] And it was Mendoza who won the crucial support of Panama's popular neighborhood of Santa Ana. In a photograph from the time, Mendoza sits in wooden armchair and Morales stands next to him;

both are dressed in the dark suits of early twentieth-century lawyers and sporting the thick mustaches fashionable at the time. They look intently at the camera, perhaps aware of the symbolic importance of a picture with a black politician alongside a white one. While one city after the other declared Panama's independence, nine US gunboats began to arrive in Panama's ports (the *Nashville,* the *Dixie,* the *Atlanta,* the *Mayflower,* and the *Maine* arrived in the Port of Colón and the *Boston,* the *Marblehead,* the *Concord,* and the *Wyoming* in the Port of Panama). Although Colombia did not recognize Panama's separation until 1914, it did not have the military power to regain its former territory.[26] Panama was now its own independent country.

Perhaps nothing captures the contradictions of Panama's independence as much as the combination of US gunboats and the independence declarations of Panamanian municipalities. There was a clash between two political visions of Panama's political identity and political future. On the one hand, Panama's independence declarations represented an old political tradition that began in the late eighteenth and early nineteenth centuries when the former English and Spanish colonies declared their independence. Panamanians at the turn of the twentieth century saw themselves as rightful heirs to that republican tradition. On the other hand, the gunboats represented the new imperialist policies of US president Theodore Roosevelt, who saw black people from the Caribbean as backward, inferior beings who needed an American guiding hand. Which one of these perspectives would frame the relationship between the United States and Panama?

Panama's government presented its country as a smaller, less powerful but equal nation. Panama and the United States were equal partners in the construction of an important work that would benefit humankind. Panamanian diplomats like Eusebio A. Morales belonged to a generation of lawyers from regions outside of Europe and the

United States who adamantly sought to establish the equality of their nations under the rule of international law. The rules and principles of international law of the early twentieth century divided the world between regions that fulfilled what was then called the standard of civilization and regions that did not. The first deserved to be treated as equals by other civilized nations under the rules of international law and nations, while the second did not. It is worth noting that in the same year that Panama and the United States debated who controlled the ports of the Panama Canal a new edition of the famous British scholar John Westlake's book on international law appeared. Like the previous edition, it divided nations according to their level of civilization. However, Westlake now considered Japan "a rare and interesting example of the passage of a state from the Oriental to the European class," while states like Siam, Persia, China, and Turkey could only be partially admitted to the international society and remained subject to consular jurisdiction.[27] Where would Panama stand among this group of nations?

It was a bad time to defend Panama's status as a civilized nation. The increasing popularity of scientific racism and other ideas that understood civilization as white made it difficult for a tropical nation with a majority black population to keep its place among civilized nations entitled to equal rights. Would Panamanians be seen as people capable of retaining control of their country's international ports, or would they be portrayed as backward tropical people who needed to be guided and controlled? Books like Benjamin Kidd's *The Control of the Tropics* increasingly popularized the idea of "the absolute ascendancy in the world today" of white people from the United States and Western Europe over "the colored races."[28] Kidd's book was published in 1898, when the United States was taking over the Spanish colonies of Puerto Rico, Cuba, and the Philippines, and it justified US political control of tropical regions south of its border as the natural result of white people's alleged historic role as agents of civilization in backward regions. Or, in Kidd's words, the United States had the responsibility to govern them "as a trust for civilization."[29] Other books echoed this view. For example, in *An Introduction to American Expansion Policy*, published in 1908, James Morton Callahan argued against tropical people's ability to live under democratic institutions. Moreover, he continued, "the trend of modern history seems to be toward colonization and protectorates for less civilized peoples; and that it will be futile for any first class power to fold its hands and stand aloof from regions which, although they cannot perhaps be colonized by whites, must be governed by a base in the temperate zones—by the United States and other nations whose duty is to undertake work in the interest of all as a trust for civilization."[30] The idea that Latin American republics and the United States could be sister republics, having once fought for republicanism against European tyranny, was becoming an increasingly implausible proposition.[31]

Books advocating US control of its tropical neighbors were part of a larger cultural shift that changed ideas about civilization. At the turn of the twentieth century, historians developed a new concept that dramatically altered the understanding of world history. This concept was Western Civilization. It is important to highlight that the building of the Panama Canal coincided with the development and popularization of this concept and that it influenced the United States' understanding of its relationship with Panama. Contrary to what is commonly believed, the idea of the West is a relatively recent historical invention that can be traced to the late nineteenth and early twentieth centuries. In this new concept, the history of the West was the culmination of all developments in the humanities, from Greek philosophy to Enlightenment ideas about freedom, from Egyptian geometry to the technological changes brought about by the Industrial Revolution. England and the United States were part of this tradition and its rightful heirs.

In this peculiar version of history, action and movement resided solely with Western culture. Other cultures, like ancient Egypt's or ancient Sumer's, might have contributed to its development, but having done so they then ceased to be actors in the history of human progress. In the Western Civilization narrative, the input of other regions, like Spanish America, to the scientific, technological, and political changes of the nineteenth century was erased. The idea of Western Civilization made it increasingly difficult for Spanish-American nations—the nations that along with the United States made the ideal of republicanism a concrete reality in the nineteenth century—to maintain their place among that century's political innovators. Moreover, the idea of Western Civilization had created a new cultural geography that distanced the United States from its southern neighbors and fellow ex-colonies. While the notion of civilization had originally applied to any society, regardless of its race or religion, that fulfilled certain standards of social organization and complexity, historians of Western Civilization located true civilization only in the United States and Western Europe. In doing so, they realigned European and American cultural geographies. On the one hand, Eastern Europe was excluded from the West. On the other hand, the previous European colonies of the Americas were divided between the United States, which now became part of the West, and Latin America.[32] Within these new categories, it was increasingly difficult for places like Colombia or Panama to see themselves as sister republics of the United States, and common members of one shared American Continent.

In this context, much was at stake in defending a nation's "civilization." If Panama was a civilized nation, it deserved the full protection of international law. And if the United States did not comply with those laws, it would not be behaving according to the standards of international law. If Panama was not "civilized," however, US control and unequal treatment was justified. Like lawyers from Japan, Argentina, Russia, and China, Panama's lawyers sought to demonstrate that their country complied with the standard of civilization and therefore deserved to be treated as an equal.[33] What was at stake for Panama was keeping its place among the select group of constitutional governments with equal international rights. According to Panama's government, the 1903 canal treaty was a "bond of perpetual unity that linked two nations over whom the eyes of the universe rested." Thus, the Republic of Panama was "an independent and sovereign state that has the right to be respected even by the world's most powerful nations."[34] Panama expected from her "natural ally," the United States, "not only reciprocal respect, but the especial and deferent treatment that it deserves."[35] Panama counted not only on keeping control of its ports, but also, as we will see, on sharing control of the Zone with the United States.

In many ways, the controversy over the Port of Panama was a debate about Western Civilization. As we have seen, Panama's historical experience did not fit the Western Civilization narrative. Panamanian negotiators refused the idea that their country was incapable of being an important actor in global trade and unable to control infrastructure of global significance. For Panamanians, to be true to their sense of history and identity, to be able to fulfill their economic vision, Panama had to control its port. And by the Port of Panama, the Panamanian government meant the port at the entrance of the Panama Canal. For Panamanians, the canal ports were only the latest development of Panama's 400-year history as an international port. According to Panama's diplomats, "the port adjacent to this city is . . . the only one that has been used for foreign trade since the foundation of Panama, and

FIGURE 1.3 The entrance to the Panama Canal at La Boca
Credit: I. L. Maduro. Reproduced from the author's collection.

even though it is located inside the Zone, it is not part of the concession."[36] To lose the Pacific and Atlantic ports would mean that Panama
City—and Colón City—would lose their commerce and "the importance
that they had always enjoyed as places of transit."[37] The Port of Panama
could move from one place to another, as it had already done for the past
four 400 years, without changing the fact that what defined the port was
its location on the Pacific side of the Panama route and the location of the
docks for international ships. In the view of Panama's government, "the
port of Panama is only one." It included "all the coasts that surround
the city, the nearby islands, and all the waters that wash over this part
of the national territory." The Port of Panama thus included "the place
known as La Boca. As part of the port of Panamá, *La Boca is excluded
from the Canal Zone*" (see Figure 1.3).[38]

Behind this definition was a spatial conception of the canal and its
zone that was very different from the one that would become dominant after 1914. It was an idea more in tune with nineteenth-century

historical precedents that kept political and legal jurisdiction over the ports in the hands of the Republic of Colombia. Early twentieth-century Panamanians imagined that the implementation of the 1903 treaty was based on the historical precedents to the 1904 canal construction. There was nothing in the history of Panama that could have prepared Panamanians for the United States' interpretation of the treaty and the way in which the United States would make the Zone into a territory under its exclusive control. Recall that the US canal was the third largest infrastructural project that a foreign power had undertaken in Panama since the 1850s. US capital had built the Panama Railroad in the 1850s, and French capital had begun the construction of the Panama Canal in the 1880s. Both projects had required enormous amounts of labor and radically transformed Panama's isthmian region. But none had taken away from Panama the political control of the towns and lands adjacent to the canal. When a private American company built the Panama Railroad, Colombia kept political jurisdiction over the towns and territory crossed by the railroad and over the railroad's Atlantic and Pacific ports. Similarly, when the French began to build the Panama Canal, Colombia also kept jurisdiction over the ports and the territory. Why would the United States behave differently? An examination of these early years indicates that the United States' interpretation of the 1903 treaty took Panamanians by surprise. To take away Panama's ports was to provincialize it, to make it lose its global significance. It was one thing for Panama to give away the Zone and control over the new canal. It was a completely different thing to give away the ports. Of course, the government of Panama argued that under Panamanian jurisdiction the United States could use the ports as needed.

The arguments made by the government of Panama problematized the idea that building the Panama Canal would bring progress to Panama. The secretary of foreign relations agreed that the canal had the potential to boost Panama's economy, but only if Panama kept control of its international port and customs. Panama had given the United States "all that it could give" to build a project that "would benefit the world." But it had not given the United States the right to "establish an independent commercial center that would ruin the two main cities of the Republic." If this were to happen, the "predictions about Panama's progress and prosperity due to the Canal" would prove to be wrong.[39]

Significantly, the United States did not claim to want the Port of Panama or to have taken away Panama's port. It claimed that the docks at La Boca were not part of the Port of Panama but a separate port that belonged to the Zone and to which they had given the name of Ancón. Through the power of naming, they created a separate port outside of Panama's jurisdiction. In the view of Panama's diplomats, the United States could not take away a section of the Port of Panama "only by employing the fiction of a different name, like the port of Ancón."[40] Yet naming mattered. The power of naming and the power of jurisdiction now resided in the United States. A new spatial geography was created that took away from Panama any control over its international port. Ancón would not only become the new name of Panama's international port, but it would also become the site of a new town, located only one and a half miles away from Panama City but inside the boundaries of the Zone. Ancón would become the political space from which Panama's international ports would be ruled. While the French canal administration building had been located in Panama's main square, the new American administration building would be located in Ancón. The fact that the Pacific port of the Panama Canal was never called the Port of Panama—it was first named Ancón and later Balboa—reflected the initial tension and lack of clarity over who owned the port. If it had been named the Port of Panama, it would have belonged to Panama. The naming of Ancón erased part of Panama's modernity. It provincialized Panama. It ended, at least temporarily, its political control over ports of global significance. The Port of Panama became a port for local fishermen and local trade. Panama had been nativized. In other words, it had been transformed into a place incapable of controlling a port of global significance.

The conflict over the ports was part of a larger conflict over the interpretation of the Hay-Bunau-Varilla Treaty. The year 1904 was an important one. The question of who was entitled to sovereignty over the Canal Zone became the object of strong negotiations between Panamanian diplomats and the US government. The main point of contention was the treaty's third article; it gave the United States control over the Zone as "if it were sovereign." According to the interpretation of General Davis, the Zone's governor, the United States had the powers of a sovereign government, which included, among other things, the right to print postal stamps and to establish customs between Panama and the Zone. These measures separated the Zone's markets from Panama's markets, forcing Panamanians to pay import duties if they wanted to profit from the Zone's growing market. The Panamanian government had a very different interpretation and contended that Governor Davis had far exceeded his rights over the Zone.

Eusebio A. Morales developed a sophisticated defense of Panama's rights in the Zone. The thrust of his argument was that Panama had not given away its sovereignty over the Zone. The treaty had only given the United States what it needed for the construction, maintenance, and defense of the canal. Any government role not related to canal functions—customs, trade, and so on—remained in the hands of Panama. He defended Panama's position by challenging the United States' interpretation of Article III of Hay-Bunau-Varilla. Morales argued that it could not be interpreted without the antecedents of the

Herran-Hay Treaty, which never mentioned the issue of sovereignty. According to Morales, the objective of both treaties was to "facilitate the construction of a canal." It was never the purpose to sign a treaty "about the cession of a territory" or "the renunciation of absolute sovereignty."[41] Herran-Hay had explicitly recognized Colombian sovereignty and rejected "all pretention to undermine it in any way or to increase its [US] territory at the expense of Colombia or any of the sister republics of Central or South America." According to Morales, this declaration had the objective of assuaging any fear of absorption that the Central and South American republics may have had; and "it had a decisive influence in my government decision to approve without reserve or modification the Varilla-Hay [sic] convention."[42]

According to Morales, both the Herran-Hay and the Hay-Bunau-Varilla treaties gave the United States rights over the Zone's land and waters only for the "construction, maintenance, operation, sanitation and protection" of the canal. It was never the intention to give away "absolute dominion over the territory, much less the transference of sovereignty." Morales argued that this kind of concession could have been given to any private company, without it entailing anything but the rental of land. The relationship established in the treaty was that of a renter and a tenant, the only difference being that in this case the renter was another republic, which, he argued, caused the confusion.[43]

Morales further argued that if the treaty had given the United States sovereignty over the Zone, many of the treaty clauses limiting US rights over the Zone would be inexplicable and superfluous. One such clause was Article VI, which established a Joint Land Commission composed of Panamanian and US members in charge of adjudicating compensation for lands and property expropriated for canal purposes. No less important were Articles X, XII, and XIII, in which Panama agreed not to tax anything related to canal construction, to allow all the workers needed for canal construction to immigrate to the Zone, and to give the United States the right to import any machinery or implements needed for canal construction free of duties. If the United States were sovereign and if Panama did not have any rights over the Zone, none of these articles were necessary, Morales argued. He concluded that treaties "cannot admit the existence of clauses that are useless or contradictory; those that appear as useless, should be interpreted in a manner that produces some effects; and those that appear as contradictories should be interpreted taking into account the tone of the last ones, because one should assume . . . that they express the last idea or thought of the parties." From this followed the idea that the United States did not have any rights to control customs or to establish its own mail in the Zone.[44]

Moreover, because the economic life of Panama resided in the transit zone and its ports, Panama was not in the position to give away its ports and its fiscal sovereignty, because no nation can give away its own survival: "nobody enters into a contract knowing that it would bring them incalculable damage." And conceding those rights would only bring "commercial and economic ruin." Far from progressing, Panama would be "in an inferior condition from what it was before the treaty upon which it had placed its hopes for betterment and progress." If the United States continued to have jurisdiction over the ports and enforce its protectionist tariffs in the Zone, the commerce that had "always flourished would completely disappear" or be reduced. Without economic control of the Zone and ports, it was not clear what Panama would gain from the canal construction. Its status as an international trading center would be handed over to the United States and it would become a provincial city catering to the "impoverished towns of the countryside."[45]

Morales's argument is a forgotten attempt on the part of the Panamanian elite to keep its resources, to remain a modern economic player in a global economy, and to avoid being provincialized. It is a lost counter-narrative both to the idea that the canal brought progress to Panama and to the histories that portray local elites only as weak tools of American imperialism. In the 1904 protest to keep Panama's international ports and to limit US rights over the Zone, we see an economic vision of the canal that was lost: one that left Panama with its ports and with economic control of the Zone. The United States would build and run the canal and protect Panama from Colombia but leave to Panama control of its international trade, which was not possible without the ports. The ports were part of Panama's identity as a modern, sophisticated, commercial hub. We tend to forget that the questions about the future of the ports and the Zone were far from settled in 1904. Morales's interpretation reflected the ambiguity of the moment and the problems of justifying jurisdiction for construction and sanitation purposes in a region with a complex political, urban, and agricultural life. This problem would haunt Zone authorities during the first years of canal construction. It would eventually be solved with the depopulation of the Zone.

Alas, the governor of the Zone had a very different opinion. By the time the US federal government gained control over the Zone, the rhetoric of transforming a complex historical space like Panama into tropical wilderness had a long tradition. Nineteenth-century travel narratives had familiarized the American public with the idea of Latin America as the land of caudillos, disorder, and instability. Hector Perez-Brignoli calls this view the "legal frame of the Banana Republic."[46] Moreover, during the war of 1898, the United States had developed sophisticated legal and political tools that transformed the former subjects of the Spanish Empire into primitives in need of help. As

Paul A. Kramer has shown, Americans recast Hispanized *Ilustrado,* or enlightened, Filipinos and their Philippine Republic into "an impossible 'eighty-four tribes' and Aguinaldo's government as merely the hegemony of a 'single tribe' of Tagalogs."[47] Filipinos were characterized as divided into a "cacique" elite that was "corrupt and exploitative" and a "passive, backward and superstitious" lower class. Having deprived Filipinos of their modernity, Americans were now able to create a series of benchmarks that needed to be achieved to earn self-rule and entrance to the community of civilized nations.[48] A similar process took place during the US occupation of Cuba. Americans opposed the Cubans' goal to decree universal manhood suffrage with arguments that denied the abilities of most Cubans to govern themselves because of their race and climate. Newspapers used the example of other Spanish-American republics, which were caricaturized as regions where "tropical conditions," "Indian admixture," and a "strong Negro element" led to constant chaos and warfare.[49]

Yet, there were important differences among Panama, Cuba, Puerto Rico, and the Philippines. Since Panama was already a republic, it could not be given benchmarks that it needed to acquire before gaining total independence. The United States did not occupy the entire territory of Panama, but only a small part of it, and that small part was held in perpetuity. But Panama was not recognized as an equal republic. It was a "young republic," in need of the mentoring and example that the United States would set in the Zone. The term "young republic" would gain popularity. Even today we can see the term applied by the *New York Times* to republics whose origins go back to the 1810s. Spanish-American republics are eternal "young republics." Panama was a perfect location to develop this trope, because it was technically a young republic, which made it easier to erase the fact that it had enjoyed a republican form of government since 1821, when it became a province of Colombia, one of the world's oldest republics.

The response of General George W. Davis, the Zone's governor, was revealed in his view of Panama's history and its place in the world. He countered Panama's perspective with three main arguments. First, he was "surprised" that Panama's interpretation of the treaty was "so ridiculously contrary" to the United States' interpretation. It was an "inevitable necessity" for the United States to establish its own ports in the Zone. The word *ridiculously* is indicative of a cultural perspective that saw the idea of Latin America being a protagonist in the creation of global modernity as not just untenable but laughable. The notion that a country like Panama could control international ports of global strategic importance had become absurd. This idea would survive for a good part of the twentieth century. Modernity would become not something that Latin American countries already had but something to which they could eternally aspire or reject as an alien imposition.

The second part of Davis's argument was that concerns about sanitation justified US control of the ports. Yes, it was true that Panama had been the center of intense trade and shipping, but this only intensified the danger of infectious diseases coming through its ports. Thus, it would be more efficient for the United States, which the canal treaty had put in charge of sanitation, to handle both the ports and the quarantine.[50] It is interesting that the justification for this control was not based on military or political needs, or canal defense. That sanitation needs justified US control of the ports speaks to the importance that sanitation had already acquired as a justification for political control. This is the beginning of the division of the world according to indicators of modernity that are not only political or cultural but also based on technologies of health and urbanization. Indeed, to Panama's argument that if it lost its ports it would lose its chance for economic progress, Governor Davis replied that the sanitation benefits would provide compensation for Panama's losses. American sanitation programs would not only clear Panama's reputation as a disease-ridden location but also "increase the wealth and prosperity of the republic's capital city to a degree that today is not easy to calculate; and its merchants, its business men, its professionals, its working class and all in general would enjoy the benefits brought by this change."[51]

Finally, Governor Davis dismissed the importance of historical continuity. He rejected the notion that the wealth and prosperity of the Republic of Panama depended on its historical connection to the sea. He argued that although many considered maritime trade to be crucial for the wealth of a nation, there were many exceptions to this rule. "Switzerland, which had never had a sea port," was nevertheless rich and prosperous.[52] One can only imagine the bewilderment of Panamanians at being told to follow Switzerland's example. The idea symbolized the displacement of nineteenth-century Panama as the heir of Spanish imperial trade. Now the heir was the United States. The city of Panama had been deprived of its international port, and like Switzerland, it was landlocked, not by mountains, but by the Zone. In the histories of the Panama Canal, the nineteenth century would become a century of failure: the French failure to build a canal and the Colombian failure to provide peace and prosperity. Only American technological expertise was able to fulfill the old Spanish dream of building a canal through the Isthmus of Panama. Yet there are other alternatives to this history.

The 1904 diplomatic conflict over Panama's ports resulted in the Taft agreement, which gave Panama some concessions while keeping the canal ports under US jurisdiction. The negotiations over the interpretation of the 1903 treaties and the resulting Taft agreement are a clear example of ambiguities of the relationship between the United States and Panama: two nominally equal nations with unequal power. The official US response to Panama's complaint came in October 1904 from Secretary of State John Hay, who refused Panama's argument and reaffirmed the United States' absolute control over the Zone. Soon after, however, President Roosevelt sent Secretary of War Taft to Panama to negotiate with the government of Panama. In his letter to Taft, Roosevelt expressed the importance of assuaging any doubts about the United States' future intentions, making clear that the US government had no plans to create a colony in the middle of the isthmus. Taft's visit resulted in the revocation of the Executive Order of June 1904. Now Zone officials could only import merchandise for canal purposes; the tariffs between Panama and the Zone were eliminated; the products that the United States could sell duty-free to boats passing the Zone were limited to coal and oil. Panama's merchants were relieved. They had not lost access to the markets of the growing population of the Zone and to the ships using the canal and its ports. At the banquet in Taft's honor, Panamanian politician and future president Belisario Porras exclaimed, "Our Republic will not perish."[53]

The Port of Ancón remained as a separate port under American jurisdiction, but in practical matters it continued to organize the space around the Bay of Panama as a single port. In terms of sanitation, customs, and postal service, the ports of Panama and Ancón were a single port. The United States gained "complete jurisdiction in matters of sanitation and quarantine in the maritime waters of the ports of Panama and Colon." Yet, at the same time, the US government agreed to unify Canal Zone customs and postal system with those of Panama and to import to the Zone only goods needed for the construction and maintenance of the canal. Finally, given "the proximity between the port of Ancón and the port of Panama and the port of Cristobal and the port of Colon," ships entered or cleared at the Port of Panama could anchor and dock at Ancón and vice versa.[54] The Port of Panama kept many of its previous uses; what changed was the political and military control of the port, which for the first time in its history was not in Panama City. The Port of Panama was now shared between two republics. This division reflected the beginning of international power relations that, on the one hand, emphasized the nominal equality of republican nation-states, while, on the other hand, highlighted their differences in modernity. One nation had superior technology and superior democratic traditions, while the other was still catching up.

What we see in this debate is not the struggle between an imperial power and a native elite, in which the latter tries to preserve a traditional way of life. Instead, we see a local elite trying to retain its modernity and its economic control over modern resources in the face of an imperial elite trying to erase the history of that control and transform the local elites into "natives" in need of stewardship and help. Although excluded from the West, Latin American nations remained independent republics that continued to be formally treated as equal nations. In this context, a new formulation of power relations among nominally equal states that enjoy Westphalian sovereignty emerged.[55] On the one hand, the nominal equality of Latin American republics was recognized. On the other hand, the region's role as a protagonist in the history of nineteenth-century politics, science, and technology was erased. Latin America was seen as a region that could not control its destiny without the help and guidance of more advanced nations.

Panama was at the center of these cultural and ideological changes. In the relationship between the United States and Panama there is a reformulation of power relations among states that enjoy Westphalian sovereignty and are nominally equal.[56] These relations would become common after World War II, when most European colonies became independent nations, but they were experienced for the first time in the Americas. New relationships among nations would require new hierarchies. Differences would now be framed initially by the dichotomy of the civilized and the non-civilized and after World War II by the dichotomy of the developed and the underdeveloped. The post–World War II success of these dichotomies would require the erasure of the "underdeveloped" country's modernity. At the beginning of the twentieth century, Panama—like other regions of Latin America—did not yet see itself as not-modern, and, thus, tried to reassert its own economic and political modernity.

2

The Canal Zone in 1904

WHAT DID THE OLD Panamanian towns of the Zone look like when the United States took control of the territory in 1904? It is hard to tell. For the thousands of pictures taken of canal construction and of the American side of Zone towns, there are very few pictures of the private houses and businesses on the Panamanian side of the Zone. Travelers' accounts can also be profoundly misleading. Filled with jungle stories and stereotypes about native huts and towns, they are of little use for understanding the long commercial history of most Zone towns. Nor can the historian return to the towns to understand their history through their remains, because the towns have been either completely demolished, as was the case with Chagres; transformed into a defunct bomb range, as happened with Emperador; or partially flooded by Lake Gatún, as happened with Gorgona. However, through a careful examination of many travelers' narratives, local geographies, official accounts, and archival records, it is possible to recreate an urban geography. The archives sometimes hold surprises, like the 1905–1906 tax records of Gorgona and an early map of its saloons, which can help us reconstruct a profile of Gorgona during the early years of canal construction. Any attempt to recover Panama's historical connection to the isthmian route and any attempt to challenge the idea that the canal was built over a barely habited jungle requires reconstructing the lives of these lost towns.

Gorgona and the Chagres River

When American canal construction began in 1904, Gorgona had a long history of international commerce. Located on the southern margins of the Chagres River, nineteen miles from Panama City and thirty-three miles from the port of Chagres, it was the most important town between the ports of Chagres and Colón, on the Atlantic Ocean, and Panama, on the Pacific.[1] Situated on a high bank above the Chagres River, the town was described by one mid-nineteenth-century traveler as being "alive" and "substantial."[2] The first geography of Panama described it as a pleasant and healthy town at seventy-six meters above sea level, where Panamanian families went to spend the dry summer season.[3] The urban layout, the architecture, and the population of Gorgona clearly reflected Panama's long history as a node of global commerce, as well as the historical changes in land use and transport that had shaped the town since the eighteenth century.

In 1904, this small town of 2,000 to 3,000 people had a Catholic church, at least one—perhaps two—Protestant churches, and a "Chinese" temple. Its tax records show that its habitants had Spanish, French, English, and Chinese surnames. There were several hotels and even a Chinese bakery. When Gorgonans walked up and down their main street, they walked from one means of transport to another. To the north were the Chagres River and its port, where river boats like *bongos* and *cayucos* left their passengers and merchandise. They reminded Gorgonans that for most of Panama's history the most efficient way of crossing the isthmus was by mule or by a combination of mule and river transportation, and that Gorgona used to be the hub where travelers ended their journey over the Chagres and began their journey over the Gorgona mule trail. To the north were also the local religious and political centers: the Catholic church, the *plaza,* or main square, and the public school. As in many nineteenth-century Latin American cities, Gorgona's main square had a bandstand. The town's market was also in the north, close to the river. If Gorgonans walked to the south of the town they would find the railroad tracks and the railroad station that transformed Gorgona from a river town to a railroad town with the construction of the 1855 Panama Railroad. To the southeast, close to the railroad and the canal buildings, was a section of the town called Pueblo Nuevo or New Town. It was the American side of town where the ICC built the YMCA building and the ICC hotel.[4] To the southwest, a bit distant from the town, was the cemetery. To the east were the buildings that remained from the French attempt to build a canal in the 1880s, a reminder of Gorgona's importance as a center for machine repairs during that period (see Map 3.1). In 1886, the town was destroyed by fire, but given its value, the governor of the then-Department of Panama issued special provisions as an incentive to rebuild.[5]

Gorgona's street names also reflected the town's different technological, political, and cultural influences. To help reconstruct Gorgona's urban layout and street names, one can use a 1908 ICC map and a 1906 property tax census. The ICC map shows that by 1908, Spanish street names had been replaced with letter-marked avenues and numbered streets. Only two streets had names and both were in English: Rocky Lane and Shady Avenue, both of which were located in the new American section of town. The 1906 tax record, however, shows a different and more complex pattern of street naming. Property owners mentioned both the new street numbers and letters and the old names. According to one property owner, Avenue A used to be Núñez Street

(Calle de Núñez), after the Colombian president Rafael Núñez, a name that brought back Gorgona's recent political past as a municipality of the Republic of Colombia. Another property owner mentioned that E Street, which connected the Chagres River to the railroad tracks, was called Calle de los Rieles or Railroad Street, perhaps signaling that Gorgona had originated as a river town and that the railroad was a new addition to a longer history. Second Street was called Calle de Pueblo Nuevo, a name that stressed that American presence in the town was, indeed, new. Many houses were located in a Calle Principal that the 1908 map does not mention. It paralleled the river and was probably the town's most important street before the construction of the Panama Railroad. It was now replaced in importance by First Street, which paralleled the railroad. The neighbors also mentioned the existence of a Barrio de Chagres, or neighborhood, and a Barrio del Cementerio, cemetery neighborhood.[6] The erasure of the old names, now present only in local memory, symbolized the replacement of one political system for another.

The structure and material of the houses also reflected the town's history. A large number of houses were built of wood frame and galvanized roof. According to the 1904–1906 property records, fifty-nine houses were made of this material. The material of these houses was similar to those in Colón City's houses. The pictures that survive of Gorgona show a town with streets and frame houses like Colón's and those of many other nineteenth-century railroad towns. In 1903, however, according to Captain H. C. Hale, the majority of Gorgona's 390 houses were "huts." The rest were "frame houses."[7] What Hale and many others before him described as huts were thatched roof houses made with local materials, following traditions of house construction along the Chagres River. These "huts" varied in size and materials. Some were made of bamboo walls, some had the new wood frames, and others were adobe. Some houses even had a mixed thatch / galvanized roof.

Who were the people living in the towns on the isthmian route and how did they interact with Panama's international trade? Most nineteenth-century travelers described the towns of the route— Chagres, Gorgona, and Cruces—as black towns. According to the French diplomat and explorer Gaspard Théodore Mollien, "Gorgona was a town populated solely by blacks" and Cruces "was populated by men of color."[8] Unfortunately, we do not have the residents' own stories and must rely on travelers' accounts that described in detail the dangers and incidents of their trips and the habits of local boatmen and muleteers. Their descriptions have to be read carefully, however, since most of them shared common racial and geographic prejudices of their times and could not see tropical peoples and landscapes as anything but primitive and exotic. Mollien, for example, ridiculed the people living along the Chagres as unfit to be the protagonists of such an important route. Their "huts" were "dirty," and they "disdained any work that was not very lucrative."[9] Twenty-five years later, Lady Emmeline Stuart Wortley would repeat what had, by then, become common descriptions among American and European travelers in the tropics: "the natives" had been "rendered indolent by their climate, and apt to depend almost entirely upon the abundant yield of tropical production for their livelihood."[10] Also, they had a "characteristic laziness and nonchalance."[11] She also used rhetorical tropes that distinguished between "eager, bustling, rapid, impatient Yankees" and "quiet, deliberate, and inanimate natives."[12] Her account repeated common nineteenth-century stereotypes about the tropics and tropical people that described and ridiculed "half-naked" black Panamanian "natives" whose primitiveness seemed only confirmed by their tropical surroundings.[13] A rhetoric that emphasized the connection of black Panamanians to a timeless tropical nature helped silence the economic and technological modernity of people who lived and worked in a region that had been at the forefront of transportation technology since the sixteenth century.

A careful reading of travelers' accounts from the nineteenth century, however, tells a different story: a route filled with towns and people well adapted to global traffic and with a long local history of labor practices and technologies. The black men and women living in Gorgona were not naïve "natives," disconnected from global political, cultural, and economic changes. They were deeply familiar with the route and its commerce and resourcefully used available technology and local natural conditions to handle increased trade. The people of Gorgona had for generations provided the skilled labor that made travel across the isthmus possible. They were the descendants of slaves brought by the Spaniards to the isthmus to work as muleteers, boatmen, and laborers who built and fixed roads in the countless jobs required for the isthmian trade. Before the abolition of slavery in 1851, both slave and free blacks provided the great amount of labor required for navigation on the Chagres River and for mule travel along the Panama route. The fact that as late as 1846, when Panamanian slavery was in serious decline, the parish of Gorgona still had forty-seven slaves, the same number as the parish of San Felipe, in the elite walled center of Panama City, reveals the importance of slave labor and the importance that Gorgona had acquired by the 1840s.[14]

Working and Living at a Tropical Crossroads

It is hard to gain a clear picture of how boatmen, artisans, local peasants, and small merchants participated in the trade economy, but some sources give us a glimpse at how they dealt with the vagaries of international commerce. Already in 1748, the Spanish scientists Jorge Juan and Antonio de Ulloa had described how black people took advantage of the international fairs of Portobelo, which were famous around the world as one of the few official and legal trading posts in the Spanish Empire. There Peru's legendary silver was exchanged for European merchandise destined for South American markets. Juan and Ulloa described the economic activities of Guinea, a neighborhood on the outskirts of the Caribbean port city of Portobelo where the "free and slave blacks live." During the Portobelo fairs, the black neighborhood of Guinea grew substantially because of the many artisans who came from Panama to offer their services and the "poor people and mulattos" of Portobelo who moved there to rent their habitations in the city to the many foreign merchants looking for a place to live.[15]

During the first half of the nineteenth century, Panama continued to be a well-traveled highway.[16] People going from the Atlantic to the Pacific Ocean arrived by sailboat and steamer to the Port of Chagres. There they negotiated with local boatmen, who used their crafts to take them upriver to Gorgona (or Cruces), where they had to find a place to spend the night before traveling by mule to Panama City. The river section of this route took from two to four days to travel and often required spending nights on small settlements located on the riverbanks. Travelers going in the opposite direction would travel first by mule and then by boat.[17] In the 1820s, Mollien described the economic activities along the Chagres River and the Atlantic Port of Chagres. British merchants brought textiles and took back Colombian gold and Mexican and Peruvian silver. Americans traded in salted beef, cod, and onions; and South American merchants traded in various items.[18] Mollien saw "more money circulate [in Chagres's port] than in any other place of the Republic" of Colombia. The small huts of Chagres "stored prodigious riches" and were used as warehouses that rented at "400 franks per month."[19] Like many travelers before and after him, he complained about expensive prices and expensive labor. According to him, few of Chagres's black citizens earned less than sixty to eighty pesos per week, which suggests the ability of free blacks to negotiate to their advantage during these years. Writing in 1843 for a British steamship company, William Wheelwright described how people in the river towns along the Chagres River took economic advantage of the route by selling fowl, eggs, and fruit to travelers.[20] He also mentioned how muleteers tried to steer him toward Cruces, where they had "their relations and friends," even though by then the Gorgona Road was considered the best land route between the Chagres River and Panama City.[21]

Stereotypes about tropical peoples also hid the important and fascinating story of how the people of Gorgona lived through some of the most significant social, political, and technological changes of the nineteenth century. The number of people migrating across the world had increased dramatically, and technologies were changing fast from muscle power (human or animal) to coal power. Living in the center of one of the world's most important routes, the people of Gorgona were at the heart of it all. The four years before the 1855 inauguration of the Panama Railroad were an interesting transitional moment. With the onset of the California Gold Rush, traffic along the Panama route dramatically increased as forty-niners began to arrive in droves to Panama, which was one of the easiest and most popular routes connecting the East and West Coasts of the United States. Each steamer brought hundreds of people. Passengers described several steamers and sailing boats arriving at the same time. One traveler calculated that the several ships landing in Chagres brought together "about one thousand passengers."[22] In addition to the California steamers, there were steamers from Peru and from other parts of South America. The mules and traditional boats seemed to have reached their capacity just before the advent of the Panama Railroad. Travelers recounted seeing hundreds of boats waiting for the steamers at the Port of Chagres and the Chagres River, filled with passengers and merchandise, mules everywhere on the Gorgona road.[23] The history of these years is the history of how the people of the Chagres River adapted to the increase in traffic across the isthmus to provide transport, lodging, and food to thousands of travelers.[24]

By the mid-nineteenth century, below the town of Gorgona, by its river shore, there was a large American encampment where many travelers from California waited to arrange a trip to Panama City. According to one such traveler, many of them preferred to wait for ships to San Francisco in Gorgona rather than in Panama City, where lodging was more expensive.[25] Everything became dearer. Fruit vendors sold their fruits to the thousands of travelers who passed through their town. Butchers used a method that allowed them to sell meat quickly and efficiently to busy travelers. They cut the meat in three-inch-wide strips of various lengths and hung them on rails, so that buyers could purchase their meat by the yard.[26] Foreigners arrived in Gorgona to open hotels, stores, and restaurants. In 1850, a British woman described how her party could find food and sleeping accommodations in any small settlement along the Chagres River if they had to stop for the night. Small settlements like "Dos Hermanas" offered houses made of bamboo walls covered with mats and hides.[27] In Gorgona, the range of possible accommodations had expanded. It included an American Hotel—Mr. Miller's—and at least two local hotels, or *posadas*. Other people opened gambling houses. Porters and hangers-on, idlers and thieves, gamblers and dancing women all tried to profit from the thousands of people who stopped to rest and wait for transportation in Gorgona.[28] By the mid-nineteenth century, Gorgona was a bustling river port with merchants, boatmen, and muleteers. Because of its growing importance, it had started to replace Cruces as the main transition point between the Chagres River and the mule path that led to Panama City.[29] A reflection of Gorgona's new status was its transformation from parochial district to municipality in September 1855, a change that increased its rights and powers.[30]

The work of people along the Chagres River was made increasingly difficult by travelers' constant demand that they hurry. Passengers did not seem to understand how difficult and exhausting it was to row a long, canopy-covered *bongo*, and they resented any stop made to eat and rest, or even to spend the night. Americans seemed particularly annoyed that boatmen had to fix and rethatch the canopy of their *bongos*. It rained constantly, and thatched canopies required frequent maintenance in order to keep passengers and goods dry. Yet, when the *bogas*, or boatmen, were busy doing this work, passengers would not stop gesticulating, imploring, or threatening to make them stop their work and start rowing right away. Muleteers and restaurant and hotel owners were similarly harassed. Sometimes Panamanians took revenge by mocking and mimicking Americans, telling them, *"Vamos, go-ahead!— ho! poco tiempo, poco tiempo,"* as they walked or rode from Gorgona to Panama City.[31]

Travelers' jungle narratives also concealed the technological sophistication of a road that had developed over three centuries of global trade. Mules and mule paths were uniquely adapted to the muddy and forested hills of the isthmian route. The mules that carried passengers and merchandise were the creatures of a complex trading and breeding process from colonial times, when mules were imported in large numbers from Nicaragua, El Salvador, and Honduras.[32] The mule paths required regular upkeep, for which the Spanish Crown, and later the Colombian government, dedicated considerable resources.[33] Because of the town's location as a transition point between a river road and a mule road, mules had always been an important part of its life. A large number of Gorgona men were expert muleteers, and important people in town owned large mule packs. By the late 1840s mules were everywhere in Gorgona. The number of mules had increased dramatically with the influx of thousands of California travelers. Their number was so high that the road between Gorgona and Panama was sometimes littered with mules that had died on the road carrying the passengers and baggage of the California trade.[34]

Travelers navigating the Chagres River during the Gold Rush did not voyage alone amid the tropical beauty; they moved along a busy river filled with *bongos* and *cayucos,* single-passenger boats, carrying travelers between the Port of Chagres and Gorgona. Lady Stuart Wortley described how as her boat got closer to Gorgona, she passed "more and more boats, till the river seemed alive with them. Occasionally, passengers broke out into a cheery shout of "Ho! For California!"[35] The men who worked in the *bongos* that transported passengers traveling between Chagres and Gorgona were very skilled at their trade. Well acquainted with the river's turns and fast currents, they knew that not using the rhythms of the Chagres to the *bongos'* advantage could make all the difference between being trapped in a sand bar or rowing along quickly.[36] It is important to remember that the Chagres was not a pristine river left untouched by human intervention. The Colombian government scheduled periodic upkeep and cleaning, which made the work of boatmen a little easier.[37] *Bogas* knew well the advantages and disadvantages of the different boats navigating the Chagres. The *cayucos* were the smallest and fastest boats on the river. A light and "graceful-looking craft," the *cayuco* fit only one passenger carrying a mule load—"two trunks and a bed."[38] Some *bogas* worked carrying solo passengers who had the money to pay for the speed and convenience of a *cayuco,* which took only eighteen hours to travel from the Port of Cha-gres to Gorgona—or Cruces.[39]

Other *bogas* worked in the larger *bongos.* They had a carrying capacity of 400 to 500 quintals and took forty-eight hours to travel be-tween Chagres and Gorgona.[40] Apparently this type of boat did not fully develop until the eighteenth century.[41] Jorge Juan and Antonio de Ulloa described them as "things of admiration."[42] The *bongo* was long and narrow, and its broadest part could be eleven feet wide.[43] Passen-gers traveled in the back, which was covered with a thatched roof, while merchandise was covered with protective cowhides. *Bongos* were manned by a crew of twelve boatmen and a captain, who was very ex-perienced in the ways of the river. Boatmen performed difficult and arduous labor. They used a "broad paddle" for the faster parts of the river and changed to *palancas,* or poles, as the *bongo* went upriver and moving against the current became more difficult. To propel their *bongos,* the rowers had to carefully coordinate their movements. They rose simultaneously, stepping up on a seat. After signaling with a cry, they threw themselves back on their oars and returned to their seats. One California traveler was impressed by how they worked in "uniformity as if they were an entire piece of machinery."[44] The *bogas* of the Chagres River had also developed their own culture and traditions. *Bogas* mocked and yelled at the crews of slower boats, who returned the mockery in kind. The river also had its songs. Just as the boatmen changed their rowing instruments with the currents, they changed their songs, which transformed their pace and tone from fast and high-pitched to a "doleful and quivering drawl" as the river cur-rents became stronger and more challenging.[45] Just like its towns, the songs of the Chagres River are now lost.

If men found economic opportunities working as *bogas* and mule-teers, women worked as cooks making breakfast and lunch in the local hotels or diners. In one eatery, perhaps a typical one, passengers sat at a large table covered with a green oilskin cloth, while two or three cooks prepared a meal that consisted of fried bread with pork, followed by a soup made of beef and roots. The meal also included large amounts of rice and jugs of molasses and treacle for sauce, as well as coffee and tea. Chickens and eggs were difficult to find and very expensive. They were a luxury that only a few travelers could afford, and not every hotel was able to serve them. Those that did would hang a chicken sign to identify themselves.[46]

The inhabitants of the Chagres's river towns also saw firsthand the passengers traveling along the river. They saw American women coming back from California dressed like men. They might have been shocked at the fact that the women rode their mules like men and wore pants, flannel shirts, and boots. After a while they probably got used to them, as they had to the frantic pace of the travelers moving through Gorgona.[47] Every so often a famous foreigner or an important Colombian general would stop in Gorgona and the entire town would try to catch a glimpse of the important person. Constant contact with international trade also influenced home décor. In the mid-nineteenth century, most houses along the Chagres were made of bamboo and reed walls and had a high thatched roof. Some people covered their interior walls with blue and red calico, which was fashionable and available. Houses were divided into two floors connected by a ladder. The upstairs was for sleeping. Some homes had a few expensive luxury items like muslin pillows trimmed with lace. The ground floor usually had a table, a couple of hammocks, and a trunk with valuable possessions. Onions and other provisions were also stored downstairs.[48] Some people would earn extra cash by allowing a traveler to sleep in a hammock on the first floor.

With the construction of the Panama Railroad in the early 1850s, Gorgona became a railroad town and a railroad stop. The people of

Gorgona most likely did not have any input on the concessions that the Colombian government gave to the Panama Railroad Company (PRR). However, the granting of municipal land for railroad construction required an agreement with the local *cabildo*, or town council. The PRR also had to reach agreements with individuals over the use of their private land. The agreements show how the people of Gorgona understood their geographic location at the center of the isthmian road and the economic opportunities it provided them. The contract between the municipality and the railroad company indicates that the municipality shared the central government's view of the railroad as a "public utility." It claimed that it was the town council's duty to "foment enterprises of public utility that . . . favor the region under its domain."[49] It reflected the belief that the railroad would increase the value of nearby lands and thus the income of the town council. Gorgona's municipality ceded to the PRR free of charge all municipal lands that it needed for the construction of the railroad line—120 feet wide—and for railroad buildings. Importantly, the town council made sure to protect local economic rights by explicitly forbidding the company, or its successors, from establishing on such land any "stores, houses of commerce, hotels, or places for buying or selling agricultural products, or other places of private interest."[50] This claim echoed the sentiments previously expressed by the private owners of land needed for railroad construction, who signed an agreement to sell their improvements (buildings, cultivations) and to cede their lands without cost (while maintaining ownership) for the construction of the railroad. Like the town council, they forbid the company from establishing "any type of *ventas*, *mesones*, or other commercial establishments of commerce, now called hotels, or stores, or warehouses *(almacenes)*, or any other merchant or agricultural business without first buying the land for its fair price from the legitimate owner." They made clear that the land concessions were only for the building of the railroad.[51]

The Gorgona railroad agreement provides a window into how a local town council of the Panama route understood the concept of public utility that granted rights of eminent domain to an international company. Gorgona granted the land to the railroad free of charge but made sure to safeguard some of the town's commercial vitality by exempting stores, hotels, and commerce in general from the concession. The agreement reveals how the people of Gorgona envisioned their future during the early years of railroad construction in 1851 and 1852. They expected Gorgona to continue to play a historic commercial role like other important towns along Panama's isthmian route.

From Citizens to Natives:
The Problem of Black Republican Politics

In addition to experiencing important economic and technological changes, the people of Gorgona also participated in some of the most important political changes of the nineteenth century. In 1821, they witnessed Panama's independence from Spain and union with the Republic of Colombia. At a time when the institution of slavery was still prevalent in the Americas and most of Europe remained under monarchical rule, the constitution of 1821 created a new republican system that provided for the equality of all free men regardless of color.[52] Thirty years later, the people of Gorgona saw the culmination of the midcentury civil war between liberals and conservatives in the 1851 abolition of slavery and the 1853 declaration of universal manhood suffrage. (During the last decades of the nineteenth century some suffrage rights were rolled back when Colombian laws became increasingly centralized and set literacy requirements to exercise the right to vote.) They also witnessed black men becoming a crucial sector of the local Liberal Party, with some of them reaching powerful political positions.[53]

The Gold Rush and the thousands of Americans crossing the isthmus coincided with one of the most radical times in Colombian politics: the abolition of slavery and the declaration of universal manhood suffrage. In places like Gorgona, the most important political authority was the *alcalde,* or mayor. In the mid-nineteenth century, this position was often occupied by black men who exercised political and police authority over local people and over the thousands of travelers passing through. The *alcalde* governed from a courthouse that resembled the town's other bamboo and reed structures. His skin color and the courthouse where he worked were often mocked because a copious travel, historic, and scientific literature had taught the American and European public to associate certain places and peoples with modernity and others with savagery.[54] Panama's black citizens did not fit within these dichotomies, and white Americans often clashed with the black mayors of Gorgona, resentful of their self-respect and political power. Mary Seacole, an educated black woman from Jamaica who spent a year between Cruces and Gorgona, provided detailed commentary about the racial tension between Panamanians and American travelers. According to her, "Yankees had a strong prejudice" against "the negroes, of whom there were many in the Isthmus, and who almost invariably filled the municipal offices, and took the lead in every way."[55] Local mayors had to constantly assert their authority over travelers. For example, Panamanian soldiers arrested an American who had robbed some Chilean travelers. When a rowdy mob of Americans gathered to protest the imprisonment of their countryman and began to hurl insults at the black authorities who had dared to judge one of them, the local black *alcalde* ordered his soldiers to control the riot. He then gave an angry and passionate speech about his determination to make all foreigners respect the laws of the republic and to imprison and punish anybody who committed a crime. He also explained that the arrival of Americans had increased robberies and disorder in the isthmus.[56]

Seacole tells of another instance of conflict between Gorgonans and US travelers. The conflict began when the town was awakened by the screams of a slave woman who had been severely lashed by her American owner. The mayor of Gorgona intervened and enforced Colombian laws—slavery was already abolished in Colombia—that allowed him to free the slave woman. (Although most slave owners were permitted to travel with their slaves without losing them, apparently Panamanians would sometimes whisper to the slaves "that they could easily escape and be free."[57]) The tensions between black Panamanians and American travelers reflected nineteenth-century political conflicts. At a time when the United States was acutely divided over slavery and over the legal status of free black men, Panama's "black republicanism" represented a challenge to American race relations. It also questioned the idea that the United States was freer or more politically advanced than Colombia and Latin America.

Far from appreciating Colombia's pioneering republicanism, American travelers mocked it. Their ridicule set the first stages of the tropicalization and nativization of local republican politics and the erasure of Panama's nineteenth-century political modernity. Travelers described "Black Republicans" as indolent and supine.[58] Even a sympathetic black writer like Mary Seacole could not help making fun of the fact that the "court house was a low bamboo shed" and that the mayor, "a negro, was reclining in a dirty hammock, smoking coolly, hearing evidence and pronouncing judgment."[59] When she wrote her book, tropical travel narratives had already taught a large reading public to associate thatched huts and tropical forests with primitiveness. Seacole knew that her readers would find this contradiction amusing and interesting.

Americans found it odd, if not ridiculous, that blacks thought of themselves as republican citizens of the nineteenth century. This language erased the important political innovations of the Republic of Colombia, reflected in the presence of black mayors. It also obscured the fact that abolition happened in Colombia more than a decade before it did in the United States and that black Panamanian citizens disapproved of the continuation of this practice among US travelers. Through ridicule, travelers managed to transform innovators into imitators. This was the first step toward the nativization of Panama's black citizens.

Finally, travelers and observers from abroad often transformed political conflicts and civil wars into examples of native backwardness through the use of tropical metaphors. According to Willis J. Abbot, "It would be idle to describe, even to enumerate, all the revolutions which have disquieted the Isthmus since it first joined Colombia in repudiating the Spanish rule. They have been as thick as insects in the jungle."[60] Abbot's metaphor tropicalized Panama's politics and made it one with its surrounding jungle. In his view, civil wars were caused by climate and race, not by the political differences over centralism and federalism, slavery, or church and state relations common to most nineteenth-century nations in the Americas, including the United States. Latin America had become a region where climate and race made political modernity a joke.

Empire and Gatún: Railroad Towns and Tenements of la Línea

Unlike Gorgona, Empire was not an old river town but a nineteenth-century railroad town. It was one of the largest towns located along the Panama Railroad—what contemporaries called "la Línea," or "the Line." During the French construction era, and even more during the

American one, la Línea became an area densely populated with towns along its forty-mile length. A Zone policeman described it in 1912 as "lined with villages of negroes and all breeds and colors of canal workers . . . Never a mile without its town."[61] The forty-one towns along la Línea had a combined population of 62,018, which was larger than that of Panama City.[62] The towns were densely populated, filled with tenement houses similar to the popular neighborhoods of Colón City and Panama City (see Map I.1).

Empire was the second largest of the la Línea towns. It was twenty-one kilometers from Panama City and sixty meters above sea level. As with Colón and other railroad towns of la Línea, the land of Empire was owned by the Panama Railroad, which laid out the lots and streets. Property owners possessed only their buildings; they had to rent their lots from the railroad.[63] During the French period of canal construction, the town grew in size and the arrival of many, mostly non-native, people fed the growth of an animated commercial life. Because of its importance, Empire became a municipality of the Republic of Colombia. According to Valdes's *Geography,* it already had 5,740 people in 1904.[64] In 1903, an American surveyor considered it the best place for a large permanent camp because of its high ground, natural drainage, and clean water supply from Camacho Creek. When American canal construction started, the French had already built in Empire houses for 4,000 men and many officers. Many of the "better houses" had shower baths. The town also had a large bathhouse with a swimming pool constructed of concrete and cement.[65]

Empire continued to grow during the American construction period and became the second largest town in the Zone. By the time of the Zone's 1912 census, the population of Empire had reached 7,152. Descriptions of the canal construction era suggest that Empire was a noisy industrial town, where immigrants from all over the world lived together in the local private tenements and in the ICC laborers' quarters. It was "the most cosmopolitan and thickly populated district" of the Zone.[66] It was the "metropolis of the Canal Zone."[67]

Like other Zone towns, Empire was divided between an American side and a "native side" (or "private owned town"). The former had the ICC buildings privileged by canal narratives and canal pictures. It was where the white American workers lived, and it also attracted many visitors to the Zone who wanted to see how Uncle Sam treated US citizens in the tropics. Most of the Zone's inhabitants, however, did not live there. They lived in private houses in Zone towns on the native side. It's hard to tell where the native side was located. According to *Policeman 88*, the native side of Empire was located behind the police station hill.[68] Empire consisted of thirty-one blocks divided into 547 lots, most of which were in old, or native, Empire: 444 lots divided into twenty-nine blocks. New Empire had only two blocks divided into 103 lots.[69] Each lot had at least one building, if not several. Descriptions of the era portray a lively, crowded, and cosmopolitan space.

Many private owners actively participated in the economic boom brought by canal construction and the arrival of thousands of new immigrants who needed food, clothing, entertainment, and lodging. For the entire construction period, these private businesses not only coexisted with commission commissaries, restaurants, and hotels but were also a central part of the Zone's economy and, as such, were taxed by the ICC. Walking around the streets of Empire, workers would see a lively business community that offered its services to the thousands of canal workers living along la Línea. In the streets of Empire workers could buy insurance, clothing, or hire a lawyer. Empire was important enough that one of Panama's three branches of Banca Moderna, from International Banking Corporation, was located there—the other branches were in Colón and Panama City.[70] Some people advertised their business during games or official parades. A 1913 picture of a baseball park shows advertisements for insurance from Henry Seymor's insurance and suits by Billy Evans. In Empire you could buy bread or other baked goods from small bakeries run by women.[71] You could also eat at one of the many small restaurants that catered to canal workers. These restaurants were the predecessors of contemporary Panama's omnipresent *fondas,* which serve office workers and manual laborers a daily menu of rice, meat, and soup. People selling their goods and services in native Empire belonged to all nationalities. There were Chinese merchants, smartly dressed in Western clothes, and Bengali peddlers. Local farmers sold their goods at the new public market built by the ICC. In many ways, Empire was a small version of Colón City.

Although elections were not allowed in the Zone, people in Empire found a way to show their political inclinations. Republican Chinese merchants wore the image of their new president on their lapels; anarchist Spaniards found the time to write, print, and publish a newspaper in Gatún and another in Miraflores. Probably inspired by the 1910 victory of Jack Johnson, who became the first black boxer to win the world heavyweight championship, West Indian workers hung pictures of famous black boxers on their walls.[72] These were years of great political change across the globe. A revolutionary movement had overthrown the emperor in China and declared a Republican government in 1911. W. E. B. Du Bois had organized the Niagara Conference in 1905 to demand an end to all forms of racial discrimination, and the Mexican revolution was in its first year in 1911. That year, Marcus Garvey had also arrived in Colón City, where he published a newspaper. One can only imagine the conversations among the many workers and merchants who came to Empire from all corners of the world.

Many buildings in native Empire were tenement houses. According to the description of a Zone policeman, "Tenements and wobbly-kneed shanties swarming . . . monopolized the landscape; strange the room that did not yield up at least a man and a woman and three or four children." Some tenements and houses were built three feet above ground, following the new sanitary regulations. Others were built earlier, during French canal construction or perhaps during the railroad period. Most workers lived in windowless rooms that measured six by eight feet. A calico curtain divided the room into two sections: a parlor in the front and a slightly larger bedroom in the back. They furnished their rooms with any furniture they could find or afford and enlivened their space by decorating the walls with pages from illustrated magazines. They cooked on a tin fireplace on the porch or veranda.[73]

Because the ICC thought Empire would be a permanent town, it erected many public buildings, carefully laid out streets, built a sewage system, opened public schools, and built a public market. Together these improvements represented US civilizing powers in the tropics. There were many social events and public activities: bands played on town squares, workers played in baseball leagues organized by the ICC, and churches of different denominations catered to the religious needs of local workers. Depending on their political taste or inclination, canal employees could join masonic lodges or anarchist groups.

If Empire was the largest town on the Pacific side of the Zone, Gatún was the largest town on the Atlantic side. Situated at the confluence of the Chagres and Gatún Rivers, Gatún was once a Spanish fort. Originally it was located on the western bank of the Chagres and became an important stop during the California Gold Rush. Later, the Panama Railroad Company built a Gatún station on the opposite shore of the river.[74] The town acquired some commercial relevance during the French construction years.[75] In 1908, canal authorities relocated the town to the east site, because the original site of Gatún would be used to build the Gatún locks.

The new town of Gatún grew to become the largest Zone town during the American construction period. It started off small, as a tent encampment that housed 500 gold and silver workers. In 1906, it had a total of 150 tents of different sizes, but most—134—were eight by ten. Gold workers also had access to a tent for shower baths. There was also a mule corral, two water towers, and a blacksmith shop. It soon became clear that a tent town was untenable. ICC officials knew that as the site of the Atlantic locks, Gatún would become one of the most important work sites of the canal. John F. Stevens, who was then the chief engineer, considered it necessary to start "work at Gatún as early as possible and with the largest force that can be used."[76] ICC officials also knew that the work would be difficult and dangerous and that attracting workers, always a difficult proposition, would be even more difficult without adequate housing. ICC officers worried that they would have to keep "throwing in new men every two weeks" because "on account of its being a tent camp the men will not remain there after their first pay day."[77] Keeping workers would be a challenge because the "West Indian is not particularly partial to tents. The rainfall at Gatún is excessive, and together with other disadvantages will tend to make Gatún a very undesirable point, at least for some months to come, to the average laborer."[78] They thought that the ICC should make it a priority to start building bachelor quarters in Gatún.[79]

With so many immigrants arriving to work on canal construction, providing housing, food, clothing, and entertainment for them became a source of great profit, and private investors began to build their own rental and tenement houses for the thousands of workers living in Gatún.[80] According to the ICC's chief sanitary officer, a house containing twenty-eight rooms yielded an income of $100 to $200 per month. He also calculated that one year of rent returned to owners 50 percent of their original investment.[81] One tenement house after the other was built in Zone towns, the majority of them in Gatún and Empire. Members of Panama's elite participated actively in this business, but they were not the only ones. A 1914 list of property owners in Gatún shows that established Panamanians, as well as newer immigrants, had invested in tenement houses and businesses.[82] Clearly standing out among property owners are those who had the largest number of rooms. Ricardo Arias owned seven buildings, with a total of 109 rooms, or an average of 15.5 rooms per building. The Toledano family owned five buildings, with a total of 111 rooms; Frank Ulrich owned only two buildings, but one of them had a total of fifty rooms while the other, probably a house, had only four. The Stilson family owned eight buildings with a total of sixty-five rooms. Many small-scale owners of different national origins also owned one or two buildings ranging from one to twelve rooms each.[83]

Industrialization in the Tropics

Since the times of French canal construction, Empire and Gorgona had been the industrial centers of the Zone. Centrally located between the work sites on the Pacific and the Atlantic sides of the canal, they provided an ideal place to repair the steam shovels and other machinery used for canal construction. In 1912, an American census enumerator described Gorgona as "the Pittsburgh of the Zone with its acres of machine-shops."[84] In Empire, the ICC had greatly expanded and modernized its old French repair shops, and it was the town's role as a machinery shop that led to its growth. Its landscape was dominated by these shops, which consisted of thirteen new buildings with approximately 160,000 square feet of floor space. These shops could repair any of the 101 steel steam shovels—of three sizes and two makes—and the steel cars of the canal (see Figure 2.1). The noise and smell of these shops

FIGURE 2.1 A general view of shops in Empire
Credit: National Archives photo no. 271 C.

must have been a characteristic of the everyday life of Empire's town
dwellers and workers. The distinct sound of this town was probably
the noise of the machinery of the repair shops mixed with the many
languages and accents of its workers.[85]

Zone periodicals, like the *Panama Canal Record,* proudly commented
that Empire's shops were "equal to any similarly equipped shops in the
United States," and that the skills of its 361 mechanics were "first class."
However, despite its celebration of the shops' technology, the *Panama
Canal Record* continued the nineteenth-century tradition of considering
the tropics incompatible with technological modernity. The efficiency
of the American mechanics "was a trifle lower than that of a similar
force in the States, due to the general decrease in effectiveness that
results from residence in the tropics." The 570 Spanish and West Indian mechanics who worked in the shops were not even given the

title of mechanics, but were merely called "helpers." The *Record* also alleged that they suffered from the same tropical malaise as their American counterparts: "their efficiency is likewise lower than that of men of the same class in the States."[86] As with the *bogas* before them, the skilled labor of the black workers of the Panama Canal was not fully acknowledged or recognized. Their location in the tropics made them inferior to the industrial machinery with which they worked and that often maimed their bodies.

Similarly, the technology that was so completely altering Panama's landscape by damming its rivers and digging up its land did not completely fit in a tropical landscape. One picture of the canal after the other taught the general public that modern canal machinery was incongruous with the tropics. Photographs of canal machinery conveyed two general messages. The first was to show the size and scale of the project with images of the canal's giant shovels, giant dams, giant locks, as well as the tons of land dug up. These photographs demonstrated US technological might as an engineering colossus and justified the claim that the canal was one of the seven marvels of the modern world.[87] The second message was to highlight the contrast between modern machinery and the surrounding tropical jungle. This was done in two ways: first by portraying the struggle between tropical nature and modern technology with pictures of industrial machinery covered by tropical jungle, and second, by contrasting the modernity of US machines and towns with pictures of Panama's natives standing next to their primitive thatched huts. These photographs usually depicted the natives alone in the middle of the jungle.[88] In this way, they provided the illusion that Panamanian natives were isolated from the canal's technological environment even if they lived next to it and participated in its construction and economy. The huts were also intimately linked to the canal. They were the houses of towns that had served isthmian traffic, first as river towns and later as railroad towns. Moreover, their construction changed over time and adapted to the cost and availability of new materials. By the time canal construction got under way, many had been replaced by clapboard houses with corrugated roofs.

The contrast between the tropical jungle and canal technology enhanced the wonder of canal construction. The glory of building the canal was largely based on the alleged feat of conquering tropical nature and its dangers. This ideology had important implications for the tropical spaces and peoples that were part of it. Panama and Panamanians did not become members of a shared technological modernity; the Zone was only an outpost of US technology in the tropics. The "native" workers and "native" landscapes continued to be part of the jungle. Even though the people of the Zone were participating in canal construction and dying of industrial accidents, they never quite became members of the age of steel they helped create.

There is something perverse about the idea that nineteenth- and twentieth-century technology seems natural in the North Atlantic countries and out of place in the countries of the South Atlantic. It robs tropical spaces and their peoples of their historical connection to technologies that greatly altered their landscapes and dramatically affected their lives. Telegraphs, steam-powered machines, railroads, pesticides, and fertilizers were part of the everyday life of the inhabitants of Central America, yet they remained other peoples' technology. This way of imagining the world puts tropical people outside of their historical times and locates them in some atemporal native time. For them, the acquisition of modern technology is always something that will happen later. This is particularly surprising given that the history of Panama—and other Latin American countries—has been intimately connected to the history of European technology since the Spanish conquest of the Americas. But one of the powers of the rhetoric of tropicality is its

FIGURE 2.2 A worker at the Panama Canal during the French construction period
Credit: Panama Canal Authority, Image Brochard-25, Biblioteca Roberto F. Chiari.

ability to erase the history of tropical peoples. If the goal of creating "modern democracies" erased almost 100 years of republican politics, the goal of bringing technology to the jungle erased the modernity of the people who had built the Panama Railroad in the 1850s and contributed to French efforts in the 1880s (see Figure 2.2).

Agriculture in the Tropics

Just as nineteenth-century travelers could not see Panama's black republican citizens as members of a shared nineteenth-century political culture, they could not see tropical agriculture as equal to the agriculture of temperate zones. Sometimes, they could not even see it as agriculture. Even a long-time foreign resident like Tracy Robinson could describe local farmers as "stray nomads of the colored race, who have established squatter sovereignty here and there."[89] As far as he was concerned, Panama had no agriculture "as the term is understood at the north and in Europe. . . . Neither in the manner of doing it, nor the extent to which it is done deserve the name."[90] Any potential that Panama might have had for agriculture was only a thing of the future.

Why did Robinson have such a bleak view of Panama's agriculture? For him, as for many other observers, agriculture fell into two categories: it was either the European-style agriculture with which they were familiar, or large-scale tropical plantations. And Panama had neither. Panamanian farmers were neither small European farmers nor large plantation owners; they worked small and medium-sized farms in the tropics. They could have been praised for fulfilling Jefferson's ideal of a republic composed of small farmers, but Panamanian farmers could not be described in this way.[91] When local farmers cultivated export products, Robinson criticized them for not doing it on the right scale. Panama did not have "large states for the growing of any kind of produce, such as sugar, coffee, cacao, or any of the numerous tropical fruits—not even bananas." They were grown "almost entirely by small planters, who [would] rarely have more than ten acres each in cultivation."[92] And when farmers cultivated food staples for local consumption, they did not count as agriculture because they were not European products, and they were not cultivated in the appropriate manner. Tropical products for local food consumption were scorned as the "bill of fare" of black people.[93] Once the types of cultivation undertaken by Panamanian farmers were deemed inappropriate, it was easy to come to the conclusion that Panama had no agriculture.

Of what, then, consisted the agriculture of the isthmian corridor that Robinson so despised? As the most densely populated area of the country, and one close to its main urban centers, the towns of the Zone

FIGURE 2.3 Farmers of the Chagres River
Credit: Published by the American News Company. Reproduced from the author's collection.

had a rich agricultural history that went back to pre-conquest times. The traditional farming areas of the isthmian corridor were located on margins of the Chagres and the Río Grande Rivers (see Figure 2.3). They were the lands of many haciendas, some of which dated back to Spanish colonial times. Here most farmers were the tenants of large hacienda owners. In the mid-nineteenth century, a new agricultural region developed along the tracks of the Panama Railroad, particularly near the new railroad town of Empire. This was not an area of large haciendas but rather one of small and medium-sized farms. In both historic regions farmers combined small-scale cattle ranching with the cultivation of export crops like bananas and coffee and the cultivation of fruits, roots, grains, and vegetables for local markets, as well as the cultivation and processing of sugarcane for *aguardiente* (firewater).[94] In 1894, for example, Buena Vista, one of the districts on the Chagres River, exported 22,000 bunches of bananas, and its six distilleries produced *aguardiente* of "good quality," some to be consumed locally and some to be exported to Colón City.[95]

Unlike other rural areas of Panama, the Zone did not have large cattle ranches.[96] Moreover, large plantations did not seem to be the norm there. Most of the banana cultivation was done by small farmers who sold their product to American companies—like Frank Brothers and Aspinwall Fruit—that controlled the export of local bananas. There were a handful of plantations in the Zone. One was the Las Cascadas Plantation Company, which had 1,500 hectares of land planted with 61,485 rubber trees, 40,000 coffee trees, and 69,794 cacao trees.[97]

Far from being isolated in jungle huts, the farmers of the Chagres River had a long history of supplying food to travelers crossing the isthmus, a fact travelers often mentioned in their accounts, if only to complain about the high prices they had to pay. Crossing Panama in 1823, Mollien missed the hospitality of the Andean people and denounced what he saw as the greed of local people on the isthmian route. Chickens, water, and wood were all too expensive.[98] Writing in 1843 for the British Steamship Company, William Wheelwright also described how people in the river towns along the Chagres took economic advantage of the route by selling fowl, eggs, and fruit to travelers.[99] Isthmian farmers might have also sold some of their products to the steamers traveling from South America to California. Captain Pierson of the steamer *Oregon* recalled in his memoirs that in the late 1840s, he "could get salt beef, jerked beef, hard bread, beans, and rice" in Panama.[100] After the construction of the Panama Railroad, local farmers began to peddle fruit to passengers during their brief train stops. A few minutes to sell fruit was all that was left of a 300-year-old tradition of selling provisions to travelers forced to spend several days crossing the isthmus. But with the loss of this market, a new one emerged in the new railroad port of Colón. By the late nineteenth century, farmers along the Chagres River and its tributaries—Gatún, Gatuncillo, and Trinidad—were increasingly cultivating for the market of Colón City, using the river to transport their products because the railroad was too expensive.[101]

The farmers of the isthmian route came from different parts of the world. Many immigrants who came to work on the French canal project in the 1880s remained as farmers after the project failed. The large majority of these immigrant farmers were from the West Indies, but there were also Chinese farmers and farmers from other regions of Colombia. A typical contract sale around Empire tells us something about the multinational composition of these farmers. In 1888, Antonio Maestre, residing in Empire but originally from Cartagena, sold his 300-by-800-meter farm plot with eight heads of cattle, three horses, and several types of poultry to another Empire resident, also from Cartagena, for 2,000 pesos. One of his neighbors was a Chinese farmer.[102]

According to Tracy Robinson, immigrants had "changed the appearance of the country through which the railroad passes."[103] Indeed, they had. Neither isolated nor traditional, the farmers of this region were constantly innovating. Inventories of farms in the region around Empire show different types of improvements. One of them was the farming of imported grass—mostly Para and Guinea grass—for cattle forage, whose cultivation increased in the late nineteenth century. According to an 1895 testament, an "artificial grass" farm *(huerta de hierba artificial)* included a cartwheel to haul grass, four horses and two mules to carry grass, three small machetes *(espadines)* for cutting grass, and two straight hoes *(coas)*.[104] Barbed-wire fencing was another innovation common at small and medium-sized farms. It is remarkable how fast barbed-wire fencing spread among Panamanian farmers. Barbed wire was only patented in the 1870s, but by the 1880s it was frequently mentioned in the sale records of the farms located around Empire. But perhaps it should not be surprising that in a region so well connected to global trade, traffic, and technology, barbed-wire fencing was spreading at the same time as it was among US farmers.[105] Finally, the production of *aguardiente,* another important product of the region, had also undergone modernization. Farmers who processed sugarcane into *aguardiente* often used various types of distilleries, or *alambiques*—some imported, some local. Indeed, a government report of the area between Colón and Panama City shows the presence of many types of distilleries: "American," "French," "modern French," "steam," "Comin," "simple," and finally "made in the country."[106]

Another important aspect of the farm inventories of the Zone is that they allow us to understand some of the characteristics of the Panamanian diet at the turn of the century, one that Zone administrators considered unsuitable to the palate of "the better class of Americans."[107] The 1913 inventory of the farm of Anasario Martínez is a good example. Located on the margins of the Bailamonos River in the district of Gorgona, Martínez's farm included four thatched houses (two large and two small), three cows, and three horses. Martínez sold his products in the nearby markets of Gorgona and Matachin. Especially notable about the farm is its cultivation of a wide variety of fruits, staples, and vegetables, some of which are still typical Panamanian fare. This medium-sized farm had 12 different types of fruit trees, which show the important role that fruit played in Panama's diet. It had 200 banana trees, 10 pineapple plants, 117 orange trees, 15 mango trees, 10 avocado trees, 9 guava trees, 8 cashew trees, 1 mamei tree, 4 caimito trees, 7 lime trees, 2 lemon trees, and 3 soursop trees. Martínez also cultivated various types of roots, grains, and vegetables. His farm had 2 pixbae trees, 15,000 yucca plants, 9 calabash trees, and an unspecified quantity of corn and rice, as well as other vegetables. Martínez's farm also had 150 coffee trees.[108]

Like many farmers of the region, Martínez did not specialize in one or two products, but preferred to cultivate a large variety of foods. This custom allowed farmers to diversify their risks. If prices fell on one product, they might be able to recover their loss with another one. The same was true of plant diseases, which caused less damage on farms dedicated to several products than on large plantations.[109] Although farms like that of Anasario Martínez probably played a role in feeding the workforce and the population of the Canal Zone during the construction period, the importance of local farmers was never acknowledged among canal officials, who continually repeated statements like, "Natives never look beyond their present necessities, no surplus food supply ever accumulates."[110]

Canal administrators never considered local fruits and vegetables as equivalent to those of the temperate zones and went to great efforts to feed white Americans the fruits and vegetables to which they were accustomed. Thanks to new refrigeration technology they were able to do something that neither the French nor the Americans who built the Panama Railroad could do: keep their diet by importing food from 2,000 miles away. By 1905 the Zone government had created an impressive import chain that included steamers equipped with refrigerated plants, refrigerator cars, and cold-storage plants that connected the markets of the United States to the stores of the Zone.[111] By 1909, Zone commissaries included cooling rooms that consisted of a "freezing room for poultry, and articles that must be carried at low temperature; chilled rooms for meats and a vegetable cooling room."[112]

Of course, it is common for any immigrant group to try to keep their dietary habits to the extent possible. And the problem of feeding the large workforce of the Zone was not trivial. The agriculture of a country with a population of around 300,000 people could not easily feed a sudden influx of tens of thousands of immigrants, particularly when the quarantine measures against the bubonic plague closed the Port of Panama to the usual shipping of provisions from neighboring provinces.[113] Moreover, as administrators complained, the relatively high wages paid for canal work led many agricultural workers to abandon their farms.[114] This was not the entire story, however. What stands out in the descriptions of US observers, administrators, and agricultural experts is their inability to see any connection between Zone peasants and the commercial and technological history of the route. Instead of trying to understand or explain how local peasants had adapted to their region's historic role as an international hub, they insisted on portraying Zone agriculture as "most primitive and transient."[115]

Racial ideas about black tropical people played a crucial role in the US understanding of Zone agriculture as primitive agriculture, even among experts. The weight of ideas about tropical peasants becomes very clear in a little booklet written by two experts from the US Department of Agriculture, Hugh H. Bennett and William A. Taylor, who traveled to Panama for a little more than a month to examine the Zone's agricultural characteristics and possibilities.[116] For them, the land in the Zone was "largely unused," a surprising characterization of the most densely populated and most traveled region of Panama. They described it this way not because they did not notice the peasants who lived there; on the contrary, they gave detailed descriptions of local practices. They considered the land unused because in their view it was the "most primitive patch of agriculture." And they could not think of anything "primitive" as a valid form of agriculture.

Americans of Bennett and Taylor's era had clear ideas about the distinctions between primitive and civilized agriculture, ideas that they understood as unquestionable inherited truths. One important element that separated primitive from non-primitive agriculture was the use of the plow. This notion was so common that an obscure 1870 agricultural report by the Maine Board of Agriculture could say, without hesitation, that "the plow lies at the foundation of all wealth and of all civilization." The plow signified progress. The progress of a society was closely connected to the mechanical construction of the plow. In "barbarous countries, where no vestige of civilization or of progress can be traced," no furrows or plows could be observed.[117] Thus, for agricultural specialists like Bennett and Taylor the absence of the plow in a place where "plowing is never attempted" only confirmed the backwardness of the area and would lead them to conclude that "cultural methods by the natives are most primitive." A lack of fertilizer use, except among Chinese immigrants who used night soil, was another trait that characterized local agriculture as primitive.[118]

Order—or lack thereof—was yet another crucial distinction between civilized and primitive agriculture.[119] Turn-of-the-century agricultural experts thought of civilized agriculture as orderly agriculture, and they were disturbed by the fact that in Panama there was "no semblance of regularity" in the field distribution of peasants' plots. For them, lack of regularity proved that local agriculture was effortless and involved little, if any, labor. And lack of labor was another characteristic that separated primitive agriculture from civilized agriculture.[120] By the late nineteenth century, the idea that tropical forests were so fertile that they required little labor and encouraged the natural indolence of tropical people was so popular that it had reached the writings of famous novelists like Emilio Salgari and Jules Verne. When Bennett and Taylor described Panamanian tropical crops that were "planted and thereafter allowed to care for themselves," they only reinforced ideas that were already popular.[121] And when they wrote about a Panamanian rural scene of a "dwelling, usually a palm-thatched shack . . . hidden from view by a luxuriant tangle of tropical fruits, vegetables, and ornamentals, such as papayas, chayotes, bananas, yams, sugar cane, roselle, antigonon," they were sharing with their readers common ideas that associated a palm-thatched dwelling with fertile, disorderly tropics that required little work from local inhabitants.[122] They saw the lives of tropical peasants as effortless, closer to that of animals in the jungle than to the lives of northern peasants. In a moment when human effort and ingenuity were what defined civilization, Bennett and Taylor helped set tropical peasants apart from their historical times by confining them to an eternal jungle time.

Within the descriptions of Bennett and Taylor, however, it is possible to see another story. They were, after all, agricultural experts who paid close attention to detail. And in these details, we can see the sophisticated ways in which local tropical agriculture had adapted to its environment. Hidden in their descriptions of luxuriant tangles of tropical fruits are patterns of cultivation and hard work. They explained how soil preparation "thoroughly by hand tools" varied "according to the nature of the plant." Depth could reach from eighteen inches to three feet and areas from "from a few square feet to 1 or 2 square yards." They also noted peasants' knowledge about which plants to cultivate together—corn and cassava and yams; taniers and eddo—and which plants to cultivate apart—sugarcane, pigeon pea. They also noted the tradition of having different plots depending on the amount of labor that plants required. Staples that required less weeding were planted in one place, and vegetable gardens that required more work were planted "near shack dwellings," where they were "carefully tended" and "grubbed free of wild plantain and other persistent vegetation to permit the planting of peppers, beans, chayotes, granadillas, roselle, and other garden vegetables and fruits, less tolerant of crowding by other vegetation than the staple roots."[123] Following the expected portrayal of the Zone as a primitive jungle, they described the difficulties of traveling on narrow, steep, and muddy local trails, only to add later that "natives make surprisingly rapid progress over these difficult trails either afoot or on horseback." Finally, Bennett and Taylor noticed how the "native method of migratory farming . . . has held erosion injury down to a minimum."[124]

Bennett and Taylor's writing frequently criticizes "primitive" practices only to later recognize their advantages without giving local peasants any credit for their ingenuity. Through the use of words like *except* and *accidental* they could observe sophisticated agricultural practices and present them as mere natural accidents. For example, after describing how peasants did not have to work cultivating plants that cared for themselves, they would add *"except* for occasional cutting down of weeds" (emphasis added). Anybody who has done the most basic form of gardening knows that there is nothing easy about weeding and that weeding is the exact opposite of letting plants fend for themselves. But the word *except* permitted them to observe the work and dismiss it at the same time. Similarly, they wrote that "no attention is given to crop rotation" to maintain soil condition, only to add that "the growing together of crops maturing or attaining proper development for harvesting, at different times, under the native plan of agriculture, amounts to a *sort of accidental rotation*" (emphasis added).[125] The word *accidental* dismisses established practices of tropical agriculture to convey the image of agriculture that is as natural and disorderly as the tropical forest. After decrying the area's lack of plowing, they recognized that "a large portion of the arable land is entirely too steep to be plowed." But plowing "does not seem to be especially necessary for many root crops and fruit trees, such as cassava, yams, mangoes, which apparently find suitable environment wherever the soil has been prepared thoroughly by hand tools."[126] It should have been clear that in a region crossed by a railroad, where barbed wire and steam power were part of the environment, if peasants did not use the plow it was not because they did not know about it, but because they chose not to use it based on the nature of their environment.

But how much did Zone peasants produce? Bennett and Taylor spent more time complaining about the character of the "native"—"an independent person who is not always ready to work, even for the best of wages"—than explaining what the independent peasant produced. They lamented that the local peasant found contentment "upon his small clearing in the midst of sufficient fruits and vegetables to meet the food requirements of his family, with a small surplus for providing the few additional wants."[127] Would Bennett and Taylor have said the same things of northern peasants who preferred to work their own farms rather than those of others? Probably not, because 400 years of Atlantic slavery had solidified the idea that the natural place for black farmers was working for others.[128]

Perhaps it is for this reason that the language about the actual agricultural productivity of the Zone is the most ambiguous of all. It is clear from nineteenth-century reports that the French canal project had led to increased cultivation in the Zone. Was this also true of US construction there? The thousands of claims that peasants made to obtain compensation after the 1912 depopulation order and the inventories of their farms suggest it is true. One sentence in Bennett and Taylor's report even acknowledged that "the total product of these small mixed plantings . . . is considerable."[129] Moreover, when Bennett and Taylor wrote about the crops that could be grown in the Zone and even become palatable to US consumers, they relied on their observations of local peasants' production—a fact that they never acknowledged.[130] The overriding message of their reporting was that the agricultural productivity of the Zone left much to be desired. Even when they made concrete observations about specific products, like oranges, their language remained ambiguous; they were unwilling to recognize any productivity. For example, while they mentioned the presence of "several well-fruited [orange] trees . . . at a number of points within the Canal Zone," they immediately added that "little or no attempt has been made to develop orange growing as an industry."[131] But they never explained what "several well-fruited trees" means, nor how many more would be needed to constitute "an industry." For a scientific report, these are remarkably vague statements. Or perhaps not, because to provide actual details of food production would have altered the narrative of the Zone as an area of primitive tropical agriculture that needed US intervention to become modern. Eventually, what carried weight with other Zone officials were Bennett and Taylor's conclusions, not their detailed observations. It was their conclusion that Zone agriculture was "low quality and incapable of maintaining other than very primitive standards of living," a sentiment that would be repeated in future reports.[132]

The erasure of Panamanian agriculture was powerful enough that newspapers such as the *Canal Record* and *La Estrella de Panamá* could transform what had been an old Panamanian farm into a brand-new American improvement. After reading the news, the original Panamanian owner wrote indignantly to the newspaper to clarify the facts. He said: "your newspaper . . . presents the agricultural farm of Corozal as if it were a farm of the Isthmian Canal Commission." He wanted to clarify that these lands "are the same lands that I have farmed for nineteen years and that now are said to belong to the Panama Railroad Company. The banana trees, the cattle farms planted with artificial grass [*sic*], the buildings, the *galeras,* the barbed-wire fences, and other improvements are the fruit of nineteen years of honest work. All of which was recently taken away from me by the Zone's attorney Frank Feuille, who gave it right away to the employees in charge of the new agricultural farm without giving any compensation to its legitimate owner."[133]

Assessments that characterized Zone agriculture as primitive or nonexistent erased the connection between Panamanian peasants and their nineteenth-century history and technology in the same way that ideas about black tropical people had erased the membership of black Panamanian citizens in the political history of the nineteenth century. Just as black tropical republicans were not real republicans and black tropical workers were not true members of the Age of Steel, black tropical peasants were not real peasants and their agriculture was not true agriculture. While canal narratives emphasized the triumph of modern American engineering and medicine, the people of Gorgona and other towns along the route were never part of that story.[134] Quite the opposite: they were the tropical obstacles that American ingenuity had to overcome to successfully build the canal. The people of Gorgona and other towns around the canal were rhetorically stripped of their nineteenth-century political and economic modernity to fit with preconceived ideas about the primitiveness of tropical black people.[135] These ideas would have long-term effects, as they facilitated the decision to depopulate the Zone and made that process appear less dramatic than it was. If the deep historical connections between Zone inhabitants and their region had been acknowledged, the decision to depopulate would have been much harder to justify.[136]

3

A New Regime for Old Zone Towns

Picturing the Zone

A TYPICAL PHOTOGRAPH OF Zone towns during the construction era showed government buildings like the post office, the hospital, the police station, or the gold-white American bachelor quarters (see Figure 3.1). It would depict carefully screened frame buildings—built three feet above the ground and surrounded by trimmed grass—and graded streets free of mud. Pictures of the interiors portrayed a comfortable environment in which men and women dressed in summer clothing did their work while sitting in stylish mission furniture.

These pictures represented the US government's mastery of tropical nature and its ability to protect its citizens from its dangers. There might be disease-carrying mosquitoes, but the buildings are carefully screened. It might be hot, but the comfortable, screened verandas provide breezes and respite; there might be mud, but the wide and carefully graded streets help deter its formation. Perhaps the surrounding jungle is dangerous, and local politics disorderly, but this town is a space of order, sanitation, and comfort. The photographs seem like a natural prelude to the permanent construction of Zone towns and their

FIGURE 3.1 The police station in Empire
Credit: National Archives photo no. 308 B.

future image as pristine and manicured suburbs, where the US federal government provided for the wants and needs of all inhabitants. Throughout most of the Zone's existence, visitors and locals marveled at the lack of private businesses and properties; in the Zone the US government owned all the land and all the houses, and owned and managed all private businesses. Stores, movie theaters, and supermarkets were all in its hands.

What the pictures of neatly painted and screened government buildings do not show—or show only as a blurry background—is that next to this small, manicured American urban space was a larger and older local town or "native village." The images hide the fact that during the initial years of the Zone, the towns within it experienced a vibrant economic boom as a result of canal construction. Far from curtailing or forbidding private enterprise in the Zone, the ICC sought to take advantage of it by taxing businesses and properties. It is now forgotten that until 1911, people of all walks of life in the Zone thought that towns like Empire and Gatún would be permanent settlements with flourishing businesses, and that the Zone would remain one of the most densely populated and economically vibrant regions of Panama. For example, in 1907, the general manager of the Panama Railroad Company not only considered Empire to be "one of our principal towns" but also thought that it "will remain as a permanent village after the Canal is completed."[1] Indeed, in 1907 the towns of Empire and Gatún were experiencing a veritable boom as many Panamanians and other non-Americans—or "natives"—were trying to benefit from the construction boom. Zone authorities were getting "so many requests of building lots for the natives" that they considered "the matter of building native houses" pressing "at almost all the native towns in the Zone."[2]

Why were private properties and local—"native"—towns excluded from the official pictures of the ICC and the majority of postcards of the period? Why do iconic images of the Zone during the construction period only portray industrial images of canal construction, or urban images of the small American section of Zone towns? Why have local towns and private houses and businesses been so utterly erased from the visual record of this period? Perhaps it is because they reflected the internal contradictions of the US goal to bring civilization to the jungle. They would have shown that local towns were neither exotic nor "traditional." They had private businesses and middle-class houses, as well as many shacks and tenement houses. Far from being isolated in the middle of the jungle, local towns represented the messy urban realities of an industrial setting with thousands of new immigrant workers. With their dirty and crowded tenement houses, the towns of the Zone were more similar to the New York City or Chicago tenements that Progressive Era reformers were trying to eradicate. Like the tenement rows in New York City, local towns in the Zone reflected the contradictions of early twentieth-century capitalism and its ability to create enormous wealth alongside great poverty and social disruption.

Nor did official images of local towns show the ICC's inability to control and regulate the Zone and to create a model of tropical civilization in Central America during the construction period. Eventually, the ICC would achieve the goal of creating an ideal urban space in the tropics, but this happened only after the expulsion of three-quarters of the Zone's population and the eradication of all its historic Panamanian towns. Putting the "native" Panamanian towns back in the picture is necessary for understanding the process that led to the 1912 depopulation order. Like life in Zone towns, the decision to depopulate was itself messy and did not follow a clear path. Between 1904 and 1915 the Zone went through three main periods. During the first period (1904–1907), Zone authorities kept the old Panamanian municipal structure in the Zone. Zone towns had both Panamanian and American mayors. During the second period (1907–1912), the ICC eliminated the Zone municipalities, which became administrative districts, but most towns remained in their original locations and the inhabitants of the Zone were allowed to keep their properties. Between 1912 and 1915, the

ICC depopulated the Zone, eliminated its old towns, and replaced them with a new urban geography. This chapter discusses the first two periods.

During most of the canal construction period, the ICC struggled to make local towns conform to its urban and sanitary ideals. The story of its attempts to regulate and organize the old "native" towns of the Zone is important for understanding a crucial period of the Panama Canal's history, when both Zone authorities and Panamanians thought that many of the original Panamanian towns of the Zone would remain as permanent towns. The ICC's failure to regulate and order Zone towns is a crucial part of the story that led to the 1912 depopulation order.

The Municipal Experiment, 1904–1907

Between 1904 and 1907, Panamanian municipalities became American municipalities. This was an interesting moment of experimentation in Zone government, when some US officials thought they could create "a model of American Government in the heart of Central America as an object lesson to the South and Central American republics."[3] Yet transforming the Zone into an "object lesson" of modern government for other republics required two important cultural assumptions: first, that Spanish-American republics needed lessons in government, and second, that their republican systems were not modern. It required a rhetorical erasure of Panama's modernity. The words of Theodore P. Shonts, the second chairman of the ICC, provide a perfect example of this rhetoric. According to him, in Panama "conditions approximating modern development had to be brought into existence in a tropical wilderness." The United States had to create "a modern state in a ten by fifty mile stretch of tropical wilderness, scourged by deadly fevers and pestilence, and practically uninhabitable by natives of other climes."[4]

Rhetoric did not match reality. It rarely does. But it did shape how people understood this reality and the decisions they made. The most populated region of Panama had been rhetorically transformed into a tropical wilderness in need of help and intervention to become a "modern state." With those words Shonts erased the evidence of nineteenth-century technological and political modernity in the Zone. The bringing-modernity-to-the-wilderness rhetoric glorified US work in Panama in ways that would not have been possible if the ICC had stated that the United States was merely building a canal next to a railroad line and was creating municipalities where they had already existed for a long time. This rhetoric allowed US officials to present any technical intervention as progress. Perhaps most importantly, the rhetoric made local urban history seem superfluous, because that history, the municipalities, and roots of republicanism were never considered real, contradicting as they did entrenched ideas about the tropics and its peoples.

Because the Zone already had a municipal system under the government of Colombia, the initial years of transition were complicated. Panamanian public employees in the Zone stopped working as employees of their government on June 16, 1904, when "the districts of the railroad line where they function" were "separated out of the national territory." The cession of Zone territory to the United States opened many questions about the nature of this transition. What would happen to the lawsuits pending in the municipal courts of Zone towns? Would they be ruled by Panamanian courts or by American ones? How would these towns participate in Panama's elections? Because the Zone was one of the most densely populated areas on the isthmus, the answer to these questions had important economic, legal, and political implications.

The men who first came to govern the Zone and build the canal brought with them their experiences in the Philippines, Cuba, and Puerto Rico. The first two governors of the Zone, George Davis and Charles Magoon, had worked in Puerto Rico and the Philippines, while the Zone's chief sanitary officer, William C. Gorgas, had been in charge of the campaign against yellow fever in Havana. They saw the Zone as another US territory and considered it part of their duty to govern its Panamanian towns and peoples. It is not surprising that one of their first political acts was to organize municipalities in the Zone. There were five altogether. Three of them—Gorgona, Buena Vista, and Emperador—had already existed under the government of Colombia. The Zone government eliminated one Panamanian municipality, Gatún, by incorporating it into Buena Vista. The two other municipalities—Ancón and Cristobal—were new. Just as Zone authorities had carved the Port of Ancón out of the Port of Panama and the Port of Cristobal from the Port of Colón, they carved the municipality of Ancón out of the municipality of Panama City and the municipality of Cristobal out of Colón City. Magoon, who was the governor when the Zone municipalities were established, came to Panama with years of experience in the law and government of US territories. In 1899, he had worked as a law officer for the Bureau of Insular Affairs, where he was responsible for interpreting the jurisprudence of the Philippines, Cuba, and Puerto Rico and reconciling Spanish and American law. His thinking is encapsulated in his book *The Law of Civil Government under Military Occupation*. He was the perfect governor to organize the municipalities of the Zone.

The United States' initial response to the transfer of Panamanian towns to US authority was to recognize the "temporary authority of *alcaldes,"* or mayors, to continue to exercise their judicial functions until the ICC reorganized the Zone's municipal courts.[5] At first, the ICC gave the Zone municipalities extensive rights, often comparable to those of the Zone government. For example, in August 1904 municipalities had ample rights to expropriate private property for "works of public utility."[6] In September 1904, a new act set the boundaries for and organized the municipal government of the Zone.[7]

The September 1904 Municipal Government Act provides a window into how American authorities imagined the present and the future of the Zone during their first year of rule.[8] The act was written and prepared with a long-term perspective at a time when few, if any, members of the ICC thought that the entire municipal organization would end only three years later. One thing the act indicates is that ICC officials imagined that the Zone would continue to be a place where the majority of the population would be Panamanian and both English and Spanish would be official languages. The new laws required all municipal officers "to be able to intelligently speak, read, and write the Spanish or English language" and "to be at least 25 years old" and "a resident of the municipality." There were no citizenship requirements, nor was it necessary to be fluent in English. As in other US territories, the organization of the municipalities incorporated local elites into the government. Of the five municipalities in the Zone, only Cristobal had an American mayor. The other four had Panamanian mayors.[9] Significantly, the mayor chosen for Ancón, which was the most important municipality of the Zone, was a Panamanian named Rafael Neira, and he was in charge of supervising all the other municipalities. His salary was $100 per month, which was less than the $150 earned by the US mayor of Cristobal but more than the salary of the other Panamanian mayors. Neira's brief tenure was a short but significant moment in the history of the Zone when US and Panamanian municipal traditions came together under a mayor who defended the rights and autonomy of Zone municipalities as the "universal statutes of municipal legislations" to which US and Panamanian municipalities were heirs.[10] Neira was the son of a prestigious Colombian family—his father had been president of the State of Panama in 1872—and was fluent in English and Spanish. Neira's correspondence reveals a deep familiarity with US and Colombian / Panamanian customs and laws. He was the ideal person to lead a municipal structure in which both Panamanian and American authorities would govern over the multinational inhabitants of the Zone.

The municipal laws also show that the ICC initially thought that Zone municipalities would be urban spaces not too different from the towns and cities in Panama. And their economies and populations would grow and flourish. Like other American municipalities, those of the Zone had the power to issue municipal bonds. They were responsible for keeping a civil registry. Municipalities also had to "establish or authorize the establishment of slaughter houses and markets" (Ancón had a project for a market) and to "establish and maintain schools and erect schoolhouses" (see Figure 3.2). The laws also assumed that private businesses would continue to flourish in the area. US authorities in Panama had not yet imagined a Zone that looked like a company town and had only company stores. Municipalities were to tax and control expenditures on alcohol. They were expected to license, regulate, or prohibit "cock fighting . . . public carriages, cabs, carts, drays, stages, hearses, and conveyances kept for hire, cafes, restaurants, cantinas, hotels, inns and lodging houses, peddlers, hucksters, auctioneers and auction sales, billiard tables, nine-pin alleys, horse races, public dance houses, theatrical and like amusements."[11]

There were no elections in Zone municipalities. The municipal officers, including the mayor, were chosen by the governor and paid by

FIGURE 3.2 A native market at Empire in the Canal Zone in 1905
Credit: National Archives photo no. 302 A5.

the Zone government. The municipal council had to keep its regular sessions open to the public. Yet Zone municipalities retained some aspect of political life. The Zone had not yet become a space where urban issues were solely approached as technical problems to be solved by experts. In 1904, the municipalities of the Zone had functions that would later become the responsibility of the ICC. They had to defend order and the public peace and quell riots and disturbances; they were responsible for safeguarding public health and providing for the ornamentation of Zone towns. Local taxes on private property were to provide the funds to fulfill municipal obligations like the repair and maintenance of bridges, sidewalks, streets, highways, and parks" and "fire

FIGURE 3.3 Fifth Street, Gorgona, Canal Zone
Credit: I. L. Maduro Jr. Reproduced from the author's collection.

protection." Saloons were still allowed and alcohol was still legal. Opium joints and "the evil of gambling" were illegal (see Figure 3.3).[12]

How did Panamanians imagine this space and how did they approach the relationships between Panama and the new Zone at a time when many Panamanians still lived in the Zone and the Zone still retained its old municipalities? And what role did Panama play as the Zone transitioned from Panamanian hands to US hands? Among the first issues to emerge was a legal debate between jurists who faced the question of what to do with the cases pending in the courts of Zone towns. Panamanian jurists had different opinions on who had legal jurisdiction to solve them. They even had different opinions on the canal treaty's sovereignty clause. This debate was simultaneous with debates over the jurisdiction of the Panama Canal ports. Together, these debates reveal the many ways in which people at the time could imagine the Panama Canal Zone.

After the Panamanian municipalities in the Zone were transferred to the American government, the Panamanian secretary of state,

Tomás Arias, requested that the new Zone courts handle all pending and new legal cases originating in Zone towns.[13] Many Panamanian judges did so. Yet not everybody agreed with Arias. The uncertainty of the times and the lack of clarity over jurisdiction are prominent in a case that originated in Emperador. The case was pending under the judge of the Colón circuit, who ceased to review it because jurisdiction had been transferred to the Zone judges. The case remained in legal limbo because the Colón judge refused to send it to the Zone judges until he received instructions on the proper procedures for this transfer.

The case ended up in the hands of Panama's attorney general, who was supposed to provide instructions. Instead the attorney general argued that legal cases should not be transferred because Panama had not lost jurisdiction over cases that had originated before the Zone was handed over to the United States. He went even further and suggested a different interpretation of Panama's sovereignty in the Zone. According to him, Panama had only given away its sovereignty in matters relating to the canal's "construction, maintenance, exploitation, sanitation, and protection," keeping jurisdiction over all matters not related to these issues. Panama's secretary of justice, Nicolás Victoria Jaén, held a similar position. He argued that states could not give away their sovereignty, which, he argued, even the 1903 treaty recognized. The case went to Panama's Supreme Court, which refused to render an opinion because the interpretation of international treaties was in the jurisdiction of the ministry of foreign relations. The ministry of foreign relations held a similar view. According to Eusebio A. Morales, the 1903 treaty had "restricted" the United States to the judicial rights over the Zone. Panama had given the United States restricted jurisdiction over the Zone only because it was needed to resolve "the daily controversies that might arise due to the [canal] works."[14]

Panamanians also had to confront the problem of how to address the electoral rights of Panamanian citizens living in Zone towns. Although they were living in US territory, they were not American citizens but citizens of Panama. They could not participate in US elections, and the ICC had decided that there would be no elections in the Zone. This was a change from previous political uses of this space. Before Americans took control of the Zone, this area had several municipal districts that participated in national elections: Gorgona, Emperador, Buena Vista, and Gatún. Now that these towns and their Panamanian citizens were part of a US territory without elections, the Panamanian government preserved the democratic rights of Panama's citizens by allocating each of the Zone municipalities to different electoral districts in Panama. Emperador, Gorgona, and the new municipality of Ancón became part of Panama's electoral district, and Buena Vista, Gatún, and the new municipality of Cristobal became part of Colón's district.[15] The towns of the Zone became a liminal political space. They were situated in US territory, and the Zone government appointed their most important political authority—the *alcalde,* or mayor. However, the citizens of Zone towns remained citizens of Panama and could only exercise their political rights outside their municipalities on the other side of the Zone border.

Panamanians living in the Zone lost the right to participate in an active municipal political life, which was one of the cornerstones of political life in the United States and Panama. It's important to stress that all important political events in Panama—and Colombia—had started with municipal declarations. Municipalities had declared Panama's independence from Spain and its separation from Colombia, and these declarations became official only after municipalities across the nation had confirmed them. For example, the Panama Canal treaty was signed by the provisional government and then submitted for the approval of all the municipalities of the republic.[16] Even requests for US intervention sometimes happened at the municipal level. It was the municipal council of Panama City that requested American intervention in the 1906 national elections.[17] While people in Panama's municipalities had the right to elect their municipal council, people living in the Zone municipalities did not have this right.[18] In spite of the claim of setting up "a model of American government . . . as an object lesson to the South and Central American republics," electoral politics had been displaced to Panamanian cities outside Zone borders.[19] But the rhetoric about Panama's tropical wilderness made it possible to conceal the ways in which the Zone was losing an important form of modernity: its political modernity. Zone municipalities lost the franchise rights that they had enjoyed until then. They were not gaining "modern government"; rather, they would lose it with the elimination of the municipal governments by administrative districts. Republican politics had been expelled from the Zone, which had become a non-electoral space.

At the end of 1904, the Zone remained a complex space over which two nations and two visions of modernity had claims. It was also a space of strong silences and contradictions. The strongest silences converged around the new ports of Ancón and Cristobal. Ramón M. Valdés's famous *Geography of the Isthmus of Panama,* which he finished in December 1904, listed all the Zone's municipal districts, including the new municipalities of Ancón and Cristobal.[20] Valdés noted that the town of La Boca belonged to the United States, while elsewhere he listed it as one of the towns of the municipal district of Panama. The ICC municipal law also echoed the contested nature of the Port of Ancón. When the municipal law listed the boundaries of the new district of Ancón, the city included "all that part of the municipal district of Arraijan, in the republic of Panama, which is included within the limits of the Zone, also the islands of Naos, Perico, and Flamenco."[21]

Interestingly, the law did not mention the municipality of Panama, which was the most important boundary of Ancón. By not mentioning it, perhaps the ICC hoped people would forget that Panama had once claimed that the Port of Ancón was part of the Port of Panama and La Boca part of the municipality of Panama.

This complex space was difficult to organize and classify. Its borders were fluid. People living in Zone municipal towns were citizens of Panama but lived under the US government. They had their own municipal government but could not elect it. The US and Panamanian governments recognized the franchise rights of Panamanian citizens who could not exercise them in their own towns; they could only exercise them outside the Zone borders. They could own property and businesses in the Zone, or be taxed by the US government and judged by US courts, but they remained Panamanian citizens. For two years, the ICC and the newly reorganized Zone municipalities tried to function in spite of these complexities and contradictions.

Regulating the Construction Boom

Between 1904 and 1912, Zone authorities tried to regulate and organize Zone towns. The ICC's plan was not to expel local inhabitants or depopulate the Zone but to govern and organize local populations according to what it saw as its civilizing mission. The ICC even expected local towns to grow and expand.[22] Its aim was to improve local conditions. For example, the "native town of Empire" was to "be laid out in street lines, and sidewalk lines marked as early as possible. Then the houses can be, and should be kept in line and the streets graded and kept clean."[23] Because of the immense pressure on housing caused by the arrival of thousands of workers to Zone towns, ICC authorities decided to create a "common plan for all the towns" that would regulate

FIGURE 3.4 A street scene and village in Gorgona in the Canal Zone
Credit: I. L. Maduro Jr. Reproduced from the author's collection.

things like block size and street width. The goal was to create a sanitary and orderly space—or in the words of Dr. William Gorgas, to "build intelligently" (see Figure 3.4).[24]

The American engineers and doctors who came to Panama thought bringing sanitation to the tropics was a crucial part of their mission and glory. As an early health report put it, "The Isthmus of Panama has for years been known as the filthiest and unhealthiest place on earth," and "the work of American sanitation will be watched by the whole world and the methods which are bound to be successful will undoubtedly be adopted all over the United States."[25] The man in charge of Panama's sanitation was Dr. William Gorgas, a pioneer in mosquito research who had successfully eradicated yellow fever in Havana. His methods were considered so successful that in 1903, a US army surgeon describing Panama's sanitary conditions stressed that methods of protection from yellow fever and malaria "had been so well worked out by medical officers stationed in Havana, and so widely known, that it would seem unnecessary to mention it."[26] Given the importance ICC officials placed on controlling contagious diseases, urban regulations became increasingly dictated, not by the municipalities, but by the sanitation department. In 1905, the ICC decreed that municipalities could not grant construction permits for private or public buildings without the approval of the Board of Health "as to ventilation, plumbing and drainage."[27] In 1907, the ICC enacted again—and in much more detail—urban regulations for all the towns and inhabitants of the Zone.

The ICC sanitation strategy drew on ideas about the transmission of disease that combined nineteenth-century miasmatic theories about swamps and tropical mud with the newer germ theory and the latest discoveries about the role of mosquitoes in the transmission of malaria and yellow fever. Equally important were medical ideas that considered native tropical people natural carriers of disease.[28] Therefore, ICC health officials set to create and design a new urban space that would control and deter the physical and moral dangers of life in the tropics. For this reason, distance became the defining concept of urban regulations, as proper distance between buildings would achieve the goal of saving American and non-American inhabitants of the Zone from what they saw as the numerous threats posed by the local environment. The urban regulations of the Zone emphasized four types of distances. The houses had to be three feet above the ground, distant from the dangers of tropical mud; the houses had to be distant from each other, to avoid dark alleys and native garbage; American buildings had to be distant from local or "native" buildings to avoid contagion from local diseases; and wooden fences had to have enough distance between their pickets to provide visibility and necessary supervision (see Map 3.1).[29]

The distance between ICC buildings and "native" buildings was the most important of these new urban regulations and the one that would have the most significant long-term consequences. It created distinctions between Americans and "natives" that transformed local towns into "native towns" and local peoples into "natives." What had started as a nineteenth-century tradition of nativizing Panamanians by ridiculing black republicanism and black labor practices had ceased to be merely rhetorical by 1904. It acquired concrete implications for the way Americans would regulate and organize urban space in Zone towns, as urban regulations began to create distinctions that separated modern Americans from local natives. The sanitary department determined that 1,000 feet was the ideal distance between "native huts" and ICC buildings.[30]

Correspondence between ICC officials reveals the importance of notions of tropical primitiveness behind the ideology that justified the distance between "native huts" and ICC buildings. The terms "native house" and "native hut" were used regardless of the actual characteristics of the house in question. In one instance, the term *native house* referred to the house of a Chinese immigrant. The term *hut* could also refer to a frame house built with the same materials used for ICC buildings. It did not matter if the owner was a "native" or the house was a "hut."[31] The terms were important because they justified sanitation practices developed in the British colonies of Asia and Africa, which considered strict separation between "native" houses and neighborhoods and white houses and neighborhoods essential for saving white colonials from contagious diseases. Tropical-colonial medicine considered natives part of a diseased tropical landscape. They were vectors of contagious diseases, to which they had built-in resistance. In the turn-of-the-century language of tropical sanitation, "natives" were unable to fully comply with sanitary habits and measures.[32] In this way, racialized health practices transformed the local inhabitants of Panamanian towns,

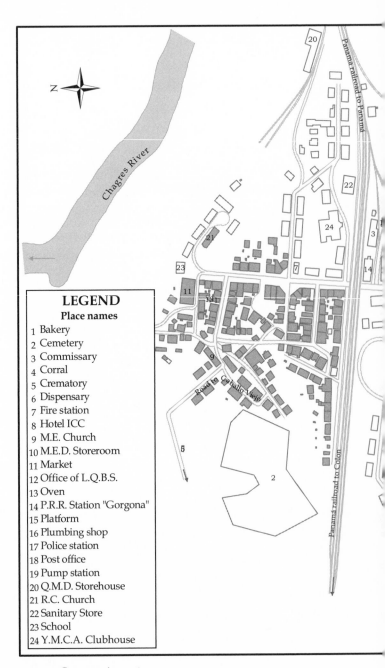

MAP 3.1 Gorgona in 1908
Credit: Héctor Camilo León Murillo.

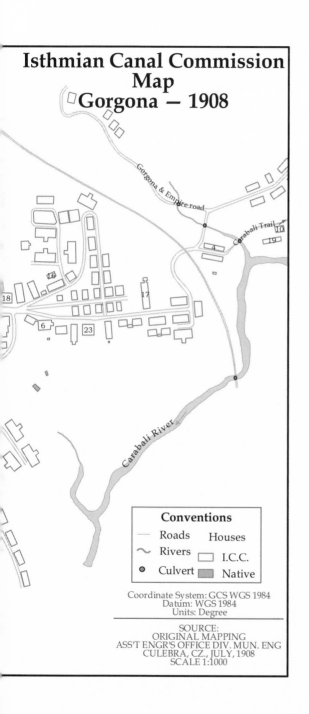

Isthmian Canal Commission Map
Gorgona — 1908

Gorgona & Empire road

Carabali Trail

Carabali River

Conventions

— Roads   Houses

~ Rivers   ☐ I.C.C.

● Culvert ▦ Native

Coordinate System: GCS WGS 1984
Datum: WGS 1984
Units: Degree

SOURCE:
ORIGINAL MAPPING
ASS'T ENGR'S OFFICE DIV. MUN. ENG
CULEBRA, CZ., JULY, 1908
SCALE 1:1000

who were of different racial and ethnic backgrounds, into "natives." Their houses had become "huts" and their towns "native towns."

This division required a major overhaul of local urban culture and spatial arrangements. For example, in 1905, the people of Gorgona still divided their town between the new town, close to the railroad tracks, and the old town, close to the river. It was a division based on technology and urban growth. The new division of Zone towns between a "native" town and an American town was based on racial segregation between "natives" and non-natives. The native side of Gorgona was located on the northwest side of town, between the railroad and the Chagres River, close to the cemetery on the historic side of Gorgona. The American side of Gorgona was mainly located to the south of the railroad, but had a section in the northeast. The railroad and Avenue A were the main division between "native" and American Gorgona (see Map 3.1).[33] Saloons were allowed only in the native side of Gorgona. Urban distance between natives and Americans was also a distance between "vice" and wholesomeness.[34] The urban segregation between the "native" side of towns and the non-native side of towns was the precedent to the future division between the towns of the "silver roll," which were non-white and non-American, and the towns of the "gold roll," which were white and American.

According to the 1906 building ordinances, houses had to be built three feet above ground. They required enough space below the house to "prevent shutting off light and air."[35] The space "beneath the house shall not be closed to furnish space for the keeping of chickens or animals or for storage purposes but must be free at all times for ventilation."[36] What was the origin of this particular ordinance? It seems specifically developed for tropical houses. Did it have the purpose of protecting all Zone inhabitants, natives and non-natives, from the dangers of the tropical landscape?

The regulation combined old fears of mud and swamps based on miasmatic theory with new fears based on germ theory. The American public had first become familiar with Panama's tropical landscape through the many travel narratives written by Gold Rush travelers in the 1840s and 1850s. Influenced by the miasmatic theory popular at that time, they believed that Panama's infamous pestilence derived from the bad fumes coming from tropical swamps, mud, and filth. Robert Tomes's description of Colón as a dirty and unsanitary "settlement over marshy pools corrupt with decaying matter" is a typical example of this narrative.[37] The sanitary ideas based on new germ theory developed in the 1870s and 1880s built on previous miasmatic notions. Germs, like harmful fumes, came from filth. The three-feet-high regulation, however, seems a holdover from previous miasmatic theories, not from germ theories, or the very new mosquito theories. A building height of three feet had no effect on mosquito control. It did not offer any protection against germs, either. It only created a distance between houses and tropical mud.

Finally, distance between houses also served the purpose of eliminating small alleys, which Zone health officials considered the cause of all kinds of sanitation problems. People chose them for throwing out slops, and at night they became urinals. Moreover, because they lacked air and light, small alleys remained constantly damp, thus increasing the problems of tropical humidity. Writing in 1906, the chief sanitary inspector considered a distance of ten feet between houses inadequate to prevent these problems. He proposed thirty feet as the mandatory distance between houses. He thought it better to create an urban structure that would eliminate alleys altogether instead of punishing people who were caught throwing trash.[38]

It was one thing to devise regulations and another to enforce them. Many of the towns that were built prior to the decrees followed spatial traditions that favored urban density; houses in such towns were built close to one another—with a distance of four or sixteen feet between them—on narrow streets. Health officials had to deal with the fact that, regardless of the tropical wilderness rhetoric, the Zone was not a blank slate. The new regulations, which privileged distance over density and sanitation over convenience and community, faced opposition from multiple fronts.[39] Joseph Agustin Le Prince, who was the chief sanitary inspector, found his task daunting. His lamentations give us a sense of the difficulty of enforcing sanitary regulations in the Zone towns when officers were faced with violations at every turn. He complained about "sloppy and filthy conditions that had existed for years about the houses in Empire." He observed that the "building boom" in Empire and the great profits that private owners could make with rental properties conspired against proper building conditions. Structures were built everywhere, including on grounds with unsatisfactory sanitary conditions. Where land was valuable, he continued wistfully, his own health department had allowed "builders to shut out light, air, and ventilation from houses," which made it difficult "to provide that the ground in narrow spaces and alleyways shall not be kept at all times damp."[40]

Other conflicting needs also worked against the enforcement of urban sanitary regulations. For the railroad, which owned the town's land and leased plots to private owners, more space between houses meant fewer plots to rent. It was also difficult to impose sanitary regulations on ICC buildings that were hurriedly built to fill the urgent need to house the thousands of workers constantly arriving to work on the canal.

During the first three years of canal construction, enforcing sanitary regulations in the midst of a building boom was further complicated by differences between Zone mayors and health officers. In 1906, the health department sent the Zone building regulations to the mayors of the Zone for feedback.[41] The mayors' responses reveal that their urban vision for the Zone differed in significant ways from the priorities of health officials. The mayors had different ideas about their responsibilities toward local towns and local citizens. They raised questions and suggested modifications to the proposed regulations. The mayors' answers provide a sense of the complexities of enforcing new building regulations that completely altered notions of distance and housing structure in local towns. They also show the conflicts between municipal political traditions and the technocratic mandates of health officers.

The mayors of Zone towns saw it as their duty to defend the interests of "native" town dwellers. George Johnson, the mayor of Empire, wanted to avoid unnecessary disruption. He thought that issues like street width should not apply to the old part of town. Similarly, the American mayor of Gorgona worried about the hardships that new regulations would impose on local "natives." His tone reflected a compassionate, but also patronizing, understanding of what the new rules would mean for locals. In his view, the new regulations should not apply to existing Panamanian towns: "I do not think that the old towns should be remodeled, excepting in extreme cases, such as the moving of a few houses to open up streets." He felt that the new ordinances should only cover new buildings or the establishment of new towns.[42] If they were applied to existing houses, they would impose great hardship on "natives, and others, who are poor and have been living in their little houses for years." Such people would "be compelled to pull their only shelter down and carry it to another site and reconstruct, as many of them have absolutely no means with which to carry out such a regulation."[43]

The mayors objected to what they saw as a double standard in the enforcement of the new ordinances. Gorgona's mayor wrote: "I do not see why the native population should be compelled to carry out a regulation of this nature [a fifty-foot distance between dwellings], when the Commission is erecting married and bachelor quarters with front balconies only 25 feet from the rear balcony or porch of adjacent quarters. This is being done in Gorgona, in fact, over the entire Isthmus." The mayor of Empire also defended his citizens against what he considered to be unfair burdens. Many houses were being built next to hills, and the regulations required a distance of six feet between the houses and the hills. Who was supposed to excavate the hills to leave the necessary distance? If a person was given a plot large enough to build a house, was that person supposed to excavate a hill on public lands or on somebody else's property? He also thought imposing regulations on private citizens was unfair when "none of the ICC labor camps will fill the requirements of these regulations . . . and it will be rather difficult to compel private persons to conform to regulations that are ignored by the Commission."[44]

In general, the mayors of Emperador and Gorgona thought that the proposed regulations were unnecessary and needlessly cumbersome. They envisioned a greater degree of continuity between the old towns and the new ICC towns. They imagined a closer, denser urban space, a space not ruled by the fear of contagion. The mayor of Emperador thought that in the old part of towns it was important to avoid "moving any more buildings than are made necessary for alignment." The desire for wide streets should be subordinated to this need. He allowed for wider streets in the new parts of town but believed that the width of the streets should be six feet narrower than proposed (twenty-four feet instead of thirty) with wider sidewalks (six feet instead of five). The mayor of Gorgona also contended that the distances between buildings and structures proposed in the new regulations were exaggerated. He suggested less distance between buildings. The mayors also paid attention to local needs and geography and were less inclined to accept a one-size-fits-all regulation. They provided many examples of situations in which local conditions—different types of soil, ground, and houses—warranted different distances between houses and between the ground and the houses. The mayor of Empire used his experience to suggest that the great distance between houses proposed in the sanitary regulations (fifteen feet of empty space) was also unnecessary. He thought that a space of two feet without windows or doors toward the adjoining house would be sufficient. He had noticed that there was "practically no refuse or filth of any kind deposited in passages between houses that are very close together, for the reason that refuse is usually thrown from the window at night." He also thought that the provision that required fifty feet between the back side of one house and another was "out of proportion to the width of streets."

Along with the distance between houses and the division of Zone towns into "native" and non-native sections, sewage treatment received a great deal of attention. It is hard to imagine how revolutionary it was to organize urban space and housing space around dirt closets. For Progressive Era reformers, there could be no civilization without sewers. Perhaps a bit hyperbolically, in 1905 a Baltimore engineer exalted Paris sewers as the source of art and science. He stated that, "completely sewered, with a low death rate," Paris is "the center of all that is the best in art, literature, science and architecture and is both clean and beautiful. In the evolution of this ideal attainment," he continued, "its sewers took at least a leading part, for we have only to look at conditions existing prior to their construction to see that such a realization would have been impossible before their existence."[45]

Sanitation officers and Zone mayors most likely had a similar sense about the importance of sewers and thought there could be no civilization in the tropics without a proper sewerage system. After all, canal construction coincided with the building of sewerage systems in cities across the United States. Between 1880 and 1907 almost every city in the United States had built a sewer system.[46] Yet Zone mayors sought regulations that imposed less disruption on local people. They also seemed to have more trust in the ability of town dwellers to keep their dirt closets clean. The mayor of Empire thought that the distance between houses and closets was unnecessarily wide. "A closet properly built and properly taken care of is no worse 15 feet from the house than 25 feet from the house." The mayor of Gorgona had a similar view. He noted that "at least two thirds of the houses" had closets, which indicates that by 1906, dirt closets were already a predominant urban feature. Gorgona's mayor thought that a distance of twenty-five feet between closet and house would "compel the removal of practically every closet throughout the Zone," which would entail an expense that the "native population" was not able to stand. He was of the opinion that people could properly keep closets clean and sanitary. But he thought that until a "proper sewerage system is constructed," houses should not be required to have a closet but "two large public closets erected in each block, at suitable places to be selected co-jointly by the mayors of the respective municipalities and designated sanitary officials, these closets to be properly partitioned for the sexes."[47] He also thought that the commission should provide more infrastructure before demanding more changes. The ICC could not request a closet in every house until it had constructed a proper sewerage system.

The End of Zone Municipalities

In 1907, ICC authorities eliminated municipalities and organized the Zone into several "administrative districts."[48] It is not clear why the ICC did so, but the comments of Le Prince, the chief sanitary inspector, about the mayors' objections to the 1906 regulations suggest an answer. Le Prince argued that "the Mayors evidently had not read the regulations carefully; as may be seen by comparing their answers with the regulations proposed." Moreover, because he had heard that "the nature of the office of the mayor is to be changed somewhat," perhaps it was not necessary to heed the mayors' objections.[49] Le Prince's position reflected the ICC's new ambivalence about the municipalities and also the view that mayors—particularly if they took seriously the defense of their towns' interests even when they conflicted with ICC rules—were a hindrance to the Zone's technical administration. The solution was to eliminate the municipalities altogether.

With the end of municipalities, sanitation became the main organizing principle of urban regulations. It is not an accident that the end of municipalities in 1907 coincided with increased health regulation and an emphasis on the distance between native huts and Commission buildings. According to contemporary political ideas, citizens needed municipalities, but "natives" could—and perhaps should—be governed by colonial authorities who organized their territory into administrative districts. Zone towns went from being political spaces to technical spaces ordered by sanitary concerns. It was the end of a municipal tradition that went back to Spanish colonial times. With this measure, the towns of the Zone lost the last vestiges of municipal republican life. Civic pride was replaced with company pride. It was one step forward in the disconnection of Zone towns from Panama's urban and political history. In 1904, Zone towns went from being Panamanian municipalities with full political rights to becoming American municipalities with limited political rights. This narrow view of modernity—only sanitary, not municipal or electoral—anticipated future development projects, which were guided by a few indicators that simplified the politics and complexity of the location where they were implemented. In the early twentieth-century Zone, decisions were placed in the hands of a few technical experts.[50]

The Administrative Districts

With the end of the municipal experiment, the power and responsibility of monitoring private owners to ensure that they followed urban regulations rested in the hands of sanitary authorities. Enforcing regulations continued to be difficult.[51] The internal correspondence of sanitary authorities reveals their anguish at trying to find a balance that would allow them to impose sanitary regulations without creating too much disruption and hardship for home owners, a balance made more difficult by the continuing boom in the construction of private buildings. Sanitary inspectors were instructed to study the building regulations and to "note all building operations in the villages of the Canal Zone and to report any violations." One goal was to catch violations at the beginning of construction, which would obviate the difficulties of asking private owners to demolish their buildings "after completion at great expense."[52] In the middle of "considerable building going on in the New Village of Gatún, and in several villages between Empire and Culebra," the Panama Railroad asked the engineering department to help put an end to private owners' habit of building houses that extended beyond the limits of their lots.[53]

The sanitary department also asked for the help of the engineering department to approve construction plans before the sanitary department provided the construction permits. The hope was that this measure would prevent the construction of unsafe buildings "due to faulty construction" in the "native towns" of the Zone.[54]

Despite the measures to regulate and control private construction, the ideal sanitary space envisioned by Gorgas and Le Prince proved impossible to create. As the mayors of Zone towns had pointed out earlier, the history of their urban spaces had to be taken into account. Sanitary officers constantly faced the problem of how to deal with houses built before the new regulations or on lots whose leases were signed before the new distance regulations. The case of Luis Bosque was typical. He was asked to stop construction because his house was too close to the Paraíso station, thereby violating the rule against building "native" houses that did not comply with the mandatory distance of 1,000 feet from ICC buildings. Yet eventually he was allowed to complete his construction because he was building a better house to replace an old one and using a plot lease that had "been in existence so long." In the view of the sanitary authorities, he had to be allowed to proceed with his construction project because "if made retroactive the one thousand feet rule . . . will work hardship in many cases if rigidly adhered to in the case of rebuilding."[55] In other instances, sanitary authorities faced the question of whether it was better to authorize repairs on the buildings that violated current regulations or to let the buildings deteriorate until it was necessary for the owner to carry out "such extensive repairs that he would have to conform to building regulations." Such were the cases of Took Woo Chong, from Empire, who wanted to repair his veranda, and Rosanne, also from Empire, who wanted to repair her bathrooms and water closets and line them with zinc. They were both allowed to make their repairs, even though they violated the new regulations. Sanitary authorities decided that it was better to allow owners to fix them than to leave the buildings in disrepair.[56]

In addition to the formal native villages, ICC sanitary authorities had to regulate the many informal settlements that sprang up around the railroad line near sites of canal construction. Some settlements were created by people whom construction had made homeless. Such was the case of a settlement formed "to the West of the Garbage Incinerator of Culebra," which was made up of people who had to move from an old settlement on the east side of the railroad to a new place located between the Río Grande watershed and the new dump to the west of the Panama Railroad.[57] Other settlements emerged as people built houses near the labor sites of Pedro Miguel and Miraflores. Other places like the "old village of Jamaiquita," located on the "border of the railway line at Gatun," had been informal settlements for some time.[58] In these settlements, the houses were built without supervision or permits and following the owners' own sense of space. "The houses are fairly close together and face in many directions . . . as may be seen near most towns on the zone."[59] Even in these informal settlements, some owners built rental property for canal workers, as was the case near the Culebra incinerator, where four houses—two with cement floors, two with wooden floors—had been erected.[60] Others squatted to farm and sell their products in the markets of Zone towns.

Canal authorities feared informal settlements because they could easily become permanent. Some thought it best to transform them into properly organized villages before they grew without conforming to sanitary regulations. Others, like the legal department, argued that the houses should be torn down to make an example of people who allegedly built "where the country is sufficiently thick so that they are protected from being seen until the house has already been erected, and they feel reasonably certain after the house is once erected that the

Commission forces will not cause it to be removed."[61] The ICC's law department feared that people would build in places needed for canal construction, and that the ICC would have to compensate them for houses built without a permit. Sometimes the squatters were fined, other times they were imprisoned. Even when the ICC claimed that squatters had no permits, they were not completely outside the Zone's legal system. In some places, they paid taxes even if they had built without a permit. In other places, they built in places officially leased to somebody else. Sometimes, squatters created an informal real-estate market where they bought and sold land over which they had no official rights.

Private owners' resistance to the new regulations also made it difficult to enforce them. Some owners, like David Carrillo from Empire, used lawyers to defend their rights. Carrillo wanted to keep a recent addition to his two-story house, even if it violated the new distance regulations. His lawyer argued that since he had built the addition with permits granted before the new regulations had come into effect, Carrillo should be allowed to keep it; if not, he should at least receive some compensation for his expense.[62] Others, like Felicia Armiens, a black "French-speaking woman" from Bas Matachin (near the town of Gorgona), persisted in writing letters to various ICC authorities, hoping to keep a house she had recently built. The records do not say much about her. She presented herself as a "poor widow with two helpless daughters and two sons" who had built her house with great effort and with the help of her son. The ICC inspectors, however, described her as the owner of several houses in the Zone, which she rented. In their view, she was not a poor woman who could claim ignorance.

The source of her conflict with the ICC was an old French building that she had purchased with the intent of using the material to build a new one on a different site. She argued that she had done so following instructions from inspectors. The inspectors disagreed, saying she had purposely ignored their instructions and had started construction without following the distance regulations. In the end, she managed to obtain a personal interview with Goethals and to elicit his sympathy. Although he did not allow her to keep her house, he ordered that she be given a new site for her building. Eventually, she was even given a choice between two sites offered by the ICC. She settled on the higher one.[63]

In other instances, owners expressed their frustrations more forcefully. F. A. Lynch was overheard saying on the streets of New Gatún "that if any party was arrested for violating sanitary regulations, he would furnish legal advice free to such parties."[64] He was the owner of a furniture, hardware, carriage, and harness store in Colón City. Like many people with money to invest, he decided to take advantage of the Zone's economic boom in New Gatún. He was terribly frustrated with the sanitary inspectors, who, he complained, were harassing him. They constantly asked him to dump water from the barrels he was using to make concrete. Although he understood the need for regulations "for the good of all," he asked for reasonable treatment. Yes, it was important to eradicate sources of water where mosquitoes reproduced, but he was using water from a faucet. And how could he possibly make concrete without water? This was not his only disagreement with sanitary inspectors. He had already received a warrant for not cutting down the weeds on his lot.

Mr. Lynch, Felicia Armiens, and the other violators had their own ideas and priorities about the Zone's urban spaces. They saw Zone towns as places to live, manage businesses, rent, and find economic opportunities. Their cases show the complexities, difficulties, and impossibility of having a perfectly regulated space in a complex urban environment, a fact hardly surprising to any student or observer of cities. But the Zone was not an ordinary urban space. It was a highly symbolic space where the US government aspired to show the world its mastery over the tropics and its ability to run exemplary towns in Spanish America. However, it was difficult, if not impossible, to build a perfect symbolic space in a densely occupied region, where people had their own sense of their history and their rights. Urban regulations faced the opposition of mayors and urban dwellers. The first step of the ICC was to eliminate the office of the mayor and the municipalities. Eventually, urban dwellers would be expelled as well, but that decision was a few years in the future.

Screening Battles: Or the Impossible Task of Making the Jungle Mosquito-Proof

If distance was a crucial element of the urban layout of Zone towns, mosquito screens were a crucial element of the architectural design of ICC housing. A goal of the ICC's sanitary department was to prevent malaria-ridden mosquitoes from entering ICC buildings. One of the glories of canal construction was its sanitary campaign, and to triumph over something where the French had failed was an important proof of the United States' stature as an economic and technological power. The best-known part of the campaign was the destruction of the yellow fever mosquito habitat. Since these mosquitoes reproduced in clean water, Gorgas organized gangs of workers to oil water depositories and to destroy all types of water pools and ponds inside and outside homes. The arrival of mosquito control gangs in Panama City remained a traumatic event among locals. The gangs destroyed the traditional water repositories that held drinking water inside the houses and the barrels and cisterns that collected rainwater outside. The goal was to replace them with piped water.[65] Another, less known aspect of this campaign was the dramatic architectural change required to make every Zone house mosquito-proof.

Ideally, every house and every building in the Zone would be screened. In 1905, Gorgas had an ambitious goal: to screen all laborers' quarters with "copper bronze wire or similar material of not less than 16 meshes to the inch."[66] Yet this was expensive and difficult, and Gorgas's proposal provoked the immediate backlash of ICC managers involved in the construction process, who considered his goal "extreme or idealistic." It was costly, and not everybody thought that to "reduce illness to the lowest possible percentage" warranted its cost.[67] The controversy over what and what not to screen would continue throughout the construction years and be laden with strong racial, social, and even aesthetic components. At the end, only a small percentage of commission houses were screened. Screening all ICC buildings was an impossible goal, and the shortcomings showed, yet again, that "bringing civilization to the tropics" could happen only by focusing on a few selected spaces, leaving most inhabitants out.

The ICC created a board in charge of "the general question of screening." The board was chaired by Dr. Henry Rose Carter, the director of hospitals and sometimes the acting sanitary officer. One of the board's first goals was to develop mosquito-proof building practices. In 1905, Le Prince commented that despite having mosquito screens, none of the buildings in the Zone were mosquito-proof. There was too much space left under or above the doors. Moreover, the doors were not supplied with springs (later this would become standard practice), making screening "practically useless," and corrugated roofs could not be made sufficiently tight to keep mosquitoes out. Gorgas suggested that the sheathing of the rafters would provide additional protection and make the buildings cooler.[68] Sanitary officers also realized that screening verandas and porches, instead of windows and doors, was more efficient and cost effective. Soon this design would become standard for the porches and verandas of commission houses.[69]

Screening also had strong social and aesthetic components, which became apparent during the discussions over whether the two most important hotels in the Zone during this construction period—the Culebra and the Tivoli—should be screened. The Culebra was located in a town of the same name, next to the most important digging sites at the canal: the Culebra Cut. For most of the construction period, some of the ICC main offices were located there. Visitors and gold-roll employees waiting for housing were often lodged there. The building had three floors with galleries, and Gorgas thought that its galleries should be screened. Not much attention was given to the aesthetics of this hotel.[70] It was a work-site hotel.

The Tivoli Hotel was a very different thing altogether. Located on the slopes of Ancón Hill, next to the border with Panama City and not too far from the administration building, the Tivoli was Panama's most important and luxurious hotel, the first choice of important visitors. It was not clear how mosquito screening would fit the Tivoli. In the opinion of Dr. Carter, screening was ugly. Compared with other hotels, the Tivoli was "a much handsomer building and anything that injures its appearance, as we think screening galleries would do," should be avoided. He approved of screening doors and windows but not the galleries. Gorgas was of a different opinion. Screening was important because should any of the "important visitors" contract malaria, "it would seriously injure our reputation for health, and thus affect the ease with which we can get employees to come to the Isthmus."[71] Carter used social and racial considerations to support his position against screening the Tivoli's galleries. Its location was distant from mosquito breeding places; it was located on "the top of a considerable hill" and far from "unscreened colored quarters." Moreover, the guests "are the class of people who will be careful to take precautions necessary to protect their health."[72] Carter's opinion reflected a mix of the sanitary ideas that had developed over the past century: that distance from infected natives would protect whites from infection and that good habits protected people from disease. It also revealed that the second medical authority at the Panama Canal perhaps considered the Tivoli's symbolism and aesthetics more important than mosquito control. His opinion shows that even at the head of the sanitary department there was tension between the goal of controlling mosquitoes in every possible way and in every possible place and the goal and desire to adjust sanitary rules to local social and racial conditions.

The attempt to adjust screening to social and racial conditions was also apparent in internal correspondence from 1907 among the members of the sanitary department over the question of which ICC buildings should be screened. Some members advocated a case-by-case approach, just as had been done with the Tivoli. One internal letter suggested that it was important to weigh "the risk avoided by screening" against "the cost of screening and keeping it in repair." A number of variables could be considered. Was the building "in a very malarious locality" or not? Were the apartments occupied only during the day or used as sleeping apartments? As for "the class of people who occupy" a building, would they benefit from screening, and were they "so valuable a class of employees that it is especially desirable to protect them from malaria or not?" No less important a consideration was the number of people that a screened building would protect.[73] These suggestions provide a candid assessment of a sanitary social scale that weighed cost against "employee" value. It was also a proposal that would require a careful examination of each ICC building.

But this was an impossible proposition. The construction of the Panama Canal was an industrial enterprise, and providing lodging for workers was a massive, industrial undertaking that benefited from standardized practices. A small debate over building different doors for white and black laborers reveals this fact. The acting chief sanitary officer requested that the master builder equip the white and black barracks with different doors. He argued that while black workers kept their batten doors closed at night, white workers opened them to let the air circulate and, therefore, needed screen doors. The master builder's response shows his exasperation at this request:

> As a matter of fact, we have not distinctive "white laborers"
> quarters. Our barracks are all known as "laborers" barracks
> and are all of the same type. The fact that some of them are
> used for European laborers and others for colored laborers,
> is entirely controlled by the Bureau of Labor & Quarters, and
> I have no means of knowing when barracks are built, to what
> use they are to be put, and in fact, the barracks now in use,
> have been used for both classes of laborers, as conditions
> require.[74]

This response is indicative of a standardized building process that needed broad guidelines. It was one thing to examine in detail the needs of a special building like the Tivoli Hotel, and another thing entirely to pay attention to the specific details of each ICC building.

One of the biggest disagreements between Gorgas and the quartermaster's department, which oversaw the construction of barracks, concerned the question of screening the school and living quarters of silver-roll married employees. At first it seemed that Gorgas's goal to screen all buildings would become the rule. The 1907 regulations included among the buildings to be screened "all white barracks, black barracks, bachelor quarters, married quarters, churches, lodge-rooms and all other buildings."[75] These regulations reflected Gorgas's comprehensive approach to screening. Ideally, he would have liked to screen not only every ICC building but also all private houses in the Zone located within 500 yards of ICC houses. However, he conceded, "inasmuch as the matter has gone so far and so many houses have gone up along the line, it would be very difficult to require this." The debate over whether to screen married silver-roll housing became intimately linked to the screening—of lack thereof—of the "native" (or private) side of towns.

While the screening of married white quarters was never questioned, the screening of married black quarters became linked to the screening of "private housings" in the "native villages" of the Zone. As the sanitary department and the quartermaster's department argued, both sides reinforced a spatial division between ICC housing and non-ICC housing that further contributed to the nativization of local towns and houses that were alternatively defined as "the bush," "native villages," and "huts." For example, when R. E. Noble, the acting chief sanitary officer, defended a proposal to compel "the screening of all buildings used as eating and lodging houses," he hoped that it would lead to the closing of a large number of private lodging and eating houses in the Zone, "and cause to return to ICC quarters most of the employees who are now quartered in the bush."[76] Although his goal was to have most West Indian workers live and eat in screened commission quarters, his statement, by transforming local private housing into "the bush," reinforced an urban division that separated the commission side of town from the local side of town. The chief quartermaster, who opposed screening silver married quarters, also reinforced the division between "native" and ICC spaces. He argued that since the great majority of West Indians employed by the ICC lived outside of its quarters—23,411 out of the 29,095—it was futile to screen the quarters of the few non-white employees living in ICC housing.[77] He also mocked the sanitary inspectors' attention to detail: "the importance which appears to be attached to the minor defects in these old buildings" and the great importance given to "minute details." He was exasperated by the fact that cracks three-eighths of an inch wide are "considered serious enough to be made the subject of an official report," when four-fifths of West Indian laborers were housed in private buildings that had "no screening, and frequently, no doors or windows."[78] The constructing quartermaster thought that it was an "evident waste of money" to keep married silver-roll quarters mosquito-proof for two main reasons. First, the occupants' habits made them unworthy of this protection since "natives cook on the porches; and in fully 50% of quarters screened . . . the doors were propped back with boxes or chairs as in most of these quarters." Second, it was pointless to protect a few families when "no attempt is made to protect other silver families living in the Native Villages in the vicinity of our Married Silver Quarters."[79]

The sanitary department strongly disagreed. Gorgas wanted to screen all ICC quarters and dismissed the aforementioned reasons against screening non-white quarters, arguing that it should follow that gold quarters should not be screened either because "the Tivoli hotel and the Hotel Central and other private buildings in Panama are not screened."[80] In the end, the sanitary department lost the debate. A resolution adopted in an ICC meeting resolved "that the screening of married silver quarters will be discontinued."[81] The participants in the meeting had asked whether there was a middle ground between "the carefully screened authorized quarters of the ICC employees and the great number of various huts and houses, unscreened, in which the families of the greater part of West Indians live."[82] The answer was that West Indians' living quarters were not a right, like gold quarters, but a privilege. There were only "about four thousand occupants of these quarters and probably forty thousand men, women, and children, more or less, connected with work on the Canal" who lived on private quarters.[83] Moreover, neither the poor conditions of the old housing stock where West Indians lived nor their "method of living—cooking in small charcoal pots on the porches" and keeping the doors open—made screening viable. Thus, if West Indian married quarters were screened, "considerable money would be expended, with practically no beneficial results."[84] Two years later, in 1911, a similar debate took place over the screening of the schools for the children of silver-roll employees. This time the opposition argued that silver-roll married quarters were not screened, so it was pointless to screen the schools. Gorgas vehemently disagreed and argued that it was better to protect the children while they were at school than to offer no protection at all.[85] Again, he lost. The same meeting resolved "that the screening of married silver quarters and the screening of schools for colored children be discontinued."[86]

The mutual exasperation of Gorgas and the chief quartermaster reflected the contradiction between the goal of creating a model sanitary space and the budget realities of construction. The solution was to create two spaces: an ICC space for white workers that followed sanitary ideals and a space—ICC and not—of non-white workers that was associated with "the bush," an uncivilized native space. This was one of the first steps toward excluding these urban spaces from the Zone. Local towns became part of "the bush," the space that could not be transformed to the ideal sanitary and urban space that many ICC officials aspired to bring to the tropics. Yet as the correspondence reveals, this was largely a matter of resources. Building ideal urban conditions was expensive and to do so for the entire Zone population was never part of the budget. Commission housing for white employees was screened, and non-white ICC houses were not screened. But this was not the ideal; it was the outcome of budget restrictions and an adaptation to urgent construction needs. The medical staff never agreed.

The debate over screening paralleled a debate about grass cutting that took place during the same years. On one side, Gorgas and the sanitary department thought of grass cutting as a form of mosquito control. Because tall grass provided a good habitat for malaria-carrying mosquitoes, the sanitary department sought to keep the grass cut in crucial places—housing and work sites—close to mosquito habitats. Since their concerns were not about landscaping but sanitation, they did not care if the grass was short enough to fulfill ICC landscaping standards. They only worried about the grass when it reached a height of one foot or more. One the other side was the quartermaster's department, whose primary concern was that a well-kept landscape of trimmed grass created a comfortable and manicured space for white workers. The quartermaster's department did not care if the grass was close to mosquito breeding grounds. What mattered was its proximity to the space occupied by gold-roll white workers.[87]

The decision to screen only the white quarters contributed to the creation of urban divisions that were not part of the initial political and sanitary goals for Zone towns. Non-commission houses were the "bush" and non-white ICC houses were associated with it. But what commission officers referred to pejoratively as "the bush" contained, in reality, the many private houses and tenements located on the non-ICC side of Zone towns. According to ICC estimates, three-quarters or more of its West Indian workers lived in private buildings on the local side of Zone towns. The use of the term "the bush" to refer to the "native side," or to the private houses of the Zone, was a way to represent the native side of towns as an uncontrollable wilderness. It played a role in spatial segregation between ICC space and non-ICC space. Transforming non-commission areas into an uncontrollable "bush" was an initial ideological step toward transforming native towns into areas that did not rightfully belong in the Zone and could be erased and depopulated.

During the same years that US engineers found technical solutions to the many challenges of building the Panama Canal, ICC administrators faced insurmountable obstacles to achieving their initial goal of creating perfectly regulated canal towns that would showcase US urban modernity to the world. Their biggest challenge was an industrial setting of forty-one towns and 60,000 people. With ordinance after ordinance, ICC officers tried to contend with the challenges of this urban reality. Their first major modification sought to reorganize the existing municipalities with new regulations. Yet when the US mayors of Zone towns who took their office seriously and defended the interest of their town's dwellers against cumbersome regulations, the ICC eliminated the office of the mayor. In spite of this dramatic change, which erased the region's long municipal history, controlling and regulating the towns remained difficult. Far from being a blank space, the Zone had its own sophisticated economic and political history.

The ICC's decision to eliminate local towns altogether was neither simple nor easy. It required a certain way of looking at the world that made it possible to separate the Zone from its history and its people. By drawing on ideas about tropical places, ICC officers were able to divide Zone towns into native and non-native sections. The ICC section of Zone towns became the space of screened houses and trimmed grass. The native section became "the bush," the area that the ICC could not completely control. But to have a disorderly local section in the Zone, a section more similar to the tenements of New York City than to the carefully planned US suburbs of the early twentieth century, was not the goal. Eventually the ICC would build a few model towns for a few permanent workers, and screening and trimmed grass would become standard features of all Zone housing. But that would come only after the Zone's depopulation.

4

A Zone without Panamanians

Anyone familiar with the saga of the Panama Canal knows about the important health and engineering debates among the government officials charged with the task of building it.[1] Yet during the years of construction another equally important debate got under way when canal officials began to discuss the future of Panamanian towns and populations in the Zone. Would Americans govern and "civilize" native towns or would they dismantle them and send their inhabitants to the cities of Panama and Colón? This debate concluded with the depopulation order of December 1912, which led to a transformation of the landscape as impressive as, if not more so than, the construction of the canal itself.

The decision that led to this enormous transformation was neither immediate nor predictable; it was the product of careful debates among US officials in the Zone. Neither was it the natural result of canal construction. As we have seen, during most of the work the Zone was dotted with Panamanian "native towns" that did not look very different from the nearby cities of Panama and Colón. US officials did not try to dismantle them but instead sought to regulate, civilize, and tax them. Yet the idea that native towns did not belong in the Zone slowly began

to circulate among Zone authorities. This debate had two crucial moments: the January 1911 discussion about the future of the native town
of La Boca and the visit of a US congressional delegation to Panama in
December 1911, during which the question of whether or not the Zone
should be populated was carefully examined.

The Future of Balboa

In August 1910, the ICC Town Site Committee met to discuss the future
of the Balboa district in the Pacific port of the Panama Canal. It had to
decide what to do with the residents of the town of La Boca—also called
the "native town of Balboa" or "Old Balboa"—because the town had
to be evacuated to create space for the new port facilities on the Pacific site of the canal.[2] In 1911, La Boca was an important Zone town. It
probably started as a fishing town on the mouth, or *boca,* of the Rio
Grande. Its importance grew during the construction of the French
canal when a new port was built nearby. For a brief moment, it had
been the residence of the mayor of the Ancón municipality.[3] Although
La Boca was not as big as Empire or Gatún, it had the typical mixture
of restaurants, stores, and tenements of Zone towns. In 1911, there were
sixty-six buildings that contained approximately 410 rooms for rent.
Eleven of these buildings were used for stores, restaurants, and other
commercial enterprises.[4]

La Boca's location between Panama City and the Pacific terminal
of the canal made the city, and the entire district of Balboa, a central
sector of the Zone. Balboa would also eventually become one of the
best examples of the American urban conquest of the tropics. However,
in August 1910 it was not yet clear what its future urban layout would be.
The Town Site Committee believed that the Balboa district would
have a "white settlement" and a "native village."[5] The notion that

Panamanians would not live in the Zone or that there would be no Panamanian towns there had not yet become prevalent among US officials. On the contrary, the ICC chairman, George W. Goethals, considered Panamanians to be "inhabitants of the Zone." He thought that it was important to find "a convenient location for the residents of the Zone, who will be required to move from the land which they now occupy and which is located in the area reserved for ship's basin etc. at Balboa."[6] Thus, in January 1911, in the eyes of the highest authority of the Canal Zone, "natives" were still "residents" and "inhabitants" of the Zone. This should not be surprising since La Boca—or native Balboa—and other Zone towns were not mere labor camps that could be removed and relocated at will. They were old towns with deep histories that had only recently been stripped of their status as municipalities. Nothing demonstrates the success of the erasure of the Zone's connections to Panama's urban history more than the fact that it seems surprising today that at one point many residents thought local inhabitants would remain in the Zone.

The most important precedent for the relocation of La Boca was the relocation of the old colonial town of Gatún, situated at the intersection of the Gatún and Chagres Rivers. Gatún had served the river traffic for centuries; it even had an abandoned Spanish fort that once defended the route. In 1908, the ICC had to relocate the residents of "native" Gatún because a dam was planned for the site of the town. According to Zone officials, the residents of Gatún had complained about having to abandon the margins of the Chagres River, which for centuries had guaranteed their transportation and livelihood. However, in 1908 the ICC did not expel the residents of Gatún from the Zone but instead relocated them two miles away in the town of New Gatún, which would become the Zone's largest town. The ICC moved the church and school to the new town and provided the inhabitants of Gatún with cars to transport their goods and housing materials. New Gatún was expected to be a permanent, modern town with water, sewerage systems, and connections to transportation routes. It would be on the new line of the Panama Railroad, and there were plans to build a road that would connect it to Colón City.[7]

But the political climate changed between 1908 and 1911. The attempt at regulating local towns to make them an example of American urban modernity in the tropics was proving increasingly difficult to achieve. As the deliberations about the future of the "native" town of Balboa progressed, it became clear that not all Zone officials believed that native towns belonged in the Zone. Eventually the Town Site Committee shifted its focus to "whether there should be a native town site in the vicinity of Balboa at all."[8] To help answer the question, in January 1911 Tom M. Cooke, the chairman of the Town Site Committee, sent a letter to several members of the ICC, requesting their opinion about the future of the "native" town of Balboa.[9] The correspondence reveals different ethical values about the duties and responsibilities of the US government in the Zone. It also reveals that there was not yet an established consensus on the question of whether the current inhabitants of the Zone should continue to live there or be relocated to the nearby cities of Panama and Colón. This debate involved the highest authorities of the ICC: Chairman George W. Goethals, Chief Sanitary Officer William C. Gorgas, and David D. Gaillard, the engineer in charge of the central division of the canal.

Some of the respondents to Cooke's letter agreed with the chairman, who thought that the inhabitants of the native town of Balboa should be relocated to another place inside the Zone borders, not too far from their original town.[10] One respondent approved the building of a native town as long as it was not located on space needed, or potentially needed, by the federal government on the Pacific seafront.[11] Another response showed less concern with the location of the native town than with guaranteeing that its layout take into account that this area of the Zone "may grow into one of importance and beauty" because of its location. It recommended wide streets and sidewalks, and enough space for a public park and a mall, with flowers and trees to decorate the shoreline.[12] It mattered less who inhabited the town than whether it conformed to the aesthetic and urban guidelines appropriate to its future importance.

Gorgas did not object to the presence of a native town in the Zone either. He thought it made economic sense: "it would be advantageous to . . . locate a native town . . . on American ground, so that if a considerable population collected around Balboa, the department of Civil Government will get the benefit of the revenues therefrom."[13] Gorgas's perspective reflected a now lost economic vision of the American Zone. In 1911, it was still possible to imagine that a "considerable population" would collect around Balboa; that the Zone would continue to have real towns with saloons, restaurants, stores, and private housing; and that the US government would derive economic benefits from a vibrant and urban Zone economy. It is important to point out that during the construction period, the Zone had a department of taxation that duly collected taxes from the many thriving private businesses that catered to thousands of canal workers. Taxes were expected to play a role in the US civilizing mission. They were supposed to "educate them [natives] gradually to the requirement of a self-sustaining government."[14]

Other respondents vehemently opposed the building of a new native town near the port of Balboa. David D. Gaillard was the strongest and most prominent voice against it. Gaillard was the engineer in charge of the canal central division, which included the famous and challenging Culebra Cut. He had extensive experience in the US Army Corps of Engineers and had participated in the Spanish-American War in Cuba. Gaillard thought that "it was undesirable to have a native town anywhere near the docks: that such town would necessarily be a place for rum-selling, drunkenness and disorder." In his view, the canal's entrance was a privileged space that should be reserved for commercial purposes and, if not, should be held as "a United States Reservation *with the distinct idea of keeping slums away from the immediate vicinity of the Canal entrance.*"[15] Gaillard expressed what would become the predominant sentiment about the area around the Pacific port. It had to showcase American urban modernity to the world. A couple of years later, Austin W. Lord, a famous New York architect and Columbia University professor, would be hired to design the American town of Balboa Heights and the administration building that watched over it from Ancón Hill. The symbolic importance of the canal would even warrant a visit from the Commission of Fine Arts of the US Congress to ensure that the canal followed appropriate aesthetic standards.[16] Slums definitely did not belong in this privileged space.

Gaillard also considered the possibility of Balboa becoming an important military post, in which case he knew of "no greater curse to a military post than having squalid native villages or slums adjacent to it."[17] Only a town site reserved for "dwellings of a better class, say for dwellings costing not less than three or four thousand dollars," would be appropriate near the port. His only objection to a residential community next to a military post was "the establishment of saloons, etc." He warned the committee that if the local population of the current native town of Balboa were to be moved to the proposed town site, the prospect of having a "select residential community will at once vanish."[18] It is worth noting that not even Gaillard had completely excluded the possibility of having a native town, even if only for a "better class." As we can see, in January 1911 the ideal of a Zone without any native towns had not yet been conceived.

Gaillard also had strong ideas about the extent of the ICC's obligation toward the displaced "native" population. According to him, the "occupants of the present native town" could find housing in Panama City. He "wholly disagree[d]" with the idea that the ICC was obligated to find a suitable town for the people displaced by port construction. The ICC's only responsibility was to pay the owners the cost of the damages done to their few houses of "cheap construction and very poor repair." "Having paid them full value for property taken, the Government is under no obligation whatever to see that they are established in a town site."[19] If the ICC considered it necessary to establish a town for the laborers working around the canal terminal, it could build it on the outskirts of Panama City, where it would be absorbed by the "natural growth of the city." At a time when many workers and managers still believed that work and housing should be near each other, Gaillard argued against it, since there were "but few cities or localities where laborers do not have to ride from one to three miles to and from work." The growing importance of the new port at Balboa would surely foster the growth of public transportation between Panama City and the port.[20]

Another canal engineer, S. B. Williamson, echoed Gaillard's views. He did not think "it necessary to provide for the inhabitants of the 'native town of Balboa' when it is destroyed for wharf purposes." Like Gaillard, he thought that the residents of the "native town of Balboa" could find houses in Panama City and use "labor trains as the majority of the employees of both the Commission and the Panama Railroad do at present." If the ICC insisted on providing for the people driven out by wharf construction, a small town farther from the canal than the proposed one would suffice. Because "the houses built at the present time will be of an inferior type and owned or occupied by an undesirable class of people which the Commission will desire to remove toward the completion of the Canal," Williamson thought it was not a good idea to create a town for them close to the canal.[21]

Gaillard's view of the people to be displaced as "occupants" of a "present native town" characterized the dwellers of the Zone as temporary residents. It differed from the view of Goethals, who continued to consider them "inhabitants of the Zone" and still believed that the ICC had a responsibility to relocate them to an appropriate place close to their old location. At the heart of this difference were two conceptions of the character of the Zone and of the responsibility of the United States toward the people and places it governed in Panama. Eventually, Gaillard and Williamson's position would triumph. Perhaps they were more conscious of the Zone's symbolic function. In Williamson's words, if this land was not going to be used for defensive purposes, "a modern town site may then be laid out and buildings constructed according to modern building regulations provided for."[22] Shacks, slums, and "undesirable" people did not belong in the Zone.

The resolution of the Town Site Committee acknowledged the differences of opinion among Zone officials but nevertheless took Gaillard's position. It resolved to cancel the leases of the people living in the "native town of Balboa," and "without consideration of the relocation of the leaseholders by the Canal Zone authorities. It is the opinion of the Committee that these people can find location in the city of Panama."[23] The proposed location at the Balboa dump was considered too valuable for a "native town." After Gaillard's suggestion, the Town Site Committee did not recognize any obligation to relocate the inhabitants of the "native town of Balboa." Yet some Zone authorities retained a sense of obligation toward the people displaced by canal works. The acting chairman of the ICC was not willing to accept the Town Site Committee's recommendation without first ordering an inquiry to "ascertain and report whether such a procedure . . . will result in any hardship to the residents of the present native town of Balboa."[24]

At the end of February the Town Site Committee again considered relocating the "native town of Balboa" to a site that was less strategic than the originally proposed Balboa dump but still within the Zone's limits. The proposed new town would be located in an area of eight acres bounded "northerly by the Panama Railroad, easterly by the diversion channel, and southerly by a line approximately parallel with the Panama-Balboa road." The town site would be divided into fifty-one lots.[25] Gaillard again opposed the relocation of the residents of native Balboa to a site within the Zone. This time he gave technical and financial reasons. It would be too expensive and it would divert attention and energy from more important operations.[26] Goethals did not approve of the new proposed location but was not yet willing to refuse any responsibility toward the residents of native Balboa. Thus, he ordered an investigation to "ascertain whether the non-establishment of a new native town site in the vicinity of Balboa will result in any hardship to the residents of the present native town of Balboa who are to be driven therefrom in the near future." He would not approve any course of action until the results of this investigation were known.[27]

In response, the Department of Civil Administration produced a detailed report that listed the characteristics of the current "native" town. However, it did not take a position on the hardships that relocation would inflict on its dwellers. Quite the contrary, it concluded that "it has been impossible to ascertain what hardship will result to the residents of the present town of Balboa if they are driven therefrom. It would seem, however, that the employees could find houses in the suburbs of Panama, and could easily get to and from their work at Balboa by means of labor trains."[28] The administration's official recommendation: "inasmuch as the land on which these houses are located is required in the near future for Canal construction work, I recommend that the leases in the present town of Balboa be cancelled . . . and the owners of the buildings notified to remove their structures at once."[29] Goethals agreed and instructed that "all leases in the area in question be cancelled as of April 1, 1911 . . . that the lessees be required to remove their buildings at the earliest practicable date on account of the requirement of construction work."[30] The houses of the "native town of Balboa" had to be removed and the land made available for port construction after June 1, 1911.[31]

How should we interpret the need for a report on the hardship caused by relocation and the report's surprising conclusion that "it was impossible to ascertain" this hardship? It could be dismissed as a hypocritical bureaucratic formality that refused to deal with the social disruptions that canal construction had brought on local people. Perhaps something more profound was at stake. The contradictions of the hardship report reflected the impossibilities of what would later be called development programs.[32] The Panama Canal had become a symbol of American modernity, and Zone towns were expected to bring the benefits of modern science and technology to the tropics. The internal contradictions of this narrative were immense. The construction of the Panama Canal had brought thousands of workers—40,000 according to the most conservative estimate—who had to be housed in Panama City, Colón City, or in the many towns in the Zone. Providing housing for these workers was expensive and difficult, particularly if the Progressive Era guidelines for working-class housing were to be followed. Zone authorities did not have the resources to provide model housing for the entire Zone population, and so private tenements that rented rooms to canal workers began to sprout up in the various towns of the Zone.

Yet bringing industrialization to the tropics was marked by particularly strong silences. While Progressive Era reformers were not afraid to acknowledge the excesses of the "world of iron" and the social problems that industrialization had brought to cities in Europe and in the United States, they seemed less willing to acknowledge these contradictions in Panama. Poverty in Panama could not be the consequence of a large industrial project like the construction of the Panama Canal. To recognize that Panamanian poverty derived from the same disruptions that industrialization had brought to American and European cities would interfere with important geographies of progress that located tradition in Latin America and portrayed the American presence as a necessary and redemptive force that brought the benefits of technology and modernity to Latin America. Panama's poverty had to be explained with a history of regional backwardness and tradition.[33] But the Zone could not be a model of modernity as long as its towns were filled with tenements and slums. The solution was to relocate most canal construction workers to the cities of Panama and Colón outside of the Zone borders and to create a few model and segregated towns that would only house the canal's small permanent workforce. Only a depopulated Zone would eventually allow the US government to create a suburban landscape that closely followed contemporary urban ideals.

On December 5, 1912, a year after the ICC reached the decision to expel the residents of native Balboa from the Zone, President Taft decreed the depopulation of the Zone with an Executive Order. The alleged reason, and the only one that the Panama Canal treaty allowed, was that "all land and land under water within the limits of the Canal Zone are necessary for the construction, maintenance, operation, protection and sanitation of the Panama Canal." At no point during the 1911 debate was the "need of Canal Zone lands for canal construction or operation" mentioned as a reason against relocating the inhabitants of La Boca to a place nearby inside the Zone, as the ICC had previously done with the residents of Gatún. To understand the reasons behind the 1912 depopulation order it is necessary to look at two things: the US congressional hearings that took place in the Zone in December 1911, during which several high-ranking canal administrators gave their testimonies, and *The Government of the Canal Zone* (1915), in which Goethals gave a long and detailed explanation of his thinking.[34]

A US congressional committee visited Panama at the end of 1911, during a crucial moment of canal construction. Soon, a good portion of Zone lands would be flooded by the creation of Lake Gatún. Moreover, although canal construction was still in full swing, it was clear that in a few years the workforce would dwindle from tens of thousands of workers to a much smaller number necessary for the operation of the canal. The US government faced a major decision. Where would it relocate the people displaced by the creation of Lake Gatún? To new towns and areas inside the Zone, as had happened with the residents of Gatún, or outside the Zone, as had happened to the residents of La Boca? Therefore, the visiting congressional committee routinely asked the canal administrators two important questions about the future of the Zone. First, should the Zone be populated? Second, should agriculture be encouraged, or would it be better to allow the jungle to grow back? If the Zone remained populated, it would continue to be a densely populated region filled with towns and agricultural fields, just as it had been for hundreds of years. However, if the US government decided to depopulate the Zone, the ICC would have to undertake a costly and dramatic process of social engineering that would involve expelling the longtime residents of the Zone along with the workers who had been involved in canal construction and replacing an entire urban and agricultural geography with a new one.

The answers to the questions of the congressional committee varied. But, according to one committee member, "the consensus opinion of every witness has been, I think, that there are no tracts on this zone which are of any value in attracting any kind of *desirable population;* that American population will not come here because it cannot support itself; that it will deteriorate; and that it ought not be encouraged; that *the only kind of population that would come would be an undesirable black population,* which would deteriorate, be a menace to the welfare of the community, require expensive government and policing system, and be detrimental to the best interests in operating the canal."[35]

This summary made it clear that the issue was not whether there were people living in Zone lands or willing to cultivate them, but rather whether it was desirable to keep the current black population. Most answers shared contemporary racist views and opposed a populated Zone if that meant the population would be black. Opposition to a populated Zone could be fierce. For example, the engineer Williamson said, "My idea is this, that the zone should be depopulated, with the exception of the force necessary to operate the canal. All the others should be concentrated in the towns at the ends, where they can be policed and fumigated more economically."[36] For Williamson, natives were no better than mosquitoes; they needed to be controlled and fumigated. This perspective was taken up by a US congressman who stated, "these people are no more use than mosquitos and buzzards; they ought all to be exterminated together."[37]

Others, however, did not share to the same extent the deeply racist views of their peers. Colonel Sibert disagreed with the idea that black West Indian farmers required a more expensive civil government to "hold them in check." He thought "it would be a bigger job to hold the 2,500 Americans than the Jamaicans. The Americans need the Law more than anybody else." He also disagreed with the idea that the Zone was not suitable for agriculture and thought that native oranges and native bananas were sweet. He also thought that a cultivated Zone with its land cleared provided better protection to the canal than a Zone covered with jungle.[38]

Chief sanitary officer Gorgas also preferred a populated Zone. Ideally, he would have liked a Zone cultivated and settled by "the best class of people" because, in his view, this would lead to the drainage of Zone lands, which would have positive sanitary effects on the area. When asked, however, what he thought of a Zone settled not by "an intelligent population" but by a "different class of people," he still answered, "well, it would not aid it [the sanitation] as efficiently in that way, but I think much more efficiently than leaving the land covered with jungle and uncultivated." Gorgas did not seem to share his peers' bleak view of the tropics and tropical people. He did not believe "that the Tropics are more unhealthful than the Temperate Zone." Moreover, he acknowledged that the Zone was not fit for the cultivation of temperate products, but that did not seem to bother him much. Zone land was "adapted to the production of such things as the native produces around here. I see him everywhere as he settles in his little cabin cultivating half an acre or an acre of yams, bananas, cassava, and those things that grow that he uses." When pushed to answer if he thought that a cultivated Zone was essential for the sanitation of the Zone, he recognized that it was not. He admitted, "My interest in the zone leads me to want to see it a cultivated country. My wish for doing this is probably more of a romantic idea than a sanitary advantage, but I believe it would be a sanitary advantage too, if the country were cultivated."[39]

Eventually, the view in favor of a depopulated Zone prevailed. As is apparent in the 1911 answers, the reasons for or against a populated Zone had nothing to do with the flooding of Lake Gatún or with other engineering requirements for canal construction. The reasons were deeply racial. The question was whether it was possible to attract white settlers to the Zone and, if not, whether it was desirable to retain its current black population. For the majority, the answer to the second part of the question was no.

Although in 1911 George Goethals had not been the main voice against keeping the residents of La Boca inside Zone borders, by 1915 he had developed a complex and elaborate justification for the Zone's depopulation. He strongly argued against those who wanted to use the Zone as a colony for American farmers. He considered these plans naïve and uninformed. His reasoning can be roughly divided into three main arguments: first, the Zone's climate, soil, and legal status were not conducive to American farming; second, he did not want to see the Zone populated by West Indians and native blacks; third, the jungle was the best form of canal defense.[40] According to him, the legal and geographic characteristics of the Zone were not appropriate for American farmers because they could not secure rights over their property owing to the Zone's special legal status. Farmers could not buy tracts of land and could only obtain twenty-five-year leases, which could be revoked at any time if the land was needed for canal purposes. Moreover, the Zone's geography—its peoples and its land—were also inappropriate for agriculture.

Of course, the isthmian corridor had a rich tradition of farms that cultivated a variety of tropical fruits and vegetables. The Zone had also been an area of small cattle ranches, which experimented with new types of grass. Yet according to Goethals, "the natives were not given to tilling the Zone beyond the extent of supplying their own needs in the forms of a few bananas and yams . . . the country supplies nothing except cattle, and these only in limited numbers."[41] For him, as for many other American observers, tropical products for local food consumption did not count as agriculture. Only the tropical plantations that grew for export and the cultivation of fruits and vegetables of temperate climates to which Americans "had been accustomed at home" counted as agriculture. Goethals explained that the geography of the Zone made it unsuitable for large-scale and export-oriented plantations. Canal authorities had also conducted interesting experiments to acclimate some temperate products to the Zone, but they failed. In Goethals's language and perspective, the Zone became a barren place where Americans were unable to cultivate temperate fruits and vegetables.[42]

If local geography was unaccommodating, local people were worse. If the Zone was not an adequate place for American farmers, the alternative was to continue to have a Zone cultivated by local farmers. But Goethals "did not care to see a population of Panamanian or West Indian negroes occupying the land, for these are non-productive, thriftless and indolent." Nor could he see them as workers for American farmers. To those who proposed opening the Zone's land to "gentlemen farmers" who would enjoy franchise rights, create municipalities, and with their presence provide protection to the canal, he objected, arguing that by "such an arrangement a large population of negroes would be left within the Zone, increasing the cost of government."[43] In Goethals's view, black settlements contributed nothing and only added sanitation costs because the government would have to provide "police, waterworks, roads, fire protection and schools."

Goethals used the era of canal construction to prove his point. He admitted that during this period sanitation efforts focused mostly on American settlements and "little work . . . had been done around the aggregations of native huts even when in proximity to American towns, and nothing at all where the natives and others were living in the brush." The choice was clear: either increase government costs or continue ignoring many of the sanitation needs of native settlements and forgo the ideal of a Zone thoroughly urbanized according to the highest sanitation standards.

Goethals also thought that native towns were dirty. Getting rid of the native sides of Empire and Culebra would rid the Zone of the filthy conditions found there. And "while filth may not be the cause of disease, to Americans generally it is not pleasant."[44] With this argument Goethals concluded his case against the desirability of keeping native and West Indian settlements in the Zone.

Finally, he considered the jungle the best military protection for the canal. According to him, the jungle made the movement of large armed bodies difficult. Even if small armed groups could move through it and reach the locks, canal defense should be able to protect them from any damage. For Goethals, "the jungle would give greater protection" than a populated Zone, without the sanitation costs.[45] He concluded that "all of the arguments seemed to point to the desirability of depopulating the Canal Zone, thereby decreasing the cost of civil government and sanitation and increasing the protection of the canal."[46]

It is interesting to note that Goethals used the racist language of his era to conceal what had been a failure. This language allowed him to pass over the years when the ICC sought to sanitize the entire Zone without expelling its original inhabitants. Instead of admitting the enormous costs of creating an ideal urban sanitary landscape, and perhaps questioning some of its assumptions, Goethals transformed the local population into lazy, dirty, and costly human beings better replaced by the jungle. Only a depopulated Zone could transform the Zone towns into the urban models ICC officials had initially envisioned.

It was possible for Goethals to use this argument because it built on ideas about human progress popular among a large section of the US and Latin American public. According to this view, the world's inevitable march toward progress was unstoppable and civilized peoples were destined to dominate and transform peoples living in lower stages of civilization, particularly nomadic cultures without sedentary agriculture, those whom Darwin had characterized as "living fossils" who represented the first stages of human history. This ideology had helped justify the expulsion of Native Americans from their lands during Argentina's conquest of the desert and the US conquest of the West.[47]

The Zone was a peculiar version of this story. While the expulsion of Native Americans relied on an ideology that denied their historical and cultural connections to their lands, the depopulation of Panama's isthmian corridor required denying the many ways in which Panamanians and Americans were part of the same political and technological culture. For the story of civilization or barbarism to work in the Zone, Panamanians had to be transformed from long-time farmers who continually experimented with new forms of agriculture into jungle nomads without sedentary agriculture; and their towns had to be transformed from republican municipalities with a long political history into administrative districts without any historical and political connection to Panama. Only then could the inhabitants of the Zone become jungle natives destined to give way to a higher civilization.

5

After the Floods

The Creation of Lake Gatún

WHEN NEWS OF THE impending opening of the Gatún Dam reached the US public at the beginning of 1912, throngs of tourists traveled to Panama eager to see marvels like the Culebra Cut before water covered them. According to the *New York Times*, tourists "do not mind what they pay or what accommodation they obtain so long as they are able to see the great cut engineered by Col. Goethals before the water is let in." "The rush" had begun just after New Year's Day and had increased "by leaps and bounds," forcing companies to bring extra steamships into service.[1]

News of the dam's opening probably had a very different effect on the people who lived in the towns and lands to be flooded by Lake Gatún. What did they think about this event? How did they experience it? How did talk of the canal's grandiosity sound to their ears? What did they feel when they heard that Lake Gatún would be the largest artificial lake in the world? That it would cover an area as large as the island of Barbados? That the dam contained twenty-two million cubic yards of material, an amount so significant, according to a writer in

1913, that it "would take twice as many horses as there are in the US to move the dam were it put on wheels"?[2] What did they think upon learning that it was the creation of Lake Gatún—and the flooding of their lands and towns—that solved the project's technical challenges by allowing the currents of the Chagres River to be controlled to provide water for the canal's lock system?

Unlike US tourists, rather than rushing to see the canal before the water came, the people living in its vicinity prepared to confront one of the biggest challenges of their lives: being forced to leave their homes and lands. They had to find a way—and a place—to move while they tried to negotiate some compensation for their properties. It is difficult, perhaps impossible, to know what the people about to be displaced by the flooding of Lake Gatún thought of the canal project. There are only a few documents—a song, a letter to Panama's congress, and an anonymous letter to Goethals—that reveal how some of them felt about having to abandon their lands. What the historian can do best with the available historical record is to recreate the process through which people were forced to leave their lands and homes.

From Gorgona to New Gorgona

Of all the Zone towns flooded by Lake Gatún, the largest was Gorgona. In 1911, Zone authorities notified the town about the impending flooding of its lands. We do not know how the residents of Gorgona reacted to the news or how they talked among themselves about the enormous changes they would soon face. We do not know what rumors circulated on Gorgona's streets or what families said in the privacy of their homes. We can imagine that their conversations were sad and spirited, and concerned with plans and strategies for facing their collective and personal challenges.

What we do know is that by October 1912 the residents of Gorgona had organized to write a collective, public letter to Panama's National Assembly demanding the government's support. The letter was signed by the "organizing board of New Gorgona," which included Jose I. Vega, the board's president, and eight other men. They asked Panama's government for public lands where they could resettle and restart their lives. They claimed the same rights to vacant lands that their government had given to European immigrants and also asked for free access to public lands. The place they had chosen to resettle was a small bay on the Pacific coast of Panama in the district of Chame and four hours by boat from Panama City. They also requested assistance in the difficult process of moving from Gorgona to New Gorgona.[3] It was an effort that warranted all the help their government could provide. In this case, and throughout the depopulation process, the government of Panama would be the intermediary between the Panamanians expelled from the Zone and the US government. It would often try to defend the legal rights of Panamanian citizens; at other times it would try to convince them to accept US terms and demands.

The tone of Gorgonans' letter was sad and tragic. It was a far cry from the hundreds of publications that represented Lake Gatún as a technological triumph. Gorgonans recognized the magnitude and fame of Lake Gatún, which their letter described as the "great lake they propose to make." But the new lake brought them not progress but expulsion from their historic lands in the Zone. Instead of acquiring new urban comforts, they had lost everything. In their words, because of the lake "we shall all remain such as nomadic tribes, homeless and without bread." For them, these were "hours of anguish in the course of our life."[4]

Gorgonans wrote of "the painful hour when we shall see disappear the flourishing towns of Gorgona, Matachin, Mamey, San Pablo,

Gamboa, Obispo and Cruces." Far from characterizing the towns as the poor little jungle towns of many US accounts, the letter presents them as "flourishing" towns whose future had abruptly come to an end.[5] And Gorgonans were right. As we have seen, since its emergence as a river town in colonial times, Gorgona and the region around it had continuously grown in importance. By the time of the creation of Lake Gatún, the most important machine shops of the Zone were located in Gorgona, and many people considered the town to be a good place to invest in real estate and rent rooms or houses to the thousands who had come to work on the canal. The high proportion of property owners living outside of Gorgona is a good indication of the town's economic importance. Of the ninety-one real estate owners in Gorgona, forty-two lived in places like Panama City, Colón City, Gatún, and Empire. Some property owners lived in places as far away as Jamaica and the United States. Several owned more than one house. Gabriel Jolly, with six buildings, had the most. Others had four or five.[6]

Gorgonans' understanding of their fate dramatically contrasted with how other people portrayed their reaction to the flooding of their towns. According to David McCullough's classic history of the Panama Canal, *The Path between the Seas,* "the native populace found it impossible to imagine" that its towns would be covered up.[7] McCullough was following an old narrative from the depopulation era. For example, the *Canal Record,* which was the official newspaper of the Isthmian Canal Commission, stated that it was "difficult to persuade some of the inhabitants that the inundation will ever take place."[8] "One old bush settler," it continued, "heedlessly ventured it as his opinion that the Lord had promised never again to flood the earth."[9] The contrast between the way Gorgonans represented their fate and the way they were portrayed could not be starker. Gorgonans saw themselves as

Panamanian citizens and residents of the Zone who were forced to abandon their flourishing towns. By contrast, the newspaper depicted them as "bush settlers" unable to understand what was happening to them. While the residents' tone was tragic, the *Canal Record*'s coverage was farcical, an occasion to laugh at the locals' inability to understand the modern world. Humor erased tragedy. This narrative also set local people in a historical time different from that of the canal builders, which also diminished the possibility of sympathy. In these stories, the inhabitants of Gorgona were not portrayed as modern citizens affected by a modern technological tragedy. Instead, canal stories presented them as part of a primitive, natural time. They were people who "disappeared in the higher silence of woods creatures." Their tragedy was similar to that of the trees eradicated by the flooding and the animals that had to seek refuge further inland.[10] Even worse, local people could be seen as a natural nuisance.

In response to the Gorgonans' petition, the government of Panama founded the town of New Gorgona, to which it assigned an area of 100 hectares. There, the residents of the Zone "who live in the towns which are to disappear" would find refuge and a new home.[11] President Belisario Porras, who was a modernizer behind the urban renewal projects that transformed Panama City during these same years, wanted New Gorgona to comply with the best urban standards of the era. It was to have a well-planned layout and ample space for avenues, public gardens, parks, and squares. Given that Panamanian citizens had lost the right to live in their historic towns, President Porras sought to re-create a new modern geography, one that would have all the attributes of early twentieth-century urban modernity. It would not be along the historic isthmian route, over which Panama had lost jurisdiction, but along the Pacific coast, which would now become the backbone of Panama's new geography.

Each Panamanian head of family residing in the Zone would receive a free plot in the town of New Gorgona and rural lands outside of town, so they could start their new lives. Heads of family would receive ten hectares, while adult Panamanians without families would receive five.[12] The government envisioned a town of 3,000 people—a number similar to that of Gorgona—composed of families coming not only from Gorgona but also from other places in the Zone.[13]

In spite of the law's good intentions, nearly four months after the decree the residents of Gorgona wrote another petition to the government, this time asking that their new town be founded in a different place, closer to the Chagres River. Indeed, New Gorgona was far, very far, from the Chagres River and the historic trade corridor of the Zone. It was nowhere near the railroad line and the historic isthmian roads. It was located on the Pacific coast of Panama by the Yeguala River, not far from the town of Chame. The only way to travel between New Gorgona and Panama City was by sea; New Gorgona did not even have a port, although Panama's government had promised to build one. Moreover, the lands of New Gorgona were not as fertile as land by the Chagres River. Thus, it is perhaps not surprising that several residents of Gorgona preferred to establish their new town at Vigia, in close proximity to the Chagres River. Their main argument was that the new town was unsuitable for agriculture.

President Porras strongly disagreed. He praised the good qualities of New Gorgona: its breeze, its small bay suitable for the arrival of all kinds of vessels, its public lands suitable for agriculture and cattle ranching, and the quality of nearby rivers. Moreover, he argued, New Gorgona was only four hours by boat from Panama City, which would make it easy for Gorgonans to transport their agricultural products to the nation's capital. More importantly, he continued, Zone authorities had not approved Vigia. Although the town was above the flood line of Lake Gatún, it would be inundated with water if the United States went ahead with its plan to build a dam at Alajuela.[14] After President Porras rejected their petition, the residents of Gorgona began the difficult process of relocating away from the river and their historic home in the middle of Panama's isthmian route.

In June 1913, the depopulation of Gorgona reached a new pace when the Zone police posted the following notice around the town:

> You are hereby notified to remove or destroy your building in the town of Gorgona before August 1st, 1913.
>
> In so far as available the Panama Railroad Company will furnish care for the free transportation of the lumber and material in your house to Panama or Colon.
>
> It will be necessary for the Isthmian Canal Commission to destroy your building, if not removed before August 1, 1913.[15]

With a little more than a month to leave their town, Gorgonans still had many questions about their rights. What did moving entail? Who would pay for it? The most pressing question for homeowners was whether they should dismantle their houses or not. Most houses in Gorgona were made of tongue-and-groove industrial wood walls that could be dismantled and carried to a different location. Homeowners wanted to dismantle their properties so they could rebuild them in Panama City, Colón City, or New Gorgona. But they remained unsure about the legal consequences of doing so. Would they still be entitled to receive compensation for their properties if they dismantled their houses? What if they did not take them apart? Would they still receive no compensation and, on top of that, lose the opportunity to take some of the material from their homes? The August 1913 correspondence between Panama's authorities and the ICC authorities is filled with negotiations over this pressing issue.

As we will see later in more detail, in August 1913 homeowners were at the center of a legal dispute between Frank Feuille, the head of the ICC Department of Law, and the Joint Land Commission, which according to the 1903 treaty was in charge of awarding compensation to people who lost their property due to canal construction. The Joint Land Commission had compensated Gorgonans for the damages they suffered because of the depopulation order. But Fueille had challenged these awards before authorities in Washington, DC, because he thought that the Joint Land Commission did not have the authority to make them. Everybody was waiting for Washington's final legal decision. But what were Gorgonans to do in the meantime? The ICC had threatened to destroy houses not dismantled by August 1.

Panamanian and ICC authorities continued to discuss this issue through the mail and even during personal visits. Panamanian authorities wanted to be assured that dismantling and taking their houses with them would not affect Panamanians' rights to receive compensation from the Joint Land Commission if Washington approved the awards.[16] At first Feuille would not grant that assurance. If owners took their houses, they "must accept the legal effects of their actions."[17] He also treated differently homeowners who reached compensation agreements directly with the ICC instead of waiting for the awards of the Joint Land Commission. They were entitled to take awards and dismantle their houses. It was probably an attempt to pressure Gorgona homeowners to forfeit their claims before the Joint Land Commission and reach direct agreements with the ICC.[18]

In the midst of legal uncertainty, some homeowners decided to wait while others began to relocate their properties. The ICC had granted free transportation, by train or water, to local residents with their possessions and house materials. Yet transporting thousands of people and hundreds of houses was not a simple task. The human drama behind this fast and forced movement can sometimes be glimpsed in the bureaucratic letters arranging their transportation and trying to improve transportation logistics. It was a fast process, with a speed typical of natural disasters and war calamities.

The process of dismantling and moving a town the size of Gorgona to a new location was difficult and fraught with unknowns. As the first large town to be expelled from the Zone, Gorgona was an experiment for the future depopulation of the Zone's largest towns—New Gatún and Empire—which were not flooded by Lake Gatún. Like everything involving the canal, the depopulation of the Zone involved large numbers. Journalists and commentators loved to use examples to drive home the magnitude of the Panama Canal, but the scale of the Zone's depopulation was not the type of scale that pundits liked to advertise. A *National Geographic* article told its readers that if the amount of material excavated from the canal were to be loaded on the dirt cars used during its construction, "it would make a string of them reaching over two and a half times around the earth."[19] Yet nobody asked how many passenger wagons would be filled if all the people expelled from the Zone were put on a train. While canal stories explain in detail the complex engineering aspects of canal construction, nobody cared to explain the logistical and social challenges of the depopulation process.

The first Gorgonans to relocate to New Gorgona did so in July 1913. They got on the train at the Gorgona station, where coaches for passengers and boxcars for personal effects, household goods, and house materials waited for them. The movement was constant. Sixty people took the train on July 9. More people moved on July 23; on July 25, 176 people moved, and 115 additional people moved on July 29. By late August trains were taking 250 people a day.[20] People relocating were coming not only from Gorgona proper but also from nearby rural areas like Juan Grande, Mamey, Culo Seco, and Bailamonos.[21] This flow of people, hundreds at a time, continued until the railroad tracks to Gorgona were pulled up in early September.[22]

The process was difficult and confusing, particularly during the initial weeks. The people who took the trains to Panama City on July 9 had to wait until July 25 for the two lighters (a type of barge) that would take them to New Gorgona.[23] And while they waited they had to find a place to stay in Panama City. For some, this probably meant seeking refuge with friends and family. Others had to rent a room in a hotel. As if this were not enough, they had difficulties locating their household effects because some were unloaded at a freight house in Panama City and others at the American pier. Umberto Vaglio, the Panamanian in charge of looking after the interests of the Panamanian citizens of Gorgona, asked the ICC if in the future all household goods could be unloaded at the American wharf, so that Panamanians would have less difficulty locating their belongings.[24] We can only imagine the confusion caused by the constant arrival of hundreds of people with their household goods and house materials, and everybody trying to locate their belongings and determine whether anything had been lost.

By mid-August the logistics of the moving process had somewhat improved. On August 15, 250 people, along with seven carloads of personal effects, arrived at the Port of Balboa at 9:00 a.m. The lighters that would transport them to New Gorgona were waiting to receive them. The unloading and loading of material began immediately. It took six hours of continuous work to unload and reload the cargo. There was no time to separate any household goods; owners would do that at their final destination. Although much had improved since July, passengers complained that they had to wait on the train cars, near the docks, for six hours. In response, the railroad officer in charge asked that in the future household goods arrive twelve hours before passengers, so that everything would be loaded into the lighters by the time they arrived.[25] After a six-hour wait, Gorgona residents embarked on the lighters headed to New Gorgona. Thankfully, this time lighters had tarpaulins that afforded passengers protection from the sun. In an earlier trip, there was no roof or sun protection and some children had been badly sunburned.[26]

During these two months of forced relocation, people also had countless problems and concerns. For example, D. W. Ogilvie, a Jamaican doctor living in Gorgona, had not been able to find buyers for his livestock and wanted to know if the ICC would pay to transport his livestock, personal property, and furniture to Jamaica. The ICC's answer was no. Although the ICC provided free transportation to West Indians who wanted to return home, they refused it to Dr. Ogilvie because he was "quite able financially to take care of himself." Indeed, he owned several houses in Gorgona and had received compensation for the improvements on his Juan Grande plantation.[27]

Gorgonans also developed different strategies to make their journeys a little easier. Although the ICC provided free transportation for every inhabitant of the Zone and their property, in the middle of the chaos and confusion caused by thousands of people moving in two months, some chose to pay bribes to facilitate their relocation. For example, Francisco de Toma, an Italian carpenter, paid five dollars to secure railroad cars for his belongings, while Mrs. Victoria V. de Andrade had given a "gift" of fifty dollars to the railroad officer to secure three railroad cars for her property.[28] By mid-August, only thirty-seven occupied houses were left in Gorgona. Of the 3,444 habitants of the town of Gorgona counted in the 1912 census, only 123 remained (92 male adults, 12 female adults, and 19 children).[29]

Relocation became even more complicated in early September—after the new moving deadline of September 5 had expired—because Gorgona had lost its rail connection to Panama City and Colón City (the ICC tore up the tracks).[30] This caused problems for the many homeowners who had chosen not to dismantle their houses until receiving assurance that their claims before the Joint Land Commission would remain valid even if they removed their houses. But Goethals did not provide this guarantee until September 3, only two days before the final deadline to move![31] This created a new set of problems for property owners like T. L. Maduro. When he went to Gorgona on September 12 to start dismantling and moving the four houses he owned there, he was dismayed to learn that the railroad tracks were gone and he could not use the train to transport the components of his houses. He pleaded with the ICC, explaining that he had waited so long to move his properties not because of "neglect or indifference" but rather because only that week his lawyer had notified him that he could remove his houses without losing his claim rights before the Joint Land Commission. He added that he was not the only homeowner facing this predicament.

But the train tracks were gone for good. The ICC claimed that Maduro and other homeowners had had "ample time to remove their houses, as they were notified in June or July that the settlements would be abandoned."[32] As throughout the process, language was important. Two months full of legal uncertainties was considered "ample time." Also, the historic municipality of Gorgona was now only a "settlement." From 1904 to 1913 the town had gone from being a municipality to an administrative district to a settlement. Like so many words used to describe the depopulation of the Zone, the term *settlement* transformed permanent, historic, political towns into non-historical, transient arrangements.

The only remaining way to transport house materials was by water. Homeowners began to use rafts to cross the canal from its west side, where the town was located, to the east side, where the new railroad was. The ICC allowed them to take their houses using this process but stationed an employee at Gorgona "to see that the houses are removed in an orderly way" and with the necessary care "to prevent any of the material from going into the river."[33]

Houses and housing materials continued to be transported by train and boat. Materials were important not only because of their intrinsic monetary value but also because they helped recreate lost urban landscapes. The residents of Gorgona wanted to take to New Gorgona "some of the buildings which have been used for some time by the inhabitants of the town." In particular, they wanted to take the Catholic church, the schoolhouses, and the old municipal building.[34] With these structures they sought to recreate the communal life they were about to lose and to reclaim the political identity that they had lost after the 1907 reforms had eliminated the municipalities of the Zone.

Alas, not even this request was easily granted. Goethals explained to President Porras that he would have loved to donate the buildings, but because they were "of some value to the Commission," he did not have the authority to do so. Panama's government was welcome to purchase them at their appraised prices. The church, however, could not be purchased because the Catholic Church owned the building.[35] It is not known if these buildings eventually made it to New Gorgona. We only know that the Catholic church was one of the buildings removed from Gorgona by the Quartermaster's Department in August 1913.[36] Private parties also purchased buildings like a one-family French house, a three-family French house, an ICC hotel, and a dentist's office. Their final destination is unknown. Like the people of Gorgona, they were scattered around Panama's geography: some in Panama

City, some in Colón, some in New Gorgona, and some in the new towns that were forming on the other side of the Zone's borders.[37]

Business owners also had to relocate their establishments, hoping that their clients would follow them. That was the case with Esteban Durán, who owned a distributing house for wine and liquor. He moved from Gorgona to Bolívar Street in Colón City and advertised his relocation in Panama's main newspaper, *La Estrella de Panamá*. Since he only had until July 1 to move, he asked his clients to pick up their merchandise before June 30, otherwise he would transport all the remaining merchandise to Colón City.[38] The economic cost of this type of business relocation or its impact on Duran's client base when he left Gorgona, which was centrally located in the middle of the Panama Railroad, for Colón City is unknown. Neither do we know how many businesses failed because of relocation. With so many people moving and so many businesses relocating, real estate prices likely went up in Panama City and Colón. Some businesses might have lost established clients. Perhaps only the largest businesses managed to survive.

In the midst of tragedy, not everybody was equal. Panamanian citizens had rights that West Indian immigrants did not have, even if the latter constituted the majority of the Zone's population. To the pains and difficulties of forced displacement, West Indian immigrants added the burden of segregation. Umberto Vaglio, Panama's commissioner in charge of protecting the rights of displaced Panamanians, requested separate railroad cars for Panamanian citizens and West Indians. He complained that some of the second-class coaches intended for Panamanians were "utilized by Jamaicans and as a consequence considerable confusion resulted." The ICC complied and "orders" were "given to the railroad agents and others that cars . . . be limited to Panamanians, for whom the request is made."[39] Also, West Indians displaced from Gorgona had the rights of neither Panamanian citizens nor European immigrants, whose immigration Panama's government sought to promote. Chinese and West Indian immigrants had been prohibited since 1904, a status that was reinforced by successive laws.

Both groups also experienced Panama's growing racism.[40] Their treatment highly contrasted with the way in which the government of Panama treated European immigrants working on the canal. In 1913, when the process of abandoning the Panamanian towns of the Zone had started, Panama's government published announcements in local newspapers trying to attract "the European laborers working in the Zone" to settle in Panama as farmers. Unlike immigrants who were legally considered undesirable, European workers enjoyed the same rights as Panamanian citizens, and so they benefited from new land laws that were decreed to promote the agricultural development of Panamanian farmlands.[41] To better achieve its goal, the government wanted to create a census of European workers in the Zone, in order to know how many would remain unemployed once canal construction was completed. Like other countries at the turn of the twentieth century, Panama had developed racist immigration policies that favored some types of immigrants over others. Panama's government feared unemployed West Indian workers, saw them as a threat, and tried to ensure that the United States would do everything it could to repatriate them. In contrast, the government saw unemployed European workers as an opportunity to whiten the country's complexion. Unlike Panamanian citizens and European immigrants, West Indians were not given free plots of land in New Gorgona but instead had to purchase plots from the Panamanian government.[42] To the difficulties of forced relocation was added second-class legal status. The US government gave West Indians free tickets to move back to Jamaica, but those who had settled in Panama, who owned houses or cultivated land, were at a clear disadvantage. The ICC paid only for the transportation of household goods and housing materials destined for Colón City, Panama City, and New Gorgona, not for Jamaica. Thus, if West Indians returned to Jamaica they had to pay for the transportation of their goods, and if they relocated inside Panama, they had to confront segregation while traveling and additional expenses if moving to New Gorgona.

The Fate of New Gorgona

What happened to the people who moved to New Gorgona? What was it like to move from a railroad town in the middle of the isthmian road that had specialized in servicing international commerce for centuries to a small rural town far from any major road or city? A detailed account written by two sergeants sent by the ICC to spend a day at New Gorgona and report on its conditions provides some answers.[43] Their report describes a surreal landscape of unfinished projects and uprooted people failing to flourish in a new environment. New Gorgona was a town of forty-two buildings constructed with second-hand material from the old buildings of the Zone. The Panamanian government had promised to build a modern town that would have been the envy of Gorgona. However, when the sergeants visited New Gorgona, there were only promises and unfinished projects. The streets of the town had been laid out but the absence of grading had allowed the grass to grow back; the Panamanian government had begun to construct a pipe to bring water from the Yeguala River but the work had been suspended due to technical difficulties; the government had also begun to build a wharf using old railroad rails as the supporting frame, but the work had not yet progressed to the point where the wharf could be used.[44] From the time of the town's initial occupation, eighteen people had died from diseases caused by stagnant water found nearby; the closest source of clean spring water was a half-mile away. There was no physician, drug-store, or licensed midwife. The town had a post office but the nearest telephone and telegraph service was in the nearby town of Chame.

But nothing revealed the ghostlike nature of New Gorgona, a rail-road town without a railroad, a river town without a river, more than its abundance of stores. "Nearly every house has a small general mer-chandise store on the first story," the report noted, adding that "the number of stores in the town are out of all proportion to the popula-tion." This was quite an understatement. Gorgona was a town of mer-chants who had made a living in the middle of the isthmian route; the town had catered for centuries to travelers and laborers working for the railroad and canal projects. It now found itself with stores in a new location in the middle of nowhere, and without customers. One can imagine them passing their days inside stores filled with goods they could not sell, watching their neighbors, also with goods they could not sell, and wondering what their next move would be. They might have wished they had followed the example of their Chinese neighbors back in old Gorgona who had decided not to move to New Gorgona.

By the time of the report New Gorgona had just 250 people, children included, whereas more than 3,000 people had lived in Gorgona. The ICC sergeants learned that half of the population had left after the gov-ernment had stopped working on the wharf and the water pipe. On October 1, 340 men, mostly Martinicans, had left for Panama City. The sergeants also found a "noticeable" absence of young Panamanian farmers. People were leaving in droves. Apparently, 60 percent of the population that had migrated to New Gorgona had already left for the district of Paja (later renamed Nuevo Emperador), near the Zone's western border. Its lands were considered "very fertile," a characteristic that might have reminded its neighbors of the fertile lands of Gorgona. Paja was also located along a major road, the Empire Chorrera, which at the time was part of the main road connecting western and eastern Panama. Centrally located near the Zone and with fertile lands, Paja would be the New Gorgona of New Gorgona.[45]

The Property Rights of Canal Zone Inhabitants

On March 1, 1913, the members of the Joint Land Commission, two Americans and two Panamanians, met at Panama's National Palace to decide how to compensate people forced to leave the Zone by the depopulation order of 1912.[46] (The commission had been established by the 1903 treaty.) To ensure the fairness of the process, both Panama and the United States were equally represented on the commission with two members each. If a majority was not reached, an arbitrator would make the final decision.[47] This was not the first time the commission met.[48] It had also met in 1905, 1907, and 1908 to decide the compensation for property owners whose lands were expropriated for canal construction under eminent domain. During the commission's initial years, the awards were few and substantial. From 1905 to 1908 it made twenty awards totaling $258,000. Awards ranged from $90,000, paid to Antonio Andrade for Hacienda Andrade, to $725, paid to an unknown claimant for Barro Colorado and Frijol Grande. It was during these years that the United States acquired hundreds of hectares from the large haciendas in the Zone—for example, 126 hectares from Hacienda Cárdenas and 406 hectares from La Pihiva. Some of these haciendas dated to the Spanish colonial era.[49]

When the Joint Land Commission met again in 1913, everything was different. The commission members had to decide on the thousands of claims caused by the forced depopulation of the most densely populated region of Panama. It was a time of turmoil during which the inhabitants of the Zone had to figure out the best way to defend their property rights. Panamanian lawyers—including future president Harmodio Arias—began to advertise their services to those filing claims before the commission.[50] Some people could afford to hire his prestigious law firm, Arias and Fabrega; others had to be more resourceful about defending their case. In addition to solving thousands of claims, the members of the Joint Land Commission also had to deal with the complexity of the many types of property rights existing in the Zone. Some people were squatters on old hacienda lands. Other people owned buildings on rented municipal lots, and still others owned buildings or farms on lots they rented from the Panama Railroad or the ICC. The task before the members of the Joint Land Commission was daunting and required great legal acumen and political skills on the part of Panamanian commissioners. They would constantly refer to Article VI of the 1903 treaty, which stated, "The grants herein contained shall in no manner invalidate the titles or rights of private land holders or owners of private property in the said zone or in or to any of the lands or waters granted to the United States."

Panama's commissioners reviewed claims at Panama's National Palace. Panama's two representatives in 1913 were Samuel Lewis and Federico Boyd, the latter having previously participated in the 1905 Joint Land Commission.[51] They were wealthy and highly educated men who belonged to the intellectual world of Colombia's elite and had many years of political experience. They had participated in the 1903 separation of Panama and had been active in the political struggles of the late nineteenth century. They belonged to a generation of men who came of age after the liberal reforms of the mid-nineteenth century.

They were formed in a legal world in which slavery no longer existed and in which colonial forms of property had been replaced with modern forms that privileged private property over communal property and one sole proprietor for one property over the multiple-use rights that one property could have under the Spanish legal system.[52] Like their US counterparts, they believed in the sacred right of private property and in the relationship between science, technology, and progress.[53] Their main task was to ensure that those sacred rights of private property would apply to Panamanians, and that the legal traditions and rights that had governed property rights in the Zone during the nineteenth century would be respected.

The talents of the Panamanian members of the Joint Land Commission were put to the test on June 23, 1913, when a man named Juan Botillo submitted a claim for the property he owned in Gorgona and an ICC lawyer challenged his right to do so. Botillo's case became the hallmark case on which Panama's commissioners focused their energy because the "status of most of the claimants of the towns of Gorgona" depended on its resolution.[54] The case's legal controversy centered on the question of whether Gorgona's property owners had any right to receive compensation from the Joint Land Commission.

Like most property owners in Gorgona, Botillo did not own the land on which his building stood. He rented it from the ICC. He had previously rented his town lot from the municipality of Gorgona. There was nothing unusual about his situation. Homeowners had been renting town lots from the municipality of Gorgona since the nineteenth century, if not earlier. Their rights had been regulated and protected under multiple Colombian and Panamanian laws until, at the end of 1907, Botillo and his neighbors were required to sign a new type of lease with the ICC. Like other inhabitants of the Zone, Botillo had no choice but to sign a lease that damaged his legal and economic interests. With the end of municipalities in 1907, the ICC had an almost complete monopoly on Zone lands, and its legal office could impose any type of lease on Zone inhabitants, who simply had to accept it if they wanted to remain in their towns and continue to participate in the Zone's vibrant economy. These leases not only gave the ICC the right to end the leases at its convenience but also placed all the expenses of property removal on the shoulders of building owners and, most importantly, freed the United States from any "claim for damages . . . on account of such removal."

The section of the ICC lease at the heart of the controversy stated:

> This lease shall be revocable at will by the lessor or his successor in office; and that the lessee shall pay to the lessor, or to his authorized agent, on demand, for the use of the United States, any sums which may have to be expended after the expiration or revocation of this lease in putting the said premises or property in a good condition for use by the United States as it is at this date.

> It is further agreed that after the expiration or revocation of this lease, the lessee shall remove any buildings and other property on said premises which the lessee may own within such time as the lessor or his successor may indicate, and upon the lessee's refusal, neglect, or inability to remove the same, the lessor or his successor may cause them to be removed, at the expense of the lessee, AND NO CLAIM FOR DAMAGES AGAINST THE UNITED STATES, OR ANY AGENT THEREOF, SHALL BE CREATED BY OR MADE ON ACCOUNT OF SUCH REMOVAL.[55]

According to the ICC lawyer, by accepting the condition of this lease, Juan Botillo had lost his rights to be covered by Article V of the 1903 treaty, which guaranteed the rights to compensation of property owners in the Zone. In the eyes of Frank Feuille, a special attorney of the ICC, the ICC had not taken any property from owners, only their right to live in the Zone. The houses still belonged to their owners, who were at liberty to remove them. Feuille thought that the ICC had fulfilled its responsibilities toward Gorgona's residents by offering owners free transportation for the housing materials.[56] As it happened, much of the legal controversy between Zone urban and rural dwellers and the ICC centered on the type of lease that Juan Botillo had signed.

The Joint Land Commission disagreed with the legal opinion of the ICC. It argued that the ICC lease could not legally divest town dwellers of rights they had accrued under previous Colombian laws and under the 1903 treaty. According to the commission, anybody who had constructed a building or created a farm or plantation before 1907 had "acquired certain definite rights" under Colombian and Panamanian laws that neither the American Municipality of Gorgona nor the ICC had the power to ignore. Colombian laws had protected the rights of land renters. In order to recover their land, landowners had to "pay the value of the building, planting, or sowing." The Joint Land Commission further argued that the US presidential instructions for the government of the United States in the Canal Zone confirmed those acquired rights. According to these instructions, the "inhabitants of the Isthmian Canal Zone were entitled to security in their persons, property, and religion." They also guaranteed that the laws of the lands that had existed until February 1904 would remain valid unless modified by new ICC laws. Most importantly, any laws enacted in the Zone had to abide by "certain great principles of government . . . which we deem essential to the rule of law and maintenance of order . . . that no person shall be deprived of life, liberty, or property without due process of law, that private property shall not be taken for public use without just compensation."[57] On the basis of these instructions, the Joint Land Commission argued that the ICC did not have the power to eliminate the property rights that renters of town lots had acquired before 1907.

The Joint Land Commission clarified that it did not deny the right of the ICC to enforce the controversial leases, and it dismissed the claims of persons to whom the leases were issued *"at the time of their entry* upon town lots."[58] The Joint Land Commission focused on whether persons who had acquired "a definite right of compensation" under Colombian laws and were forced to accept a revocable license that denied their rights to compensation had suffered any damages. They argued that the leases themselves inflicted a "real damage" by "reason of the attempt to destroy acquired rights." Therefore, following Articles VI and XV of the 1903 treaty, the commission "recognized a right to compensation for such damage."[59]

Since the Joint Land Commission recognized that it did not have jurisdiction over the claims of people who signed leases for the first time after 1907, it recommended that claimants go to Zone courts to present their case. However, the commission pointed out that this should not be interpreted as meaning that these claimants had not suffered losses. It further added that its decision "shall not be regarded by the United States as excluding them from participation in the compensation which the United States has heretofore made, from the point of view of equity and humanity in similar cases."[60]

Although the Joint Land Commission acknowledged that it did not have the right to "comment on the harshness" of ICC leases, it decided to include a letter by George Goethals that discussed just that. The letter, written in May 1908, suggested the need to change the leases because they were making it difficult to recognize the equity of claims made by renters whose houses were demolished because of canal work. At the heart of Goethals's letter was the question of whether the leases that denied any right to compensation were fair. The letter acknowledged that it was "practically impossible to secure a lease on any but Government land in the Canal Zone." Moreover, it was "generally understood by the tenants that while their leases are revocable at short notice they may expect uninterrupted possession for a reasonable length of time" because lots tended to be assigned "only at points where there is little likelihood of interference with the work." The problem was that when the ICC recognized the equity of tenants' claims, the disbursing officer refused to provide compensation because tenants were not legally entitled to it. Goethals saw this as a problem. He understood that "the work has been greatly facilitated by the general disposition of property holders to allow their houses and crops to be removed or destroyed without notice." He knew that this disposition was based on "their belief in the desire of the Commission to make satisfactory adjustment of their claims for damage." To address the discrepancy between equity rights and legal rights, Goethals suggested that "a more liberal form of lease should be adopted."[61]

Goethals's letter reflected the sentiments of the previous canal era. It was written in 1908, before the decision to depopulate had been reached, when new leases were only issued in places not needed for canal construction and the good will of the local population was important for a smooth construction process. It was a very different situation in 1913, after the decision to depopulate had been made, when claimants numbered in the thousands and the cost of compensating them could run to millions of dollars.

Eventually the US government upheld the position of the Joint Land Commission about the rights of renters who had leases before 1907.[62] However, many people did not fit into this category, some because they had arrived at the Zone after 1907, others because they did not have formal leases prior to 1907. On the plots they rented from the ICC, people built houses or created farms that allowed them to participate in the growing Zone economy. Indeed, of all the property holders, immigrants and poor Panamanians were the most vulnerable. The 1903 treaty recognized the rights of landowners, but few people had land titles. Most property owners either rented their lands from the ICC or were squatters. Many squatters probably were peasants who at some point had arrangements with hacienda owners and had occupied hacienda lands in exchange for labor, rent, or agricultural products. Once hacienda owners sold their lands to the ICC, they probably remained in an uncertain legal position as squatters.

There were many people whose claims were dismissed because they were not protected by land leases signed before 1907. Among them were many West Indian immigrants. The letters of the British Minister to Panama, Sir Claude Mallet, offer a glimpse of their difficult situation. According to Sir Mallet, the majority of the 1,550 claimants before the 1913 Joint Land Commission (1,253 according to the Final Report of the Joint Land Commission) were small West Indian farmers.[63] Sir Mallet complained that those who had legal rights to compensation did not have their claims treated "on the same footing as Panama claims."[64] Many West Indians told Sir Mallet that they had received inadequate compensation. Sir Mallet himself had observed that Panamanians seemed to receive more than West Indians for the value of their plantations. He added that "while I would hesitate to accuse the Panamanian Commissioners [of] sacrificing the interest of foreigners in order to obtain better terms for natives, I have nevertheless formed the opinion that the tribunal . . . views the claims of West Indians as of secondary importance."[65]

During testimony before the Joint Land Commission, it became clear that many people had signed under duress the ICC leases that contained the clause denying them any rights to claim damages.[66] Mr. E. M. Robinson, the last mayor of Gorgona, testified in their favor. He had issued "permits for the occupancy of lands" in both his capacity as mayor and an ICC tax collector. He said that "a large portion of the people who signed them [the leases] already had their houses and cultivations under no contract at all, and that many who signed the leases protested at the time." In his view, claimants who had signed these leases were entitled to compensation "from the point view of equity and humanity." British claimants made affidavits to support Robinson's testimony. Lerma Lendon, who for fifteen years had owned four houses in Gorgona, testified that the agent of the Isthmian Canal Commission had threatened her. She was informed that if she did not sign the leases "her houses would be destroyed and that she would have no claim whatsoever, and that she would be compelled to vacate the premises." She was also told that if she signed "she would be fully reimbursed for such improvements, in the event of the building having to be removed, irrespective of the clause contained in the lease." She was also told that "the clause was merely a formality and did not mean anything; and . . . relying upon those representations she signed the leases." Six more people made similar affidavits.[67]

In the end, most people who filed claims before the Joint Land Commission did not receive any compensation.[68] Many of them, perhaps most, reached direct individual agreements with the ICC and received some compensation. Apparently, direct agreements with the ICC, without the interference of the Joint Land Commission, were cheap. Frank Feuille considered the Joint Land Commission's awards to the residents of Gorgona "in excess of the estimated value of the material in their houses," as estimated by the ICC Quartermaster's Department.[69] Be that as it may, what is clear is that by settling directly with claimants, the ICC retained the power to determine the amount of the award, circumventing the 1903 treaty and its guarantee that claims would be awarded by a panel composed of an equal number of Panamanian and American members.

It is difficult to know how fair these direct settlements were. Daniel Dunn, a West Indian who had leased nine hectares of farmland, complained to the British consul that the ICC inspector who went to his farm to appraise the value of his land "did not visit all the lands cultivated, as they were separated by jungle." Therefore, the $120 he was offered as compensation was "entirely below the real value of his property." He requested another inspection, one made when he was present so he could point out the lands under cultivation.[70] We do not know the result of his request. Nor do we know how common this type of error was. What we do know is that the ICC had to assess thousands of properties in little time, a situation that made mistakes likelier. Moreover, ICC inspectors were assessing tropical farms that they neither understood nor valued. A noncontiguous farm, formed of different plots intersected by jungle, was a sensible use of tropical lands, but it probably seemed primitive to inspectors who grew up with a different type of agriculture and who, as we saw, shared the prejudices against tropical agriculture typical of their times.[71]

The Pain of Leaving

The few testimonies written from the perspective of expelled people emphasize pain. They tell the story of their pain at leaving their homes and their anger at the injustice of not receiving fair compensation. One of these testimonies is a long anonymous letter, signed by "various victims," sent to Goethals on September 30, 1914, a year after the depopulation process had begun. Canal authorities considered the letter serious enough that the one copy left at the archives has a note that says "destroy duplicate."[72]

The "various victims" letter began by stating that it was the "offspring of our wounded hearts." They had sent it "knowing fully well that its sad and mournful echo will not reverberate, being smothered by the indifference with which we, the victims of destiny, are treated by the powerful and rich Government of the United States." The letter had three main points. First, it was sad and difficult to leave their homes in the Zone. Second, Americans did not seem to care about the pain they were causing; their own glory was the only thing that mattered to them. Third, there was much injustice in the way the various victims were compensated for their loss.

The letter tried to subvert the glorious story of canal construction and its heroic chairman George Goethals. Here, Goethals is no hero:

Colonel, before God there is no merit in the glory you are trying to gain at our cost by ruining us and hurling us into the abyss. The All Powerful, the only impartial judge without a salary, the giver of truth and justice will know how in good time to crucify those guilty of what we are suffering at the hands of the imperial Yankee represented by you.

Your name will win glory with the deeds you accomplish with the poor unfortunates but that will be on earth where all is ephemeral; but there in the other world where everything has to be just and right it will be different; he who makes victims of the poor unfortunate cannot be glorified by God.

With these words, the anonymous letter created an alternative narrative of good and evil, with Goethals as the villain. It sought to shame him by using religious notions of justice. Since the laws of men had failed them, the "various victims" appealed to the laws of God. For them, Goethals was a man who "busied" himself "solely and exclusively with the future and military power" of his country. He had lobbied the US Congress to approve a law for the "expulsion" of Zone inhabitants without remembering to ask for the funds needed to "indemnify these unfortunates paying them what legitimately belongs to them before God and the law."[73] Goethals, a powerful man who needed nothing, did not care about "the misery that would follow our violent expulsion from our home."

Goethals's indifference only served to underline the story of suffering at the center of the letter, something also present in Panama's official correspondence with canal authorities. In the words of Ernest T. Lefevre, the Panamanian minister of foreign affairs, the Panamanian inhabitants of Gorgona were "forced to leave their homes and lands where they had earned for many years the income to support themselves and their families; a land that gave them birth and that they never imagined they would have to abandon with such precipitation and in conditions so sad and disastrous for them."[74]

According to the "various victims" letter, the inhabitants of the Zone were treated worse than "ferocious criminals"; at least criminals were supplied with a roof and food, while they had been denied "a place to live and eat, our lands and houses being taken from us without paying us justly what they are worth." The people of Zone villages had been dispossessed of their holdings and reduced "to misery and the most awful ruin." They were "unfortunates who had the unhappy idea of settling there." They were people who had lived in the Zone for a long time until "an iron hand" had forced them to go "involuntarily" to try their "luck in another place." The inhabitant of the Zone had not been compensated for what he had gained "by the sweat of his brow." They were "dying owing to the trouble which has come to them by their expulsion and confiscation of their village and lands without just compensation for what represents so many years of incessant labor."

Again and again, the letter states that the money Zone inhabitants had received was only "alms," not fair compensation. Canal authorities had forced people "out of their houses and burning them afterwards in their very sight, who were afterwards given alms to enable them to pay their way for their expulsion to another part of the country." And the difference between alms and compensation mattered. It speaks to how differently the inhabitants of the Zone and canal authorities saw what was happening. While the first saw themselves as citizens and property owners who should be fairly compensated for their work and effort, Zone authorities saw them as people without property rights who only deserved the charity given to people who had suffered a tragedy, like a natural catastrophe.

The letter also suggests a distinction between lands needed for canal construction and lands needed for the "enlargement of the military power of your country." It argued that Panamanians were under no "obligations to contribute" to the latter. "If you [Goethals] desire the lands and houses of the Canal Zone for the exclusive property of the United States, you ought to acquire them legitimately."[75] This last sentence is important because it reminds us that it was a shock for Panamanians to be expelled from the Zone. Even ten years after the signing of the 1903 treaty and the creation of official borders between Panama and the Canal Zone, Panamanians living in the Zone considered it their land and distinguished between the canal, which was American, and the Zone, which, even if governed by the United States, was still the land of the people who had lived in its villages for centuries.

This way of thinking might have come naturally to people who had seen their land survive four different nation-states during the previous 100 years. Until 1821, the Isthmian Zone had been part of the Spanish Empire. With Panama's independence from Spain, it became part of the Republic of Colombia, which governed it for the rest of the nineteenth century. During that time, they had seen the Americans build a railroad and the French attempt to build a canal. Although both projects brought much change to the region, neither altered the basic urban structure of the region as a collection of towns that connected Panama from north to south. In November 1903, when Panama separated from Colombia, the Zone had briefly been part of the Republic of Panama until it was placed under US jurisdiction in 1904. During the first eight years of US rule, it seemed that life in the Zone would continue as usual, except for the new health regulations. The idea of being expelled from lands not flooded by Lake Gatún must have come as a shock to the inhabitants of the Zone.[76]

The letter also sought to shame Zone officials like Goethals and Feuille by suggesting that their actions went against the best instincts of the American people. Neither President T. W. Wilson nor the American people would have approved of the acts committed against the inhabitants of the Zone if they knew about them. It also said that the Zone officials who had supported the rights of Zone inhabitants and "who were disposed to make public the truth," like A. A. Greeman and Federico Wetzmbergo, were forced to leave the country.

The letter ended with a strong tone of despair. With little bargaining power, the only thing left to inhabitants of the Zone was to curse their malefactors: "from Gatun to the most remote place of the Canal Zone are uniting in a single echo the most righteous maledictions which each one of those victims is hurling upon you and your Government every day as the only consolation that remains to them."[77]

Another example of Panamanian popular views about the depopulation is an early twentieth-century version of *Coge el Pandero que Se Te Va*, Panama's famous tamborito. The tamborito was a popular musical genre in which a rich combination of drums served as a background to a lead singer and a chorus. In this version, the lead voice was that of a woman. This song was recorded around 1930, on the Victor label, by the Grupo Istmeño.[78] The fact that this was one of the few Panamanian songs to be recorded at the beginning of the twentieth century probably means that both the group and the song were very popular before they were recorded, and also that many Panamanians sang its lyrics and danced to its rhythm.

Take the kite before it flies away
　　Take the kite before it flies away

It flies away, it flies away
　　(Take the kite before it flies away)

Let's leave Panama soon
Take the kite before it flies away

If we don't leave, they'll throw us out
　　Take the kite before it flies away
Because those children of Uncle Sam
　　Take the kite before it flies away

Do not have enough with the canal
　　Take the kite before it flies away

They want to seize all
Take the kite before it flies away

And the natives of Panama
Take the kite before it flies away

We can't even breathe anymore
Take the kite before it flies away

They demand everything with liberty
Take the kite before it flies away

It flies away, it flies away
Take the kite before it flies away

Flying it comes, and flying it goes
Take the kite before it flies away

Of all the Isthmus they'll become owners
Take the kite before it flies away

Uncle Sam's little sheep
Take the kite before it flies away

From our home they'll throw us out
Take the kite before it flies away

We must all emigrate
Take the kite before it flies away

Let us all leave Panama
Take the kite before it flies away

It flies away, it flew away
Flying it comes and flying it goes

They say they are on the road
Take the kite before it flies away.[79]

—o—

Coge el pandero que se te va
    Que se te va, que se te va,

Coge el pandero que se te va
Vámonos pronto de Panamá

Coge el pandero que se te va

Si no nos vamos, nos botarán
Coge el pandero que se te va

Pues esos hijos del Tío Sam
Coge el pandero que se te va

No se conforman con el canal
Coge el pandero que se te va

    Todo lo quieren acaparar
Coge el pandero que se te va

    Y los nativos de Panamá
Coge el pandero que se te va

    Ya no podemos ni respirar
Coge el pandero que se te va

Y todo lo piden con libertad
Coge el pandero que se te va

    Que se te va, que se te va
Coge el pandero que se te va

Volando viene, volando va
Coge el pandero que se te va

De todo el Istmo se adueñarán
Coge el pandero que se te va

Las ovejitas del Tío Sam
Coge el pandero que se te va

Y del terruño nos echarán
Coge el pandero que se te va

Debemos todos pues emigrar
Coge el pandero que se te va

Vámonos todos de Panamá
Coge el pandero que se te va

Que se te va, que se fue

Volando viene volando va
Coge el pandero que se te va

En la carretera dicen que están
Coge el pandero que se te va

Échale hilo que se te va
Coge el pandero que se te va

Que se va, que se fue
Coge el pandero que se te va

Volando viene volando va
Coge el pandero que se te va

Vámonos pronto de Panamá
Coge el pandero que se te va

Que se te va, que se te fue
Coge el pandero que se te va

Por la carretera dicen que están
Coge el pandero que se te va

Que se te va, que se te va
Coge el pandero que se te va

Debemos todos pues emigrar
Coge el pandero que se te va.

The song's recurring theme is that Panama did not belong anymore to Panamanians, that "not satisfied with the canal," the "children of Uncle Sam . . . want to take it all." The United States would become owner of the "entire Isthmus," and Panamanians would have to leave their country and "emigrate." The song mentions neither the depopulation order nor the Zone. But when the song was popular, it would not have had been necessary. The depopulation of the Zone was still on everybody's mind and listeners knew what the song referred to. Like the "various victims" letter, it distinguished between canal construction and depopulation. The song stated that the canal was not enough for the United States; it wanted to take it all. If Panamanians did not leave, they would be thrown out. There is sadness, fear, and anger in this song: the sadness of losing one's homeland, the fear of losing even more, and anger over the injustice of it all.

We can imagine people in the 1910s and 1920s dancing to this *tamborito* and singing along to its words during dances and parties. We can only wonder what to do so meant for them. This might have been a song with which Panamanians of all classes identified: from farmers like Hubert Brown who found himself in court because he would not stop returning to his old farm after he had sold it to the canal authorities, to wealthy owners of real estate property who had to dismantle their properties and watch the town where their business had grown disappear under the forest.[80]

6

Lost Towns

The undersigned used to be vecinos [neighbors] of the ancient town of Old Gatún, where we were born and where we were established in our homes and fields until 1907 when the Isthmian Commission forced us to move to New Gatun, because the canal requirements demanded it. When we were given this new residency, they made us believe that we would not be disturbed again with another relocation and that we would live there in "NUEVO GATUN" in complete peace, a promise that led us to expediently organize our agricultural endeavors esteeming it to be a permanent location, but we have been notified that we have to move yet again from NUEVO GATUN. . . . We, the people of Gatún, have been the most tormented by the canal necessities, we were the first forced to abandon their original town and now we are forced to do it once again when the general situation is so bad that we, who have always been poor, feel it more than anyone else.

—150 NEW GATÚN NEIGHBORS

There is therefore no excuse for these people living longer in the Zone, except that they have been allowed to live in the Zone.

—ACTING CHIEF HEALTH OFFICER, BALBOA HEIGHTS,
CANAL ZONE, JUNE 15, 1916

New Gatún

IN THE TOWNS not flooded by Lake Gatún, depopulation must have come as a shock. Towns like New Gatún and Empire were important, substantial places by early twentieth-century standards, and Zone authorities had considered them permanent until 1912. People had invested in houses, buildings, and stores to participate in the Zone's thriving economy. Nobody could have guessed that these investments had no future. It is important to remember that, until 1911, not even the ICC had decided to depopulate the Zone. Until 1911, people were still signing leases with "the Panama Railroad Company for a period of 15 years" to build houses in Empire and Gatún. That canal authorities were giving fifteen-year leases only one or two years before the order to depopulate was a clear sign of how late they had come to the decision to depopulate the entire Zone.[1] A May 1914 letter from Mr. A. Preciado to the canal government clearly shows the uncertainty of these years and the anguish of property owners. Preciado asked the authorities "to kindly inform me as to the truth of certain reports contained in the local dailies in regard to the future of New Gatún. According to the newspapers the town of New Gatún is bound to disappear sometime between June or July." Mr. Preciado had bought two old buildings in the town of New Gatún and was about to spend a large amount of money to repair them. He wanted an answer before spending his money: "if we are to quit New Gatún in the near future it is only justice that I be informed in time so that I may suspend the repairs and avoid further expense."[2]

Canal authorities confirmed the rumors. Yes, New Gatún would be abandoned in a few months and all houses would have to be removed by the end of the year. Preciado was advised to suspend any extensive repairs and to focus on repairs that were "absolutely necessary."[3] Like

Mr. Preciado, many people saw their lives brought to a standstill. Their plans were interrupted, and they had to start thinking about what to do next. In 1907, canal authorities had already moved Gatún from its old location on the Gatún River to a new location farther to the east. After this relocation, the residents thought they would be allowed to live in *"tranquilidad completa,"* "complete peace." But they were mistaken. Forced to move twice in less than a decade, the citizens of New Gatún thought of themselves as the ones "most tormented by canal needs."

The schedule for the depopulation of New Gatún proved difficult to meet. It was the largest town of the Zone and people tried to stay for as long as they could. While Gorgona was emptied in a few months, the depopulation of New Gatún took two years. Many people did not believe that the town would actually be depopulated, and canal authorities had to repeat again and again that New Gatún would not be a permanent town. New Gatún was difficult to abandon because the town had flourished for good reasons. It was located on the railroad line, not far from Colón City, close to the new lake and surrounded by fertile lands. Because of its strategic location, Zone authorities never truly abandoned the town. But they radically transformed it from a large town teeming with private houses and businesses to a small company town.

The Zone government took the first steps to depopulate New Gatún in June 1914. From the government's perspective, it was a good moment to do so since canal work was dwindling and the area covered by Lake Gatún had been depopulated. They could now move ahead and complete the December 1912 depopulation order. In June 1914, the government of the Zone decreed that all town leases in New Gatún would be canceled by August 1 of that year. People were allowed to stay in their houses a few extra months, until December 31. That date proved unrealistic. On December 19, orders were given to "notify the occupants of the houses that the water service will be discontinued on December 31."[4] Yet in March 1915, people were still living in New Gatún, and Zone authorities did not know what to do. They had stopped collecting water bills, but to avoid health problems they had left the water on, thinking that the town would soon be abandoned. Some officials worried that "there seems to be little prospect of the town of New Gatún being entirely abandoned," and asked if they should start collecting water payments again.[5] The legal office's answer was no. To accept any payment for water use "would simply give the owners and occupants of buildings the privilege of staying there an indefinite period of time." It was better for the water department to lose money than to hold back the abandonment of New Gatún.[6]

A similar situation occurred with the electric service. On April 15, more than three months after the official date for the depopulation of New Gatún, Reverend S. Witt requested the reconnection of electric lighting in the Baptist church at New Gatún. His request was denied: "it is not deemed wise to renew any services which have been discontinued, as such action would only give rise to the false impression that the village of New Gatún is to be continued permanently."[7] Canal authorities insisted that "the town of New Gatún was practically abandoned."[8] In spite of all ICC statements and measures, New Gatún continued to be inhabited. Moreover, the depopulation of New Gatún had to be momentarily reversed when canal authorities opened 354 apartments to accommodate some of the refugees from the April 30 fire in Colón City. The ICC approved the reconnection of the water to these buildings and began collecting a $2.40 rent per month in these apartments.[9]

People tried to stay in New Gatún as long as possible and to negotiate extensions and compensation as best as they could. That was the case with Mr. Wilson, a "colored" American barber. He wrote to canal authorities "regretting I am being thrown out of my own home." He had lived in the house with his wife and from there had serviced an American clientele. He requested that his vacancy date be extended to November 1, when his wife would return to St. Louis and he would be able to move to a different location. He wanted, however, to continue his barbershop business and asked the ICC Quartermaster's Department for two rooms that would allow him to do so. He hoped that being a US citizen providing service to other US citizens would earn him some consideration. Apparently, it did not.[10] Not everybody wrote to the US government about their distress, and not all letters remain in the archives. But the case of Mr. Wilson could be multiplied by the 8,000 inhabitants of New Gatún, who, like the people of Gorgona before them, had to figure out how to start over again.

Other inhabitants of New Gatún were less respectable than Mr. Wilson but perhaps more famous. An old black man from a place called Stilton Addition, also known as "Sodom Hill," was famous enough to merit the attention, even if it was sometimes mockery, of canal authorities. He was locally known as the "King of Sodom Hill." His "palace" was "in a more dilapidated condition than any other building." He was an old citizen of Gatún who had moved with his neighbors from Gatún to New Gatún. Like others, he tried to stay in his house for as long as possible. He refused to leave even after his neighbors had abandoned the area. His house had been condemned for sanitary reasons, and ICC health officers asked the land agent to give him some remuneration, since "His Majesty" was in "strained circumstances."[11] We do not know whether he managed to move to a place where he could be near some of his old neighbors. The records do not even mention his name, only his nickname.

Homeowners in railroad towns like New Gatún and Empire did not enjoy the same rights as Gorgona homeowners. Because New Gatún and Empire were built on public land that had been conceded to the Panama Railroad Company in the nineteenth century, their town lots were never municipal property and therefore were not protected by the old municipal laws governing the rights of the residents of Gorgona. For this reason, the Joint Land Commission declared that the lands belonging to the Panama Railroad were not under the purview of the Joint Land Commission. Homeowners had to ask for compensation directly from the Land Office of the Panama Railroad or from the ICC.[12]

The ICC dealt with the buildings of New Gatún in three ways. It bought the houses that could be used for the army, official government housing, or some other government purpose. The remaining houses were either taken by their owners or destroyed. As soon as settlements were reached with homeowners, the ICC waited for the owners to take their houses with them. Otherwise the police were instructed to destroy them.[13]

In January 1916, Gatún was still inhabited and Zone authorities enacted a new measure to hasten its abandonment. On Sunday, January 16, they discontinued the operation of the daily labor train that ran between Colón City and Gatún.[14] But not even this drastic measure could achieve the desired effect. Five months later, in June 1916, health authorities complained that the census of New Gatún showed that a "large number" of nonemployees continued to live there. According to a health official, although the procedure of razing some buildings and keeping only the best ones for canal purposes had advanced, "no progress has been made in the elimination of the nonemployees."[15] He considered their presence "very undesirable" for the land office, the health department, the supply department, and the legal department. He did not explain why, but it can be inferred that their presence created a legal and social limbo. The Zone was to be depopulated; only ICC employees living in ICC housing were permitted to remain in the Zone, and government stores were supposed to replace private businesses. The presence of these inhabitants challenged this vision. With over 400 vacant rooms for rent in Colón City, why did the residents of New Gatún not leave? The health officer complained. According to him, there was no excuse "for these people living longer in the Zone, except that they have been allowed to live in the Zone."[16] Only four years had passed since the depopulation order. In that short time, the people of the Zone had gone from inhabitants of the Zone to "people allowed to live" there.

In June 1916, the ICC took the final measures to vacate all the buildings in New Gatún. The ICC gave nonemployees until June 30 to leave. Thereafter, "non employees found in these buildings . . . will be ejected by the Police." Some merchants requested a thirty-day extension to dispose of their stock.[17] They were granted two weeks so they could move their goods and close their accounts with the silver employees, who were paid between the tenth and the twelfth of the month. They still had to close their stores to the public by the original date of June 30.[18] Although canal employees were allowed to stay, soon many West Indian employees or "silver families" were also asked to leave New Gatún.[19] About 1,000 of these families were refugees from the Colón fire of 1915. Most of them worked in Cristobal, which was the Zone's section of Colón City. A year after the fire, Zone officials believed that there were "ample accommodations in the city of Colón for these families." They gave these employees ninety days to leave their quarters in Gatún. Zone authorities could now "tear down the old shacks" where they lived.[20]

After much resistance, canal authorities finally managed to depopulate New Gatún. We can only imagine the silence that fell on its streets as all the private residences were abandoned and all the private businesses closed. The Zone was now on the way to becoming a sparsely populated and immaculate company town.

Some peasants from the Gatún region also tried to stay on their land for as long as possible. Two old Jamaican men, Daniel McPherson and Thomas Lodge, who had cultivated their land for over thirty years, asked the British consul to intervene on their behalf against an order to vacate by May 1915. They had refused the ICC settlement offer because they did not consider it fair and had decided to wait for the resolution of the Joint Land Commission. After all, they had been there since French canal construction.[21] According to the British consul, they were not the only peasants in this situation. Yet the ICC denied any wrongdoing. It claimed that "no cultivator was ordered to vacate who had a case pending with the Joint Land Commission."[22] Moreover, it stated that even the cultivators who had already made settlements with the ICC were "allowed to remain for a certain time."[23] If these men were given orders to vacate it was because of "some misunderstanding."[24]

But there had never been a misunderstanding. As Frank Feuille later explained, the cultivators' land was located in an area that the ICC Supply Department wanted for cattle grazing. Feuille insisted that these peasants reach a settlement with the ICC Land Office in Colón City: it was "difficult to say when the Joint Land Commission [would] pass upon the two claims in question, but their place on the calendar would indicate that they would not be reached before some considerable time, inasmuch as the Commission is handling cases in numerical order."[25] This seems to be the heart of the matter. The ICC's schedule to depopulate and take over the land it needed for its own purposes moved at a much faster pace than the rhythms of the Joint Land Commission and the needs of Zone inhabitants.

The farmers managed to hold out for almost a year. By April 1915, they had reached a direct settlement with the ICC. Could they not wait any longer for the Joint Land Commission to adjudicate their claims? Did the commission compensate them at all? It's hard to say. In any case, after a year of waiting, they found themselves in the same situation they had initially protested against.[26] Other peasants who lived around Gatún, and whose names are not known, continued to cultivate annual crops of bananas, plantains, and sugarcane on the lands that they used to lease from the Panama Railroad, but to which they no longer had rights.[27] It was perhaps their insistence on being able to continue cultivating their crops even after losing the right to do so that eventually led to the US policy of renting small farm plots in the Zone to some former laborers during the 1920s.[28] This new policy could not recreate the lost agricultural landscape, but it was a reminder of the Zone's agricultural past.

The Multiple Relocations of New Limón

> This is taken away from us because our
> government is too generous.

—THE NEIGHBORS OF NEW LIMÓN, OCTOBER 15, 1914

If Gorgona, Empire, and New Gatún were the largest towns of the Zone, Limón was small, one of the many hamlets, or *caseríos,* flooded by Lake Gatún. In spite of its small size, Limón received special attention from the Panamanian and Canal Zone governments because its multiple forced relocations—two in four years—had made it into a symbol of Panamanians' displacement and vulnerability. The case of Limón went all the way to Panama's National Assembly and received the attention of Panama's president, Belisario Porras, and Panama's minister of foreign relations, Ernesto T. Lefevre. Its history shows the fluidity of the US–Panama border during the first two decades of the twentieth century, the differing priorities of Zone authorities and Panamanian peasants over the use of Lake Gatún, and how a small community appealed to Panama's government in an attempt to influence its foreign policy and negotiate the best possible condition for its relocation.[29]

Limoneros were first relocated in 1911 from their town on the shores of the Gatún River, which was scheduled to disappear under the waters of Lake Gatún. They sought to remain close to the water and chose the border of the new Lake Gatún, close to the Gatuncillo River, as the location of their new town. They thought it would be their permanent location: since they had settled outside the boundaries of the Zone, they thought they were in Panamanian territory. To their surprise, in October 1914, Zone officers began to appear in their town with the news that they had to relocate again, because a new border convention between the United States and Panama signed the previous month had placed their town inside the Zone's borders. The convention settled the boundaries between Panama and the Zone and gave the United States all of Lake Gatún's shore lands up to 100 feet above sea level.[30] Since New Limón was located below that level, Limoneros had to relocate despite the fact that they were outside of the original ten-mile Zone limit.

The conflict between Limoneros and Zone authorities began during their first relocation. The ICC objected to their new settlement by the lake because it was on lands that could still be partially flooded by the lake.[31] Limoneros paid no heed to this warning, probably because the advantages of their new location outweighed its disadvantages. Zone authorities proved to be somewhat right because a small part of the town was flooded by Lake Gatún. But Limoneros did not seem to care. In 1914, they were living in a town that had partially become an island. A small, ten-foot channel divided the town in two: one side was located on the mainland and the other had become a lake island. Limoneros did not seem to mind and fought hard to remain there. The town already had 400 people and had built two schools attended by seventy students.[32] Limón had about sixty families who described themselves as people who had been "thrown out by the Americans from the old places on the railroad's line."[33] The governor of Colón Province described them as "humble people." To move again would mean abandoning the fertile shores of the Gatuncillo River, where they had started their new farms.

The reasons for their second displacement did not seem clear to the people of Limón or to the governor of Colón Province, who defended them. Whom did they hurt by remaining there, close to the water, close to the old river, now a lake, where the lands were fertile and access to water easy? As the governor said, they were far from the Zone and did not bother anybody. Why make the poor Limoneros move again? The new relocation "saddens them to the point of thinking that not existing would be better for them."[34] They had built schools and planted new farms. They had settled in. Did they really have to move again? For the Zone authorities, the answer was yes. The government of the Zone and Limoneros had different priorities about the use of Lake Gatún's water. If for Limoneros the lake provided crucial access to water, transport, and fertile lands, for Zone authorities the lake was a strategic asset and Limoneros were a nuisance.

Limoneros sent a long letter signed by around forty people to Panama's National Assembly asking for protection against the new border convention.[35] The petition attracted the attention of the governor of Colón Province and Panama's National Assembly. The minister of foreign relations and the governor of the Zone shared their worries about the future of the town. Perhaps Limón received so much attention because its relocation happened at a crucial moment, with the National Assembly about to vote on the ratification of the September 1914 Boundary Convention. The outcome of the convention was not clear to many people in Panama, and it concerned many people who had relocated after the flooding of Lake Gatún. In October 1914, not even the foreign relations ministry seemed to understand the consequences of the convention. When he received the notice from Limoneros complaining that Zone officials were telling them to abandon their houses and cultivations, the foreign minister wrote, "undoubtedly, if this is true, the aforementioned canal employees must have wrongly assumed that this hamlet is inside the Canal Zone."[36] Nobody in Panama, not even the minister of foreign relations, seemed to know if New Limón was on US or Panamanian territory.

The correspondence about Limón reveals great concern about the future stability of the town. Limoneros feared being "kicked out for the third [sic] time from [our] properties, forced to abandon the fruits of our constant struggles, to leave us in the depths of our wretched misery."[37] Would the National Assembly not protect them from the new convention, which "seriously threatened" their welfare? Four concerned neighbors also wrote to the minister of foreign relations, asking if the United States had acquired the right to occupy the land where the town was located and the lands where Limoneros had their farms, or whether the Republic of Panama was able to guarantee "the perpetual stability of the town."[38] When would they be able to feel safe, to feel at home, and to think of their towns as permanent again? The US government always seemed to find a new reason to keep them moving. The letter writers wondered if the neighbors would agree to build yet another town, given that "Americans take pleasure in harassing them and in destroying their homes every time they build a town." Perhaps it would be preferable to live "scattered" instead.[39] The governor of Colón Province echoed their sentiments, lamenting "a new order forcing them to abandon their place due to the incessant need of canal works. . . . If this continues it is possible that these wretched people will never find a land where they can settle."[40] At the heart of Limón's second relocation was the pressing question of when the resettlements that began in 1912 would end. Were the needs of the canal endless?

Limoneros also chastised their government. They accused Panama of being "too generous" by giving the United States all the islands and shores of Lake Gatún. What would happen to their town? Not happy with just presenting their sad situation, Limoneros sought to shape foreign policy. If Panama's government asked for exemptions to the border convention, they argued, "The United States would undoubtedly accept them."[41] Another letter sent by Limón residents asked the Panamanian government to ensure that the United States guaranteed "free movement on the waters and shores of Lake Gatún . . . understanding as free movement the right to move at all hours of the day and night, without having to pay any taxes to the American government."[42] These letters beg the question of whether petitions from different small towns in direct contact with the government of the Zone influenced Panama's foreign policy.

It might seem surprising that a small hamlet would try to influence its government's foreign policy. Yet Limoneros lived next to one of the major engineering works of the twentieth century and had a long history of dealing with different governments and immigrant groups. Most likely, they were themselves composed of different immigrant groups. Far from being the naïve natives of US narratives, they were worldly peasants quite aware of the importance of international treaties.

And Limoneros were not the only ones trying to have a say in the future of the Zone. The people of Arraiján, a small municipality located right outside the Zone's western borders, had also asked Panama's government to negotiate with the Zone government to ensure proper clearing of the roads that connected their town with the ports of Cochinito, Pedro Miguel, and Río Grande, all located inside the Zone. Panama's minister of foreign relations asked canal authorities why they wouldn't comply with Arraiján's request. The Zone government replied that "the United States is now engaged [in] depopulating the Canal Zone of all persons not connected with canal enterprises and in purchasing their holdings. In these circumstances it is the opinion of the Commission that the trails to which reference is made will not warrant clearing."

Panama's government asked canal authorities to reconsider their position. The trails had been used "since time immemorial" to link Arraiján "with the centers of civilization." The municipality of Arraiján had cleaned the roads twice a year until 1910, when the Zone took over this responsibility. Moreover, the 1903 treaty guaranteed the rights of transit on the public roads that crossed the Zone. The Zone's legal department responded with a different interpretation. It argued that the roads conflicted with the defense plans for the Miraflores and Pedro Miguel locks. And US rights to freely determine the use of Zone land superseded any previous rights that the people of Arraiján might have had. However, since the engineer in charge of canal defense said that the Río Grande and Cochinito roads did not interfere with canal defense at the moment, the ICC had decided to clear the trails, if only for that year.[43] Perhaps requests from towns like Limón and Arraiján helped Panama's government pressure the United States to keep or build roads in the Zone to ensure the connections between Panama City and the towns on the other side of the Zone.

Eventually, Panama's National Assembly voted in favor of the new border convention; Limoneros had to relocate once again and the United States agreed to pay for the costs of this second relocation. The Assembly's special commission in charge of studying Limoneros's petition reached the conclusion that the reason for the removal of Limoneros was not the new border convention but executive decree number 46 of May 1912, which gave the United States "the use, occupation and control of the areas of land to be covered by the waters of Lake Gatún and all that part of shores of the lake up to an elevation of one hundred feet above sea level." For the commission, the border convention merely ratified the 1912 executive decree. The National Assembly recommended that the executive do everything in its power to ensure that US authorities provide all the necessary aid so that the people of Limón could relocate without incurring any expense.[44]

The last chapter of this story finds Limoneros fighting to have a say in the design of their new houses. They may have been farther from the river, and far from the lake, but they were determined to live in the kinds of houses they were accustomed to. They complained to Panama's government that the Zone government was building houses with ceilings that were too low and made their houses too hot. Years of experience living in a warm climate had taught them the importance of design, particularly a ceiling's height, in controlling a home's climate. Panama's government agreed and asked the US government to alter the design. The Quartermaster's Department refused. It said that it was following construction standards for ceiling height, so any complaints were unwarranted. As a result, Limoneros ended up living far from the water in houses that were too hot because the ceilings were too low.[45]

FIGURE 6.1 Chagres and the Fort of San Lorenzo
Credit: Detail from George P. Clarke, *View of Chagres* (New York: Stinger and Townsend), in the Panama Canal Museum Collection, George A. Smathers Libraries, University of Florida.

Chagres: Losing a River, Losing a Fort

The imposing ruins of the old Spanish fort of San Lorenzo stand alone above the mouth of the Chagres River. Located high above the river's ravines and surrounded by tropical forest, the fort invites visitors to re-member past Spanish imperial glories. Yet it is not clear what this fort once defended; there is no trace of the old town and port that were once located by the river's mouth. While it would be hard to imagine any other important Spanish port in Panama without its town, Chagres is nothing but a fort. This is particularly shocking considering the importance of Chagres for colonial commerce; indeed, in the nine-teenth century Chagres became more important than Portobelo (see Figure 6.1).[46] Although Chagres was located outside the original boundaries of the Zone, its removal is part of the history of the de-population of the Zone after the 1912 executive order. In 1915, Zone authorities declared that the lands occupied by the town and port of Chagres were needed for the defense of the Panama Canal, and inhab-itants were forced to move to the mouth of the Lagarto River eight miles away.

FIGURE 6.2 The town of Chagres
Credit: Theodore Guberman Cannelle and Robert De Meuse, *Excursions et Explorations: Colombie, Venezuela, Antilles, Etats-Unis, Canada, Tahiti*, 1881–1887, Village de Chagres. Bibliothèque nationale de France, département Estampes et photographie, 4-UA-61.

The town of Chagres had a long historical connection to the river. Until the construction of the Panama Canal, Chagres was the only navigable river on the Panama route. During Spanish colonial times, the Chagres port received European merchandise destined for the rich Viceroyalty of Peru. Its importance continued during the first half of the nineteenth century. Descriptions of the difficult travel across the Isthmus of Panama never failed to include Chagres, its river, and its boatmen. According to Mollien, the small huts of Chagres "stored prodigious riches." They were used as warehouses and were rented at "400 franks per month." He saw "more money circulating there than in any other place of the [Colombian] Republic" (see Figure 6.2). And few of the black citizens of Chagres earned less than sixty to eighty pesos per week. Mollien also described many boats in the Chagres port ready to transport British merchandise up the river.[47] Chagres's historic role as a hub for global trade ended with the construction of the Panama Railroad: it replaced the river as the primary transportation route, and the new port city of Colón became Panama's international Atlantic port.[48]

Although Chagres had lost its strategic importance, the connection between the town and the river remained strong. The residents of Chagres farmed its fertile riverine lands, collected *tagua* (ivory nuts) in the nearby forest, and fished for turtles in the sea. Chagreños also continued to use their port to navigate to Colón City to sell their products. Chagres had not lost its connection to the global economy; instead of specializing in trade and transport, the town produced for the growing market of Colón City.[49] And the town's architecture reflected its connection to the world. Some of its ninety-three houses were built with traditional thatched roofing; others had zinc roofs. The walls of the houses also varied from reed—the minority—to lumber, wood, or board. Many had the same zinc roof and lumber walls of the new constructions in Panama, Colón, and the towns of the Zone.[50] Chagres also had a Catholic church and a municipal building (see Figure 6.3).

The inauguration of the Panama Canal brought new and unexpected changes for the town and port. The first change came with the opening of the Gatún Dam, which altered the river flow. In April 1915, thirty-three distressed citizens of Chagres wrote to Panamanian President Porras, explaining that "since the opening of the Gatún Dam, which flows into this river, five of the houses that are on the river banks have been razed by the river, this is something that we had never experienced before."[51] According to them, the river's new strength threatened other houses and buildings, including the town hall. If modern engineering had caused the flooding of the town, the citizens of Chagres

FIGURE 6.3 Public prayers being offered at a church in Chagres
Credit: Theodore Guberman Cannelle and Robert De Meuse, *Excursions et Explorations: Colombie, Venezuela, Antilles, Etats-Unis, Canada, Tahiti*, 1881–1887, Interieur de l'eglise— Exposition des Saints et prieres publiques pour conjurer le fleu. Bibliothèque nationale de France, département Estampes et photographie, 4-UA-61.

thought that modern engineering could also solve it and asked for the construction of a breakwater to protect their houses.[52] They also used their political clout as voters in an important political district to request President Porras's help. They reminded Porras of his proclaimed commitment to the "needs and progress of the people he governed."[53] Porras asked the minister of foreign affairs, Ernesto T. Lefevre, to take up the problem with Zone authorities.[54] Lefevre asked Zone authorities to take some measures to ensure that the waters would not "destroy the houses still standing."[55] After sending a commission to study the damages, the Zone authorities promised to build a breakwater.[56] It seemed that the people of Chagres would be able to continue their lives as before.

However, the final outcome was not what citizens of Chagres and the Panamanian government had expected. On December 8, 1915, Governor Goethals wrote to President Porras requesting the lands on the mouth of the Chagres River, including the town of Chagres, for the defense and protection of the Canal.[57] The government of the Zone had previously communicated to the Panamanian minister of foreign affairs that "it is the intention of the United States to occupy at once, for purposes of construction connected with the defense of the Panama Canal, certain points near the mouth of the Chagres river on land that is not privately owned, so far as the records of the Panama Canal show, but is public land within the Republic of Panama. It is requested that the local municipal authorities of the town of Chagres be advised of the proposed occupation."[58]

A few things stand out about the letter. The first is the blatant dismissal of the Chagreños's rights to their lands. The second is the characterization of a historic municipality like Chagres as "public lands." Chagres had not been recognized as a historic town that would be destroyed. For Goethals, Chagres was only a small agricultural village and its people only peasants and fishermen whose "habits of life would be changed very little by removing them" to another coastal town.[59] It amounted to nothing more than 280 hectares of public lands needed for canal defense. Since the United States would pay for their moving costs, he asserted, the relocation of Chagres's residents should not constitute a major hardship.[60]

The citizens of Chagres and the Panamanian government had a very different view of the town's significance. For them, Chagres was an important historic town and political district. Panama's minister of foreign affairs highlighted the "important historical significance that the Chagres Castle had for all Panamanians and South Americans" and the "sacrifice that it represented for Panamanians to cede the head [*cabecera*] of one of its best districts."[61] The citizens of Chagres had a similar awareness of their town's historical importance. Their memorial protesting their removal described the town as "the ancient and historic town of Chagres, head of the district of the same name."[62] The internal correspondence of the Panamanian government echoed these sentiments. In the words of José B. Calvo, forces of destiny compelled the people of Chagres

> to abandon with pain their dear Chagres, the place where they received their earliest and first caresses, where they saw the first light and where they imagined they would spend the rest of their lives, without ever thinking that their houses, their cultivations, and other goods they had acquired with great sacrifice would one day disappear and that they would be forced to continue their lives in a place different from the one they had been used to since their childhood.[63]

Panamanians perceived the loss of Chagres as an immense sacrifice. Indeed, the highest authorities in Panama's government—the president, the minister of foreign affairs, and the ambassador to Washington—became deeply involved in the negotiations over the town's relocation. For men like them, this might have been the last attempt to protect what they saw as an important part of Panama's history. They had already lost the ports of the cities of Colón and Panama in 1904, and in 1912 they had lost the right to own property in the Zone. By losing Chagres, they would also be losing their history.

Initially, the Panamanian government argued that, based on the 1914 border convention between Panama and the Zone, any new cession of Panamanian land required the approval of Panama's National Assembly, which would probably not approve it without appropriate compensation. The Panamanian government requested either money or lands owned by the Panama Railroad in the cities of Colón or Panama.[64] Goethals responded that the 1903 canal treaty allowed the US government to take any lands needed for the "construction, maintenance, operation, sanitation, or protection" of the canal without any compensation. Nonetheless, he explained, the United States would compensate property owners and facilitate their relocation to another area in Panama.[65]

Given the skewed balance of power between Panama and the United States, symbolic gestures became very important. President Porras convened a group of eminent Panamanian men from both the Liberal and Conservative parties to examine Goethals's response (Porras's Liberals were in power). After the group agreed to recognize the legality of Goethals's position, Porras decided that Panama's government should enact a formal decree authorizing US occupation of the Port of Chagres. The legal department of the Zone considered such a decree unnecessary, yet Porras strongly disagreed.[66] Panamanians, he said, "should not, for a single moment, allow the American occupation of the national territory without our own formal authorization."[67] Panama's government decreed to "recognize United States rights to use, occupy, and control some land near Point Tortuguilla and close to the mouth of the Chagres River for the establishment of fortifications needed for Canal defense."[68] If forced to give away an important and symbolic part of their territory, the least that Panama's government could do was to proclaim its territorial sovereignty by decreeing its concession.

While negotiations continued in Panama, Eusebio A. Morales, the Panamanian ambassador to the United States, was looking for a better deal. He wanted to exchange the Port of Chagres for the lands of the Panama Railroad in Colón City. Since Colón City had been built on railroad lands, the property owners of Colón City owned their buildings but not the land on which they stood. Morales argued that if Panama was going to renounce one of its historic ports, it should at least receive in exchange some railroad lands. He pointed out adamantly: "if the government . . . begins to relocate the town of Chagres, without demanding compensation, we will obtain nothing, absolutely nothing." He reminded Panama's government that because only the ambassador represented the US government in Panama, Goethals could not make agreements on behalf of the US government.[69] Alas, to Morales's frustration, the relocation of Chagres continued and Panama would have to wait until the 1950s before receiving ownership of railroad lands in Colón City.

In addition to their differences over the political and historical importance of Chagres, Panamanians—particularly the citizens of Chagres—disagreed with Zone authorities over the importance of local natural and economic resources. Goethals saw the area as public land that could be easily appropriated for defense purposes. The citizens of Chagres, who had close connections to the river and its port, had a very different perspective. Their frustrations, as well as the sense of inevitability with which they accepted the relocation, emerge clearly in their negotiations.

The negotiations involved several points. The first centered on the work that the Zone government would do to help establish the new town. Americans agreed to clear, drain, and level a new area no smaller than twenty-five hectares; to trace the layout of the new town; and to move and rebuild the church, the municipal building, and the school. They would also transport all the building materials of the town's residents; install a water service; and build roads that would help town dwellers bring their products to the Chagres River or Lake Gatún. Finally, they agreed to take some of the cannons of Fort San Lorenzo to Panama City.[70] This last point was perhaps the final attempt to maintain the historic connection between Panama and the fort.

The citizens of Chagres and Zone authorities soon reached an agreement over the amount of monetary compensation that residents would receive for their property. The one remaining point of contention was the location of the new town. Unlike Zone authorities, the residents of Chagres did not take this point lightly. They knew that not all coastal areas were equal and that differences in terrain, water, and accessibility by land or water could make an enormous difference in their ability to survive and thrive. The place of relocation was so important that eighty-nine "urban and rural property owners" signed a memorandum stating that although they had accepted the value of the monetary compensation, they refused to receive any compensation until they knew the location of their new town.[71]

The selection of New Chagres's location was an elaborate affair. A formal delegation composed of Panamanian and US representatives departed from Colón City in a boat that sailed the west coast of Colón Province looking for an appropriate location for the new town. The delegation included the governor of Colón province and his secretary, two American military officers, and two US government officers. The boat's first stop was the Port of Chagres, where the mayor of Chagres, the town council's president and spokesman, the municipal judge, and other important citizens of Chagres joined the official delegation. The citizens of Chagres wanted to move to the mouth of the Piñas River, where there was already a "picturesque" hamlet, because Piñas's port had decent conditions for loading and unloading. It was not as good as Chagres, but it was the second-best option.

Unfortunately, they would not get their choice. The Zone lawyer, Frank Feuille, disapproved of Piñas: it was too close to the US military presence in the area. Relocating to Piñas could "perhaps lead to frequent disputes and troubles between them and the [Canal Zone] military."[72] The citizens of Chagres had a different fear. They had found good land in Piñas but they already knew that they should not occupy that place because "they would be bothered again."[73] As inhabitants of the last important Panamanian town on the route to be depopulated, the people of Chagres knew that choosing a location that interfered with the Zone government could force them to move yet again, as had happened to the people of Gatún and Limón.

The boat continued to a new location that seemed appropriate to the US delegation but not to the people of Chagres, because it did not allow for the landing of boats. Feuille dismissed their concerns, saying that the Zone government could build a road that would connect the town to the Port of Piñas. For Feuille, if American engineers could build a road that allowed the people of Chagres to take their products to a different port, then whether or not the town itself had a good port was a minor issue. The delegates from the Panamanian government agreed. However, the Chagres delegates didn't. As the inhabitants of a 400-year-old port town, they did not consider the port's characteristics a trivial matter. Because they knew the area much better than the delegates from the Zone and Colón City, they were able to suggest an alternative location by the mouth of the Lagarto River. The official delegation sailed to Lagarto, which already had a town with 100 houses and 500 people. After forty minutes exploring the place, the delegates concluded that the river's right margin, close to its mouth, was a good place for the new town. It was high and dry and enjoyed sea breezes. Everyone agreed that the location was better than the previous one.[74]

Some official documents praised the new location. The Chagres memorial described it as an "elegant piece of land, high, flat and ventilated by the sea breezes, which for all its conditions shows to be healthy."[75] An official from the ministry of foreign affairs wrote hopeful words about its future: the arrival of the people of Chagres to Lagarto would make it "an interesting city of 1,000 people." Rich in *tagua*, it was "a picturesque region, favored by the sea breezes, which, with hard work from its inhabitants, had the characteristics to become rich and prosperous."[76]

Despite these glowing remarks, negotiations were not going smoothly, and the town of Chagres decided to send a delegation to Panama City to talk with Ernesto T. Lefevre, the minister of foreign affairs. Like many members of Panama's economic and political elite, Lefevre was a man deeply immersed in both US and Panamanian culture. He was born in Panama in 1876 but spent some of his childhood years in San Francisco. He studied at the El Colegio del Istmo in Panama and finished his education in the United States, first at a prep school in Bethlehem, Pennsylvania, and later at Lehigh University, where he studied electrical engineering. He married Oderay Arango, the daughter of the prominent Panamanian politician José Agustín Arango. His political connections, social position, and education in electrical engineering probably helped him obtain a concession to run phone and electric companies in the cities of Panama and Colón in 1904, which eventually brought him great wealth. He also invested in agriculture and speculated on urban property for suburban development. He became secretary of foreign relations in 1912, under President Porras, even though he was a member of the Conservative Party.[77]

What this white member of Panama's elite shared with the mostly black citizens of Chagres was their common membership as citizens of historic ports and their common experience with the presence and pressure of US authorities. We don't know if they thought they had something in common. What we do know is that the people of Chagres thought it was worth their time and effort to travel to Panama to talk with him. The transcript of their conversation provides a rare window into how Panama's government mediated between the United States and local communities.[78]

The Chagres delegates complained about being pressured by Zone authorities to move quickly, even though the new town was not ready for occupancy. As the conversation evolved, other worries began to surface. The land was "rugged and uneven, the river was too distant, there was no water and it was difficult to travel on horseback." When the secretary brought up the quality of the Largarto port, the delegates agreed that "after Chagres it was the best" in the area. When Lefevre brought up the new location potential, the delegates bitterly responded that "people's sustenance depended on their farms, but it was impossible to cultivate the land because of the lack of water." Lefevre then mentioned other economic activities like turtle fishing. The delegates responded that they earned a living from that and also "from tagua, but because the terrain is so rugged we cannot use our horses."[79]

Failing to convince the delegates about the benefits of the new location, Lefevre focused on the inevitability of the depopulation of Chagres. They simply had no choice. He compared their situation to that of the government of Panama. When the United States requested that Panama disarm its police, the Panamanian government could only choose between two options, he said. They could either disarm the police and obtain some compensation for the arms or disarm the police without any compensation. The Chagreños's choice was similar. They had to move from Chagres to Lagarto. All they could do was to push for the best possible relocation—which they did. They used their political clout as an important voting district to obtain the help of Panama's government in their negotiations.[80]

According to Zone authorities, the land for the new town was cleared and ready. The Chagreños disagreed. All the United States had done was cut and burn the trees, without taking out the trunks or leveling the terrain. Lefevre and the Chagres delegates agreed that the solution was to have a Panamanian engineer survey the site. The people of Chagres could trust him because he was Panamanian; the Americans could accept his opinion because he was an engineer.[81]

The Panamanian engineer considered the new location adequate and "healthier than the old town of Chagres." The new town had 104 lots, eight of which would be used for a "plaza pública." He helped translate the Chagreños's requests into a technical language of "indispensable" improvements that Zone authorities would understand and perhaps approve. The Chagreños pointed out that the creeks near Lagarto ran dry during the dry season. The engineer recommended the construction of a well that would provide water during this season. The Chagreños's complaints about Largarto's uneven and rough terrain resulted in a formal request to place a bridge on the town's main street to ease access to the hill destined for public buildings. Finally, the engineer's report included one of the town dwellers' biggest concerns: to keep open the road that connected Largarto to the old Port of Chagres "because it was dangerous for boats to land in the new location."[82] This request was a reformulation of the Chagres Act, which requested "a road from the [new] town to Lake Gatún that would allow them to take their products to Colón, as well as the conditioning of the port of Lagarto."[83]

It is difficult to know how the Chagreños felt about their displacement or what they found most difficult and painful about leaving their town. The few documents they wrote suggest that the hardest thing was losing access to the Chagres River, which had been the reason for the town's existence since its foundation. It must have been difficult to imagine a town without the Chagres River. A letter from a peasant named Simón Quintana describes the pain of moving away from the river. He had cultivated land on the margin of the Chagres River since 1906. He lamented that "today the American Government demands that we leave this place for a place so distant, abandoning what has cost us so much sweat, work and hardship."[84] If Panama City had lost its port, Chagres had lost its river. The depopulation of Chagres was the final episode in a cycle of events that took away from Panama the control of its transit route, thereby severing the connection between Panama's urban centers and its waterways and ports.

7

The Zone's New Geography

The Flooding Myth: Depopulation as a Natural Disaster

In 1962, the Panamanian writer Gil Blas Tejeira published the novel *Lost Towns.*[1] It was a heartbreaking story about Panamanians forced out of their homes by the creation of Lake Gatún. The novel describes how the lake slowly flooded the land while heartless canal policemen forced Panamanians out of their homes. Since then, both academic writing and popular lore have linked the depopulation of the Zone to the flooding caused by the creation of Lake Gatún.[2]

When I began the research for this book, I also thought that story was accurate. I imagined that the town of Gorgona—the town at the center of Tejeira's story—was somewhere in the middle of Lake Gatún. I had even heard that scuba divers could see the tower of its old church under the lake. Yet slowly, through the examination of maps and documents, it became clear to me that while the old towns of the Zone were indeed gone, they were not under the lake. As we have seen, neither Empire nor New Gatún, the two largest Zone towns in 1912, were flooded. Not even Gorgona, the emblematic flooded town, was completely flooded. Far from being in the middle of the lake, it was located on its southern, narrowest shores, and only half of its streets were flooded. There was no church tower in the middle of the lake but an old cemetery above it.[3] The town could have easily stayed in its old location if canal authorities had relocated the occupants of the streets that were flooded to lands near the town that remained dry (see Map I.1).

Why did the expulsion story, the most traumatic event of twentieth-century Panama, become submerged in a flooding story? Like most myths, this one had some basis in reality. The creation of Lake Gatún did flood much of the land, about 164 square miles.[4] But there were also other reasons for the tenacity of the flooding myth. Perhaps it gained strength because it was the perfect metaphor for a painful disaster of great magnitude over which people had no control, which is how the 1912 depopulation order must have felt to the thousands of people who lived in the Zone. The flood was also a good metaphor for the depopulation of the Zone because it happened quickly. Between the Taft depopulation order of December 1912 and the depopulation of Chagres in 1916, less than four years had passed. Like a natural disaster, the depopulation order was uncontrollable and unstoppable. People had to adapt and adjust to their new situation. More important, the flooding myth gained strength because the creation of Lake Gatún became a way for canal publications to talk about the decision to depopulate without talking about it. Lake Gatún helped explain all the landscape changes of the Zone as the inevitable consequences of canal construction, regardless of whether they were inevitable or not.

The relocation of the railroad line is a good example of how the flooding myth helped submerge the complex story of the Zone's depopulation. Like the depopulation of the Zone, the relocation of the Panama Railroad does not occupy much space in histories of the canal.[5] However, the relocation of the railroad to the east of the canal, away from the old towns of the line, had consequences that were as dramatic for the towns of the southern part of the Zone as the creation of Lake Gatún was for the northern part. When canal construction began, the nineteenth-century Panama Railroad was completely overhauled and updated so that it could service the needs of canal construction. These modifications did not alter the urban landscape around the towns of the line. This changed, however, between 1912 and 1921, when Zone authorities moved the railroad from the west side of the canal, where the old railroad towns were located, to the east side, where the new American towns would be built.[6] This change left the towns on the line without a reason to exist; a railroad town without a railroad made as little sense as a river town without a river (see Map I.1).

Why was the railroad moved from the towns on the line? Was it only an inevitable consequence of canal construction? According to Sibert and Stevens's 1915 history of the Panama Canal, the railroad was moved in its entirety from the west of the canal to the east of the canal because the main port cities, Panama and Colón, were both located on the canal's east side. Yet the history of the railroad relocation was more complex. The final shape of the railroad line had as much to do with the decision to depopulate as with the creation of Lake Gatún. It is significant that the report of the US Fine Arts Commission, which visited Panama at the beginning of 1913, when the depopulation of the Zone had not yet happened, identified the relocation of the railroad as the cause for the abandonment of the towns located to the south of Lake Gatún. According to the report, "the proposed location of the Panama Railroad entirely on the north [sic] side of the Canal means the abandonment of the present towns of Gorgona, Empire, and Culebra."[7] In early 1913, the flooding story had not yet become the explanation for the Zone's depopulation while the relocation of the railroad was still part of the story.

Indeed, Sibert and Stevens's book is a good example of how the relationship between the depopulation of the Zone and the relocation of the railroad was eliminated from stories about the canal. Yes, it was necessary to move the railroad from the area flooded by Lake Gatún. But what about the lands south of Lake Gatún that were not flooded and where many towns on the line—including Empire—were located? The decision depended on social and political considerations. If the US government had not decided to depopulate the Zone, very different decisions would have been taken in relation to the non-flooded sections of the railroad. It is important to remember that technological and economic decisions are based on social priorities, on what a society considers to be worth the price of saving and what it considers non-essential.[8] Had it been deemed important, it would have been possible to keep the southern part of the railroad line, which was not flooded, in its original location so it could continue to serve important railroad towns like Empire and Gorgona. Gorgona would have remained in its original location, and only the flooded part of town would have been moved to dry land nearby. The southern part of the railroad would have remained a branch of the Panama Railroad connected to the new railroad line by a pontoon swing bridge located near the southern end of the Culebra Cut.

Indeed, this is what initially happened. In 1914, when John F. Stevens wrote his history of the canal's construction, the western branch was in use and was linked to the main railroad line. Stevens speculated about the possibility that the branch "may be abandoned entirely in the future, as the necessity for its retention may disappear."[9] Stevens avoided the depopulation story by not exploring the issue of "necessity"—why the line needed to "disappear." He knew that "necessity" meant the presence of towns and fields on the western line of the railroad. And the railroad would disappear because Taft's 1912 executive order had mandated the area's depopulation. By not mentioning these facts, the book made it difficult for future readers to remember the importance of the depopulation order. That towns like Emperador were using a railroad line that would soon cease to exist because of the depopulation order is a fact erased from this story. The removal of the western railroad line became conflated with the flooding story. In this and other stories about the canal, the railroad relocation became a natural consequence of the creation of Lake Gatún, not a consequence of a depopulation order.

The depopulation of the Zone was also silenced in the news stories about the construction of the post-1914 towns of the canal. It began early, in coverage published by the *Panama Canal Record*, the canal newspaper of the day. While some stories celebrated and discussed in detail the design of new towns like Balboa, others mentioned the measures "to prevent further immigration of squatters into the Canal Zone, the movement of squatters from one part of the Zone to another, and the emigration of residents of the Canal Zone settlements to the jungle."[10] Although they were part of the same historical process, these two kinds of stories were never linked, which silenced the fact that the new towns were replacing an old way of life in the Zone, and that there would have been no squatters without the depopulation order. The depopulation process had just begun, but already the inhabitants of the old towns were not people driven away from their lands but squatters on lands that were not theirs. The tragedy behind the creation of the new Zone model towns was never mentioned in the *Panama Canal Record*, which instead portrayed the new towns as a natural consequence of canal construction and not of the December 1912 depopulation order. One story after another, one silence after another erased the various depopulation histories from Panama's memory until the flooding of Lake Gatún became the only story.

If the depopulation of the Zone was a consequence of the creation of Lake Gatún, it was not because it was inevitable. Rather, it was because Lake Gatún's dramatic transformation of the landscape created the possibility of completely reimagining the Zone as a place that could be reinvented *ex nihilo*. The flooding myth could be seen as a biblical metaphor for a world that was created anew. By depopulating the Zone and allowing the jungle to grow over old towns and farm fields, the ICC made visible and concrete the idea that Panama was only a jungle waiting for US progress and civilization.

A New World Emerges:
The Permanent Towns of Balboa and La Boca

A person looking at the Zone today, or even forty years ago, when it was still under US control, would never have guessed how drastically the region had changed since the early twentieth century. The post-depopulation landscape looks as though it has always been there. There are no visible markers to remind visitors of the lost geography. The old towns of the Chagres River have disappeared, and with them the towns of the old railroad line located to the west of the canal. The waters of Lake Gatún flooded some towns and farms. Other places, like Chagres and Emperador, were forcibly depopulated, and the tropical forest rapidly absorbed them along with the farms that once surrounded them. What used to be a lively urban corridor that connected towns like Gorgona, Emperador, and Culebra to Panama City and Colón City became an empty, jungle-covered area. Without towns, people, and the railroad, the western section of the Zone became an area for military exercises. The depopulation order, combined with the creation of Lake Gatún, the elimination of the western railroad line, and the policy of allowing the forest to grow back, effectively erased the traces of a centuries-old landscape. This radical transformation made it easier to forget what was once there.

The depopulated Zone offered a remarkable space for building a brand new urban geography that would reproduce US ideas about its own civilization and its role in the world. Located next to one of the most famous engineering projects of its time and in one of the most strategic areas in the world, the Zone's new towns would be the perfect companions to a canal whose construction had captured the imagination of the United States.

Unencumbered by the vagaries of urban reality in a densely populated area, Zone officials started to build the new "permanent towns" of the Zone on the eastern side of the Canal close to the new railroad line. In the process the ICC inverted notions of temporality and permanence: the old established towns became "temporary" and the brand-new towns "permanent." The new towns would be different from the previous ones. If the old towns were divided between a small American side and a larger "native" side, the new towns would be fully American and would be segregated into two types: towns for white US workers and towns for foreign, mostly black West Indian workers. If the old towns had private properties and private businesses, the new ones would have none. The US government would provide everything from food to entertainment. If the old towns sold alcohol, the new towns would be alcohol free. If the old towns had grown in ways that reflected the history of the region and the income, tastes, and priorities of homeowners, the new towns would be carefully planned to represent US urban ideals.

None were as carefully planned as the showcase towns of Balboa (for white workers) and La Boca (for black workers), which were located

FIGURE 7.1 A view of Balboa from the administration building
Credit: Library of Congress / HABS CZ, 1-BALB, 1–19.

on the Pacific side of the canal near the Port of Balboa (see Figures 7.1 and 7.2).[11] The ICC replaced the forty-one towns listed in the Zone census of 1912 with a few well-planned and manicured towns. The Zone became a new landscape with no agriculture, no private property, and fewer towns. It went from being a bustling space layered with history to an urban space showcasing the United States' urban conquest of the tropics. The jungle and the waters of Lake Gatún not only covered the old landscape but also served as background to the new one. Little by little, it became easy to think of this space as pristine.[12]

The design of the new Zone towns represented Progressive Era ideals for reforming US society. Many of these ideals had shaped the

FIGURE 7.2 The quarters of silver employees in La Boca in 1920
Credit: National Archives photo no. 185-G-26-1/2X-34 (Brady Collection).

American side of old towns in the Zone, but they would achieve their long-term expression in the new, post-1914 permanent towns.[13] For men like President Theodore Roosevelt and the historian Frederick Jackson Turner, the United States was losing its strength and character to hedonistic and effeminate elites who cared only about themselves and their profits and only secondarily, if at all, about their country's general welfare.[14] Frederick Jackson Turner famously argued that the closing of the Western frontier represented the end of American grit and innovation. Novels like *The Virginian* repeated this message, depicting a lost frontier that was home to rough and courageous men who embodied the true spirit of American democracy.[15] With the frontier gone, where could the United States recover its manly and democratic spirit? Men like Theodore Roosevelt found the answer in overseas expansion and projects like the Panama Canal. Building the canal and overcoming the challenges of tropical nature would prove that the

United States had not lost its pioneering spirit. Writers who told the story of the canal echoed these sentiments.[16] The US men in Panama were facing the challenges of tropical nature: its mosquitoes, its heat, its rains, its mud and mudslides. The canal men in Panama had "received a mandate from Civilization . . . in the interest of mankind" to police "the Isthmus in the interest of its inhabitants and our own national needs, and for the good of the civilized world."[17]

But there was a twist. The heroes who inhabited the canal towns were not the cowboys of the frontier but doctors, engineers, and other salaried middle-class professionals. With their expertise and sacrifice they had triumphed against technical and geographical challenges for the glory and common good of the United States and the world. The middle-class public who followed their feats at home could identify with them and bask in their glory and fame. If the US middle class had triumphed in Panama, it could also triumph at home. If US doctors and engineers in Panama could successfully battle yellow fever, tropical rain, mudslides, and river currents, all the while overseeing thousands of workers from around the globe, middle-class reformers back home could remedy the social malaise caused by industrial poverty, immigration, and urban squalor. It was up to them to tackle the social problems that a hedonistic elite was unable or unwilling to solve.

The new towns of Balboa and La Boca became a physical representation of Progressive social values. Balboa showed how US middle-class reformers saw themselves, and La Boca demonstrated what they thought about their role as reformers and civilizers of others, and as such they received special attention from canal administrators. The ICC wanted Balboa to be an "imposing town befitting its function as the governing center of a highly important territory of the United States."[18] Goethals hired important architects and artists. The Fine Arts Commission of the US Congress thought the symbolic role of the canal was so important that it visited Panama to supervise the design of the permanent towns.[19]

The architectural center of Balboa was the administration building. Its location on a knoll on the western slopes of Ancón Hill was of foremost significance. Situated on the outskirts of Panama City, it was the most important hill in the area and one charged with great symbolism. Since the late seventeenth century it had served as backdrop to Panama City and its ports. It symbolic value increased in 1904 when it became the most important section of the Zone's border with Panama City. Moreover, generations of Panamanians associated losing Ancón Hill with losing the Zone, and they learned to mourn its loss from a poem by Amelia Dennis de Icaza published in 1906: "I only have my heart to love you, because I cannot cry by your side anymore . . . you are not mine, idolized Ancón."[20]

The location of the administration building on Ancón's western slopes disrupted a 400-year tradition that placed the administration of the Port of Panama in Panama City, near its most important religious and political centers. Even the French had followed this pattern, locating their canal administration building on Panama's main square, facing the cathedral. In contrast, Ancón Hill served as a barrier between the administration building and Panama City. It was impossible to see Panama City from the administration building or the administration building from Panama City. Moreover, the back of the building faced Panama City while its magnificent staircase entrance faced the port, the new town of Balboa, and its palm-lined mall, El Prado. From its height, the administration building overlooked a new geography that made official the 1904 US position that the Pacific port of La Boca belonged to the United States and not to Panama, as Panama's government had claimed. Under US rule, Ancón Hill became the center of a new political power and a new canal geography that separated Panama City from its international port and transit zone.

As the architectural and symbolic centerpiece of the new Zone, the building received special attention from canal authorities. They hired Austin W. Lord, an important New York–based architect, to design it and William B. Van Ingen, who also created art for the Library of Congress, to paint its murals. Both the administration building and its murals paid homage to the glory of technology and to the new hero of the US middle class, the engineer. It is significant that the most important building of the Zone was not a military building or a political building—a governor's mansion or a city hall—but an administrative building. Its name highlighted the importance of good technocratic administration over elected officials or political and military appointments. It honored the technological achievements and hard work of canal administrators and engineers.

The design of the administration building reinforced the departure from tradition. It was not a Beaux Arts building typical of the US elite but instead incorporated a new aesthetic and sense of purpose shared by the professional, reformist middle classes. The building was impressive yet simple. Goethals requested a design that favored "simplicity," in keeping with the "massive concrete work" of the canal.[21] The building had three stories, massive walls, large windows, and an imposing set of stairs, which were the building's main architectural feature. Goethals had objected to any sculptures or bas reliefs at the building's entrance. Its only decoration was a large panel that said "Administration Panama Canal A.D. XDCCCCXIV."[22]

The Van Ingen murals were as important as the building's design. Located in the rotunda, the murals still inspire awe. Their panels tell the story of four crucial moments of canal engineering: the construction of the Gatún Dam spillway; the construction of a side wall culvert at the Miraflores Locks; the construction of a lock gate; and the excavation of the Culebra Cut. In these scenes, the enormous scale of the construction sites and the machinery dwarves the workers. The murals made visual a sentiment common among Panamanian writers who taught their readers that the canal was to US culture and technology what the pyramids had been to ancient Egyptians. Both represented the highest technological achievements of their times.

In addition to telling the story of US technological triumph in Panama, the Van Ingen murals also changed the history of the transit zone. The past is not visible in the murals: there are no Spanish roads, no Chagres River, no nineteenth-century railroads. The story of the canal is the history of US construction of its locks and dams. The history told in the murals reinforced the message of the post-1914 urban landscape. Like the murals, the new urban landscape of the Zone was disconnected from previous urban uses and traditions, and its towns were strategically organized around the new canal infrastructure. The town of Balboa was named after the Port of Balboa and located next to it; the town of Miraflores was located near the Miraflores Locks and named after them; and Gatún was located near the Gatún Dam and Locks. Gone were the names of the old towns of the Canal Zone. There was no Cruces, Gorgona, or Emperador. Only Gatún had retained its name, a reminder of the early years of canal construction when the moving of towns did not entail the expulsion of its inhabitants from the Zone.

Situated right below the administration building, the town of Balboa seamlessly complemented its message. In their way of living, their houses, and their towns, the white dwellers of the Zone conveyed what the US middle class thought about itself and its civilizing role. The town's buildings were aesthetically pleasing and well designed and planed, as befitted the professional excellence of the canal builders. Balboa's houses emphasized discreet middle-class comfort and simplicity over the luxury and decoration of the elite. They were two-story houses with one central architectural detail: a main staircase located in front of the house that connected the sidewalk to the house's main entrance. All the houses had walls painted with the same light color, and they were all topped with the same red gable roof. The uniformity and simplicity of the houses conveyed the idea that the United States had brought order to the jungle chaos.[23]

There were no privately owned houses or businesses in Balboa or in any of the other Zone towns. The houses were all company houses, but they did not belong to just any private company; they were the property of the US government. Like the canal and the administration building, they sent the message that the US government and its efficient middle-class professional administrators could act for the common good and efficiently provide for all that was needed for a healthy, wholesome, and happy society.[24] All the necessities for a comfortable middle-class life—from coffee, to US–imported vegetables, to clothing—could be found inside the well-supplied commissaries of Zone towns. The hustle and bustle of the stores, banks, and restaurants of the old Zone towns of Emperador, Gorgona, and New Gatún could only be found across the border, in Panama City or Colón City. The new towns, with clean running water, sewers, manicured lawns, and screened windows, proved that progress and sanitation could be brought to the tropics. Canal towns were places not for luxury or excess but for wholesome entertainment. Alcohol, gambling, and cabarets were forbidden—although easily available just across the border in Panama City—and the YMCA, clubhouse, churches, ball games, and other family activities provided social entertainment. Not even elitist country clubs could be found in this space. Holidays like July 4 would reflect this new life in the Zone. They would be celebrated on Balboa's main avenue or mall, right below the main stairs of the administration building. In these moments, in these new geographies, all traces of the Zone's previous Panamanian urban past were gone.

The past, however, had not completely vanished. The Zone's agricultural past came back inadvertently in the plant selection of the landscape architect William Lyman Phillips. A New Englander, Phillips had trained with the renowned Olmstead brothers (John Charles and Frederick Law Jr.) in Massachusetts. After this experience and some traveling around Europe to observe its gardens and parks, he was given the first major task of his career: to organize the landscape of the new towns of the Canal Zone.[25] Fashioning himself as a modern Darwin, he became a thoughtful observer of tropical plants and wanted to convey the incredible beauty of the tropics, where he had sensed a "fascination unknown in the pleasant northern woods, [had] been exalted by the amazing vegetal exuberance, [and] overwhelmed by the violent illumination of the lands to a degree before un-experienced."[26]

Phillips was a rare voice against common stereotypes about the tropics and prized direct observation over the "misleading nature of greenhouse collections and so-called tropical planting."[27] He understood that the tropics were rich and complex places and wanted to dispel popular misconceptions about them. For example, he challenged the idea that only the tropical rain forest or jungle represented tropical landscapes and took pains to understand the various types of forests common in tropical lands, which he classified into four types: littoral woodlands, rain forests, dry deciduous forests, and cultural forests. By "cultural forests" Phillips meant the cultivated lands that reflected the hard work of tropical farmers. At a time when the coconut tree was a stereotypical symbol of the tropics' alleged "natural bounty" and the indolent nature of tropical people, Phillips lashed out against those who thought that coconut trees required no cultivation. It was not true, he said, that coconut trees grew spontaneously. Citing the "Cingalese [*sic*] belief that coconut trees will not flourish 'unless you walk and talk among them,'" Phillips assured his readers that "the coconut grove is purely a cultural type. So great is its economic importance, so strongly is it venerated by all tropical peoples, so intensely interwoven with tropical life and almost inseparable from any thought of the Tropics than one finds it difficult to appraise its value in the landscape without bias."[28] It is perhaps no accident that this careful observer of tropical landscapes included the plants of the old Panamanian farms in new Zone gardens.

Faced with the "simplicity and businesslike character" of Canal Zone towns, Phillips envisioned a landscape design to which a "nativist approach" would add needed refinement.[29] Quite matter-of-factly, he noted that the "depopulating of the Zone has resulted in the abandoning of a great many small plantations from which plants can be taken."[30] In this way, old orchards and farms were incorporated as a "native" touch into a new Zone landscape that had no space for local farmers or local agriculture. Phillips planned to use the royal palm to outline the formal part of Balboa, not because he liked it—he did not—but because Goethals considered it "the finest tree that grows." He had wanted to use the coconut palm because it seemed to him "the very symbol and mark of the land."

In spite of his sensitivity to the tropical landscape, Phillips still wanted to appeal to a northern aesthetic and sought a compromise between tropical nature and the ideas about gardens and beautiful parks he was accustomed to. Like the houses, the commissaries, and the clubhouses, the landscape was also expected to bring a comforting sense of familiarity to the US inhabitants of the Zone. Like the red gable roofs of Balboa, tropical plants became a decorative touch of local history that didn't disrupt the Americanness of the landscape. Phillips liked mangoes and other broadleaved trees because they had a "tolerable resemblance to certain northern broadleaved associations." While in most northern trees "the foliage dominates over the woody parts, and gives the plant a definite outline and contour, in the tropics the foliage tends to be thin and the woody parts dominate." In his view, the "notable exceptions" were the mango, tamarind, lime, and the nispero, which had "round-headed forms . . . quite variable in port and often picturesque in age . . . they are all to be considered wherever a hard, definite form is desired."[31] He also lamented the lack of shrubs among tropical plants and missed the presence of plants like the rhododendron, but found in the hibiscus a good replacement. It is perhaps because of Phillips's legacy that mango trees and hibiscus—or *papos* as they are known in Panama—are ubiquitous in the gardens of the old Zone and Panama City.

The complement to the white town of Balboa was the black town of La Boca (see Figure 7.2). Canal authorities took much care in its planning because its symbolic value was as important as that of Balboa. The planning of La Boca began in April 1913, when canal authorities approved the building of a new town near the canal's Pacific port that would house the permanent West Indian workers of the silver roll.[32] The new town was to be built in the same place—the Balboa dump southeast of Sosa Hill—where the ICC had initially planned to relocate the people of the "native town of La Boca." Canal authorities considered five names for the new town: Espinosa; Lesseps; Morgan Town; Lincoln, "friend of the colored people"; and the old name of La Boca, which was the one finally chosen by Goethals.[33]

Unlike native La Boca, the new town did not disrupt the symbolic importance of the area next to the canal's Pacific port. Like nearby

Balboa, La Boca would showcase American ideals of urban modernity. If Balboa was to exemplify white Americans' ability to live comfortable and healthy lives in the tropics, La Boca was to be a "model town" for black workers. A few years after its foundation, the Zone's chief health officer proudly highlighted how

> La Boca, especially, is a model town of its kind, with wide, well-paved streets, planting spaces and lawns, screened houses with modern plumbing, and a well-supplied commissary and restaurant. By constant supervision and training the colored population of this city has been given an education in sanitation that is evidenced in their appearance and surroundings and which could well be emulated by people of a relatively higher social strata and culture.[34]

La Boca was planned so that it would satisfy modern public health standards, modern urban design, and appropriate aesthetic principles while promoting civic pride and orderly behavior among its inhabitants. The chief sanitary officer had a long list of requirements, which included proper gutters; properly graded and cemented surfaces around water taps beneath all elevated bathhouses and range closets and under all elevated buildings; self-closing garbage cans; proper wooden slats to protect mosquito screens; and barrack interiors painted a light color with an eighteen-inch black band four feet above the floor.[35] Well-paved streets and sidewalks were also standard. Even if Goethals considered concrete sidewalks excessive and costlier than those used for white settlements, the La Boca site committee disagreed: "concrete sidewalks and footpaths are really necessary from a sanitary standpoint . . . without these walks, during the rainy season mudholes would be numerous."[36] The committee also paid close attention to the town grounds. The landscape architect recommended planting coconut trees on both sides of the street, six trees—some fruit, some ornamental—around each building, shrubs in several locations, and grass in yards and parking areas. The La Boca committee agreed with the recommendations and suggested that planting begin as soon as possible.[37]

If Zone authorities were unable to tackle the "social problem" of the people of the native town of La Boca, they paid great attention to the people of new La Boca. As with most Progressive programs to improve conditions for the poor, the approach to La Boca involved an attack on popular habits and customs.[38] If, as Arturo Escobar states, "development fostered a way of conceiving of social life as a technical problem," the approach of ICC officials toward the new town of La Boca foreshadowed tactics that would later be associated with "developmental" practices.[39] A letter from the Panama Canal engineer Armand Rousseau spoke to this sentiment:

> The whole objective is to make La Boca an object lesson in seeing how far it is practicable to make the colored residents take an interest in improving their living conditions and raising their standard of comfort and observance of sanitary regulations. It will be uphill work at best. . . . So many favorable comments, however, have already been made in regard to the appearance of La Boca, that I feel it would be worthwhile to see how far we can go to make La Boca a "model city." . . . The main point is for the Panama Canal to establish the standard. If the people do not like the standard and do not want to pay the rents charged, they have the privilege of going elsewhere in Panamanian territory where they can follow their own standard to a greater extent.[40]

Two things stand out in this letter: First, the idea of making La Boca a model for civilizing West Indian workers; and second, the separation of the Zone and Panama into two distinctive places. The first was a place of standards and regulations, the second a place to expel or relocate whatever did not conform to those standards.

To tackle the goal of reforming the habits of West Indian workers, Rousseau planned to make the workers responsible for the maintenance of the town's grounds, which included cleaning and caring for the grass and plants. To encourage responsibility, he also proposed awarding monthly prizes to the best-kept buildings. Rousseau's opponents argued that the rent paid by West Indian workers entitled them to have a paid worker in charge of the grounds. Yet Rousseau's proposal was important enough that Goethals "strongly requested" the appointment of a special committee to evaluate it.[41] The result was a report on the "appearance of the town and the interests of the residents of La Boca."[42]

Typical of Progressive Era reformist ideals, the La Boca report paid close attention to two factors: whether the Zone government was fulfilling its responsibilities toward the West Indian workers, and whether it was taking the necessary measures to train and reform them so they could become the ideal black workers that Zone authorities envisioned. To achieve these goals, committee members "carefully inspected the town, consulted employees working there and others and their families living there." The report paid close attention to the needs and difficulties of La Boca's residents and to the ways in which the Zone government had failed to fulfill its obligations. It ended with suggestions for improving the habits of West Indian workers.

Its first recommendation was to install tap water and slop sinks in the many houses that still lacked them; not having them entailed "an amount of work that even energetic white people would be apt to avoid by throwing slops on the ground." It also recommended the construction of a "shadelike structure" with tables and benches near the silver-roll mess that would protect workers from the rain and sun, while at the same time ensuring that food was not left to attract rats. Other recommendations sought to deter the use of improvised structures and the disorderly appearance of the town. The report recommended that clotheslines be strung in an orderly fashion "six feet apart" in front of each row of washhouses to avoid "the irregularity" of clotheslines placed haphazardly. It also suggested that canal authorities supply kitchenettes of a neat and uniform pattern that would provide fire protection and help to end the use of "ugly kitchenettes," and also provide additional storage space to avoid the unsightly use of porches for storage purposes. It recommended the planting of shade trees, shade vines, and grass.

In addition, the committee sought to foster "civic pride." Of all the problems of La Boca, it thought that the "lack of civic pride" was "the hardest to overcome," the causes being

> as fundamental as poverty, crowding, lack of ownership or other form of pecuniary interest in the town, lack of self-government, citizenship, or other forms of political interest in it, and lack of certainty of tenure of work or other form of assurance of long residence in it.[43]

This assessment reflected an understanding of poverty as an obstacle to full political participation and healthy communal and social life. The committee acknowledged that the new Zone lacked two fundamental traits of American political and economic life: private homeownership and elections. It also recognized that, unlike Americans, West Indians born in the Zone were not entitled to American citizenship. The committee's recommendations sought to deal with these constraints. The proposal had three elements. First, there should be monthly cash prizes for "neatness and cleanliness in and about houses." Second, residents should be encouraged to grow flowers. With their goal of solving a social problem, the committee had little patience for people who objected to West Indian gardening aesthetics: "That the West Indian idea of beauty might differ from ours is here immaterial." Their goal was to foster civic pride in La Boca, not to "merely gladden the eyes of persons not living there." Third, they suggested the appointment of a "committee of inhabitants" made up of one representative from each church in La Boca, who would represent the interests of local residents and advise the governor.

Of all the committee's recommendations, the last would be the only one rejected by Goethals, who chose instead to establish regular hearings "to ascertain the desires and requirements of any resident of La Boca, acting as individuals."[44] Famously, Goethals disliked political organizations in the Zone and preferred a paternalistic style whereby workers approached Zone authorities individually.[45] The prizes for "best-kept grounds" were implemented in December 1914.[46] This practice was discontinued in 1916, before even two years had passed. Since the same families kept winning the prizes, the Quartermaster's Department considered it more efficient and cost effective to pay one man to keep the grounds than to pay for prizes.[47]

The comments about West Indians' lack of civic pride did not take into account their long traditions of organizing and petitioning, although they were important enough that some Zone officers tried to avoid actions that would lead West Indian workers to start signing petitions.[48] In fact, the residents of La Boca did not wait passively for the Zone government to provide the urban infrastructure that it had promised. In 1915, sixty-two neighbors in La Boca signed a petition requesting that Zone authorities install water and sewerage systems in the buildings that still lacked them. They mentioned how burdensome it was to carry water for everyday household uses, particularly after the arduous work they performed for the canal. Moreover, they skillfully used the sanitary concerns of Zone officials to further their point by signaling that "having to bring water . . . from such a distance" made it a "strong temptation" not to use the water required for "proper sanitation."[49]

In spite of their own shortcomings and delays in providing adequate infrastructure, Zone authorities continued to closely police the behavior of West Indian workers in La Boca. Sanitary inspectors described in excruciating detail how some residents failed to keep their premises clean. One sanitary inspector described women throwing slops in the gutters instead of in the range closets and throwing food scraps on the ground instead of in garbage cans.[50] Canal authorities also continued to be involved in an old and recurring source of conflict with workers who preferred to cook their own food instead of eating at the canal mess halls. Canal rules allowed cook-fires only in "designated places where a regular cook shed was erected." Any other use was deemed unsanitary. Yet canal authorities did not provide "regular cook sheds," arguing that the "Panama Canal furnishes good meals at a low price." West Indian workers strongly disagreed and continued to cook their own meals, while canal authorities asked the police to assist them in controlling this habit.[51] Rigid ideas about appropriate behavior clashed with the fact that canal authorities were not always willing—or able—to pay for the infrastructural investment that facilitated "appropriate" behavior, leaving West Indians with few choices and more work. A West Indian man's defense of the customs of the women of La Boca captures well the contradiction between the behavior required of West Indian town dwellers and the services provided to them. He asked the health inspector, "Why shouldn't she throw her slops in the gutter? It is too far to carry them to the range closet."[52]

Despite these tensions, La Boca became the model for the other black towns of the Zone. In 1915, the chief health officer of the Zone, citing the example of La Boca, proposed the construction of a silver-roll settlement near the Miraflores Locks. According to the proposal, "La Boca is standing proof that a negro town can be clean, decent and attractive, that negroes can be made self-respecting, that rents may be reasonable and at the same time provide for repairs and rebuilding, that the Panama Canal can and does without loss to itself provide decent housing for many of its black employees."[53]

It was June 1915, and many workers of the dredging division still lived in the private tenements of Hamilton Hill, Jamaica Town, and Spanish Town, near Paraíso. The proposal sought to replace these communities with an official black town like La Boca because "privately owned tenements in the Canal Zone are out of spirit and harmony with all of the policies and developments of the Panama Canal."[54] Nonetheless, the plans to eliminate all the tenements of the Zone and replace them with model towns for black workers had to wait a few more years. Zone authorities knew that as long as construction work continued, it was necessary to keep the tenements of Zone towns. Some even regretted the decision to depopulate the town of Empire before work at the Culebra Cut was finished.[55] Eventually the Zone government would build a series of black towns, which, along with the white towns, dotted the Zone with carefully planned and segregated government-run communities.[56] They were as important to the canal landscape as its white towns because they provided visual proof of the US idea of bringing civilization to tropical people.

Landscapes of Western Civilization

The elimination of the native town of La Boca and the creation of the new towns of Balboa and La Boca were part of a dramatic transformation of the landscape that ended an entire way of urban life in the Zone and disconnected it from the Panamanian past. The design of the new towns linked them to another history: that of US progress and technological development. The Pacific entrance of the canal had replaced the mouth of the Río Grande; the American Port of Balboa had replaced Panama City and its international port; the new town of La Boca had replaced the native town of La Boca; and Balboa had replaced Panama City as the administrative center of the isthmian route. Most Panamanians today do not even know that there was once a river on the Pacific side of the canal. Only the name La Boca retained an aspect of the previous urban landscape.

Behind the transformation of the Zone's landscape, however, was another story: the story of the failure and contradictions of Progressive Era reforms in the Zone. On the one hand, the canal provided an experimental ground for Progressive ideas about good government. Social reformers, journalists, and commentators paid close attention to US labor and social policies in Panama.[57] On the other hand, Zone authorities never had the budget to provide modern housing for the 61,000 people who lived in the Zone in 1912. To do so would have required a very different economic model and a different relationship with Panama. The depopulation of the Zone solved this contradiction. It created an urban geography of working-class housing that spanned the Panama–US borders and purged the Zone of all but a few permanent resident workers. Unemployed and temporary laborers had to move to the already overpopulated tenements of Colón City and Panama City. It is no accident that Panama's famous tenement neighborhood, El Chorrillo, developed and grew in 1913 and 1914, when the depopulation of the Zone forced the inhabitants of Zone tenements to find new housing in Panama City and Colón City.[58] Indeed, shantytowns like Chorrillo, Marañon, Curundú, and Hollywood marked the border between Panama City and the Zone.

After the depopulation of the Zone, the US–Panama border became a highly visible space in which American model towns stood next to Panamanian slums. This contrast helped naturalize ideas about the United States as the land of progress, modernity, and comfort, and about Panama as a traditional region in permanent need of modernization and technological aid. This new landscape can be interpreted as a spatial representation of the ideology of Western Civilization. Like other histories of the West, it created a contrast between Western Civilization and tropical backwardness by erasing the elements of their shared nineteenth- and twentieth-century history. A description of Panama City published in 1915 brought home, in particularly dark tones, the contrast between Panama's backwardness and US civilization: "In all the world there is no other city as depressing as Panama. Natives and aliens go through its streets with dragging feet and saddened faces. We wondered how American white men of decent tastes could stay more than six weeks in such a hole and keep their reason."[59] Such contrasts between Panama and the Zone helped to erase their shared character as global industrialized cities. The contrasts also obscured the multiple ways in which Balboa, La Boca, and Panama City remained a united urban space. The new manicured towns of the Zone could not have existed without driving the majority of canal workers from the tenements of the Zone to those in Panama City. The "wholesome" and alcohol-free lifestyle of the Zone would not have been possible without the nightlife and commerce of Panama City.

The language of contrasts between Panama and the Zone also obscured the many similarities between Panama City and the towns of the Zone. The red-gabled buildings of Balboa Heights had their counterpart in the new Panamanian neighborhood of La Exposición. Planned by President Belisario Porras, the neighborhood was the site of new government buildings and upper-class houses, as well as the home of the new and modern Santo Tomás Hospital. If Balboa showcased US ability to conquer and modernize the tropics, La Exposición was an attempt to challenge US civilizing narratives and the United States' right to control Panama. It sought to assert Panama's historic place as an equally civilized nation.[60] Even Balboa's high school had its counterpart in Panama's Instituto Nacional. Housed in a grand neoclassical building, the Instituto was for decades Panama's most prestigious high school. Located on opposite sides of Ancón Hill, both high schools were built at the beginning of the twentieth century: one as a symbol of US ability to modernize tropical Panama, the other as a symbol of Panama's ability to manage its own modernity. It is perhaps no accident that these two high schools became, respectively, the symbol of both Panama's struggles to recover the canal during the 1950s and 1960s and the United States' opposition to this goal.[61] Behind the 1960s conflict over Panama's right to control the canal and its Zone stood the questions of 1904 about Panama's right and ability to keep its international ports: whether Panama was civilized enough, and whether the canal was part of Panama's history.

The new landscape of the Zone helped naturalize an idea of historical progress that failed to acknowledge that industrialization happened simultaneously in the United States and in Latin America, and that its consequences were felt everywhere. As with the regions next to the agro-industrial banana plantations of Central America and the modern mining compounds of South America, histories of industrialization did not incorporate Panama because the Panama Canal was solely American. Panama's poverty became linked to its "traditional" history; solutions to this poverty continued to be sought in a future modernity that never quite arrived because it was already there.

Epilogue

Every time we drove by Pedro Miguel, my father used to say: everybody can return to their town but me, because my town is under water.

—DANILO PÉREZ URRIOLA, DECEMBER 18, 2016

The Ruins of Nuevo Chagres

IN 2013, I readied myself for a trip around the old Canal Zone and its borders, where I would be looking for memories of the lost landscape. This time I was not a child but a grown woman driving her own (rental) car. Neither the Zone nor I were the same. The Zone had become Panamanian and I had become Americanized. After the signing of the Torrijos-Carter Panama Canal Treaty in 1977, the slow process of transferring the Zone back to Panama got under way. It began in 1979 and ended in 2000 when the last canal structures and military bases were transferred to Panama. While the Zone was becoming part of Panamanian territory, I was slowly becoming part of America. I had left Panama in 1994 to pursue a doctorate in history in the United States, and eventually I made a life there. Neither the United States nor its way of life was a mystery to me anymore. Americans were my friends, my colleagues, my students, and my family. My own house in Cleveland Heights was built in 1915, around the same time the permanent towns of the Zone were established. I could see the obvious resemblances between my home and the old wooden houses of the Zone, and the ways in which the latter were distinguished by attempts to adapt a northern architectural design to the tropics. As much as the Zone and I had changed, the traces of our previous histories had not. More than thirty years after the end of the US Canal Zone, the landscape created after 1914 remained hard to erase, its legacy difficult to escape.

In December 2013, I drove to Nuevo Emperador and Nuevo Chagres, two small towns outside of the Zone's borders named after two depopulated towns. I did not know what I would find; these were places outside of my usual path. Unlike the old towns of the Zone, they were not located along any of the main Panamanian roads; they were not on the way to anywhere I had ever needed to go. But I was curious. I wanted to find out if the children and grandchildren of the people forced to relocate 100 years ago knew their parents and grandparents' stories.

As a historian accustomed to working with old documents in dusty archives, I found the idea of knocking on the doors of strangers intimidating. A practitioner of oral history I was not. I asked an old friend who was very outgoing to be my assistant. Having somebody by my side made it easier to knock on doors. I finally understood why Jehovah's Witnesses travel in pairs.

The first town we visited was Nuevo Chagres. I was very familiar with the Fortress of Chagres, which I first toured as a child in 1979, when all of Panama was celebrating the return of Zone lands. My parents decided to celebrate with some historical sightseeing by visiting the Spanish Fortress of San Lorenzo, located in the Zone (see Figure E.1).

FIGURE E.I A family picnic at the Fort of San Lorenzo de Chagres in 1979
Credit: Reproduced from the author's collection.

The fortress was situated on a high cliff over the mouth of the Cha-gres River. It was surrounded by jungle, isolated from the world around it. On the small road that led to the fortress one could hear monkeys howl and, if lucky, see serpents slither across the little-trafficked road. No traces remained of the town of Chagres, which once stood below the fortress at the mouth of the river. When we arrived, my family and I were the only ones in the entire fort, and we ate our sandwiches while sitting on the ancient Spanish cannons. It felt magical. As a college his-tory major I returned to the fort several times, never giving much thought to the question of what had happened to the town and the people who once lived by the fort. In 2013, the drive from Panama City to Nuevo Chagres took three hours, much longer than the old drive to the Fortress of San Lorenzo, the original location of Chagres. We had to drive north, toward Colón City; then we headed west and crossed the Gatún Locks of the canal. We continued west on a little transit road, in the opposite direction of the better-known roads to the eastern Caribbean beaches.

More so than the old Fortress of San Lorenzo with its rusted Spanish cannons and its broken walls, Nuevo Chagres is a place of ruins. Not because the town is in disrepair. Quite the opposite: when I visited, the houses were freshly painted and the park and streets well maintained. It is a place of ruins in Ann Stoler's sense of something that has been ruined.[1] The town's landscape and Chagreños's memories tell a history of what was destroyed, of everything residents lost with their expul-sion from Old Chagres.

The strength of local memory, of the town's unwillingness to forget its origins, confronts the visitor upon arrival with a "welcome to Nuevo Chagres" sign that has a painting of the San Lorenzo de Chagres Fort, even though the fort lies several miles from the new town. One hundred years after the townspeople were expelled from their original location by the Fortress of San Lorenzo, the fortress continued to be the basis of the town's identity. It was one of the many ways in which Chagreños managed to bring their old lost landscape into their new one. This sign made that history vivid on a daily basis.

My friend and I wandered around looking for somebody willing to talk with us. The streets were empty, probably because it was 2:00 p.m., the hottest part of the day. Eventually we found an elderly woman sitting comfortably in a rocking chair on her porch. We approached her, but she said she did not remember anything. Perhaps, understandably, she did not want to talk to strangers like us. Her grandson suggested we go talk with a neighbor, who used to be the town's mayor. We approached him and he invited us to sit under a thatched *joron*, where we could feel the breeze of the Caribbean Sea. There he told us about his town's history. I was surprised by how closely local memory tracked the documents I had recently read in the archives. He remembered the town's negotiation with the Americans and the reasons they had to move. But Chagreños's stories also told many things that the archives did not reveal. Slowly, after more visits, and after the local priest and a member of an NGO with close ties to the community introduced me, other Chagreños welcomed my friend and me to their porches and began to share their stories.

One of them was Domingo Becerra, who had been one of the town's *representantes de corregimiento* (town representatives) in the 1970s. He had heard many stories from his grandmother. He told me that she was already a married woman with two daughters when they were forced to leave Old Chagres. Her name was Leonarda Villalaz, and she was the daughter of a Spanish man and a Chagreño woman. When I asked him if his grandmother ever told him what she missed the most about Old Chagres, he paused for a moment and said that she missed looking at "her castle." And the *zarabanda* that happened down by the river.

Not surprisingly, what they missed the most was the Chagres River and its tributaries. Losing access to the river was the most difficult of their many losses. They missed the black fertile lands of the Chagres River, which were superior to the red lands of New Chagres. They missed the fishing. They also missed the easy accessibility to good drinking water that one of the Chagres's tributaries provided.

Chagreños also missed the convenient location of their old town and its vicinity to Colón City. After their relocation, it became more difficult to bring their products to Colón City, which was now almost three times as far away as Old Chagres had been. In the words of another Chagreño, "they went to Colón all the time. That river was their entire life."

There was also nostalgia for Old Chagres's political and historical relevance. A recurrent theme was Old Chagres's former status, the fact that it used to rival Portobelo, the other important colonial port on Panama's Caribbean coast, which was famous for its fortifications and its history as a commercial hub under Spanish rule. "Only Chagres and Portobelo had *fiestas*," Becerra said. On a different afternoon I heard a similar history. Sitting on the porch of a Chagreño woman eating her delicious rice with milk, I listened as she told me that Chagres used to be just as important as Portobelo and that San Lorenzo, their saint, once attracted as many worshipers and as many *congos* as the Black Christ of Portobelo. I felt sad, because, like many other Panamanians, I had seen Portobelo's wonderful *congos,* but I had never seen those of Chagres.

Becerra also remembered the political history of Old Chagres. During the Thousand Days' War, the town's residents had been conservatives, and every time liberals arrived, they would run to the forest. He told me that the houses of important people were all made of wood with zinc roofs, while poor people lived in houses made of wood with thatched roofs. For him, Old Chagres, like Portobelo, was a place of history, politics, and civilization. "The moving of Old Chagres brought civilization to this area," he told me. Like his ancestors in 1912, he contested the idea that his town had no history and no civilization. Far from being people who needed to be civilized, they were agents of civilization.

In addition to the memories of what they had lost with their expulsion from their old location at the mouth of the Chagres River, another set of memories focused on promises not kept. Becerra remembered his grandmother telling him that Chagreños never had any interest in leaving Old Chagres; they departed only under pressure. The "gringos" had given them $1,000 for each house and had promised that the new town would be as good as the old one, and that they would level the rugged land of the New Chagres. But they never did. Another neighbor remembered promises to build infrastructure that would facilitate access to water in the new town, where the water was scarce in the summer, but those promises remained unfulfilled until the 1970s. Another neighbor added that the Americans had not kept their word. They had promised that Nuevo Chagres "would be a marvelous town [*que iba a ser una maravilla*], but nobody did anything."

Unable to bring the Castle of San Lorenzo or the Chagres River with them and unable to stay, Chagreños brought some fragments—another form of remembrance. They brought to Nuevo Chagres a cannon from the old fort, their saint, and a bell from the old church—all symbols of the town's identity that link the town's history to its political and religious core. When I saw the cannon in January 2014, it was broken. I heard many versions of what had happened. Chagreños used to shoot the cannon on every Saint Lorenzo Feast day, but sometime in the 1980s the cannon exploded and its fragments spread all over the town. Perhaps the fragments of the cannon—and the broken bell—can be seen as symbols of the broken relationship between Chagreños and their past, between an identity and a place to which they cannot return.

Other fragments are not mementos brought from Old Chagres but ruins, in the sense that they are meant to replace what cannot be replaced. Such is the case with the local church's main mural, in which the image of San Lorenzo Castle occupies a prominent place. A Claretian priest painted the Liberation Theology–inspired mural that connects the town's history to the slave past of its black residents and compares the pain of Jesus's crucifixion to the pain of African slaves. Every time Chagreños go to church, they are reminded not only of the life of Jesus but also of their town's origins next to the Chagres River and the Chagres castle. Finally, the location of Nuevo Chagres on the shores of the Caribbean Sea by the Lagarto River can also be understood as a ruin. Like Old Chagres, New Chagres is located at the mouth of a river, but the Chagres and Lagarto are in no way similar. The small Lagarto River can be seen as a ruin of the mighty Chagres River, an attempt to replace what is not replaceable.

Chagreños tried to regain access to their old location after the 1977 signing of the Torrijos-Carter treaties, which began the long transfer—completed in 2000—of the Canal Zone back to Panama. Among the sites to be transferred was the Fortress of San Lorenzo de Chagres, which was returned to Panama in 1979. Chagreños had kept their memories and connection to Old Chagres for three generations. One resident, Bernardo Galván, had kept the documents about the town's history of forced displacement. Armed with those documents, Chagreños petitioned President Aristides Royo for the right to recover their old jurisdiction over the Castle of San Lorenzo. If Panama was recovering the Zone, then why could they not recover Old Chagres? Domingo Becerra said that when he was district representative he had asked that "our castle" become part of Nuevo Chagres's district. For them, it was natural to assume that with the Americans gone, they could reestablish their old historical connection with the castle. But, alas, that would not be. Panama's central government had decided to make the Fort of San Lorenzo a national park, and Chagreños had no place in those plans. A neighbor complained that they needed a permit to visit their old town, the place from where they had come. A military reserve had become a historical site. For the people of Chagres, it was the same. They continue to be excluded from their historical town. Their identity continues to be tied to a place to which they cannot return.

The Fragmented Space of Nuevo Emperador

During the same weeks that I visited Nuevo Chagres, my friend and I also went to the town of Nuevo Emperador. To get there, I had to drive half an hour from Panama City to the town of Chorrera and then drive north on a small road that eventually took me to the main square of Nuevo Emperador. As in Nuevo Chagres, I did not know what I would find. My first surprise was the presence of many wooden houses built in typical Canal Zone style. More than 100 years after the depopulation order, these houses set this town apart from the other towns of rural Panama. As one person from Nuevo Emperador remembered, "Years ago all the houses were wooden and came from there [old Emperador]." The connection between this town and the history of the Zone remains obvious, physical, and immediate.

The old houses are the physical fragments of an old location to which Nuevo Emperador's residents cannot return and of an old centrality that they have lost. While old Emperador—known in English as Empire—had been a strategically located town, and the second largest

of the Zone, Nuevo Emperador is out of the way, far from any of
Panama's main roads. This was not always the case. When the people
who were forced to leave Gorgona and Emperador chose this town—
then named Paja—they did so because it had two crucial advantages:
one was fertile lands, and the other was an advantageous location close
to the western border of the Zone, near the old town of Emperador and
also, importantly, on the Emperador-Chorrera road, which then connected Panama City and the Zone to Panama's western provinces.[2]
No longer able to live in the middle of the isthmian corridor, they found
in Paja a suitable and centrally located place. However, this sense of
centrality was fleeting. With the construction of the new La Boca Ferry
in 1932, which replaced the Pedro Miguel Ferry, the new La Boca–
Chorrera road became the main road connecting Panama City and the
Zone to Panama's western provinces. Having lost their centrality
twice in twenty years, the inhabitants of Paja could only appeal to history. In 1948, a group named the Acción Progresista Society pushed to
change their town's name from Paja to Nuevo Emperador, hoping, perhaps, that the name of their old bustling town would bring needed
prosperity to the new one.[3]

Nothing better represents the ruins of the old towns of the isthmian
corridor than the remains of the old Emperador-Chorrera road. Seeing
it today, you would never guess its earlier significance. When I drove
down this road in 2014 it led nowhere, except to a cemetery and a
barbed-wire fence. The fence marks the old Zone border, but now it is
guarded by Panama's environmental authority, and for good reason.
For decades, the region around old Emperador was used for US military
training, and to wander around what is an area littered with unexploded bombs can be dangerous. It would have been difficult to choose
better symbols than a cemetery and a defunct bombing range to

represent the ruined fragments of an old geography that cannot be reestablished. The transformation of Old Empire into a range of unexploded bombs can also be a symbol of the fragility of living in a border town. Many residents have felt a sense of disempowerment and lack of control when their lives have been in close contact with a much more powerful neighbor that sometimes—like the leftover bombs—would inadvertently explode and alter their lives.

If the town of Nuevo Emperador did not have the centrality of old Emperador, it retained its close connection to the Zone's economy. It was truly a border town. And the connections to the Zone were present in the memories of every person I interviewed. "Everybody worked in the Canal Zone," one person remembered. They held many positions, from construction workers to cooks and drivers. Another person said that the town had become the Zone's bedroom community [*un dormitorio de la Zona*]. A bus connected the town to the Zone. But there were also memories of a world of tense encounters with powerful neighbors on the other side of the border. When old Emperador became a military camp, American troops crossed the border and "came [to New Emperador] to have fun in one of the two towns' *cantinas*." But "fun" could be a one-way street, amusing only for those with power. One person remembered that soldiers enjoyed shooting at buses used by Panamanians to cross the Zone, not really aiming at them, only scaring them. This happened the day of this person's high school graduation, when a tank shot at the bus he was riding. He remembered this event with frustration, as something that put a damper on what was supposed to have been a special day.

At the same time, I also detected a sense of nostalgia for the old times when the Zone still existed and many town dwellers worked there. People smiled when they remembered having to walk over the Pedro

Miguel Locks to cross the canal, or take the ferry to cross the canal. One person remembered the days when one could shop at the US commissaries in the Zone and have access to high-quality products at a good price. One woman even brought out a thick rope bought many years ago in the Canal Zone to demonstrate her point. Perhaps it is only the nostalgia of old people remembering their younger days. But perhaps the recollections also reveal something about the difficulties of a community where every generation had to adapt to a radical change in their environment: first, leaving Emperador and witnessing the end of the pre-1912 geography; then, losing their centrality when the old Chorrera road was replaced by a new Panama-Chorrera road that bypassed their town; and finally, the end of the American Canal Zone, where many had worked and to which many had adapted.[4]

Of all the stories I heard, the one that surprised me the most was the Fourth of July story. Two of the people I interviewed remembered that when they were children, a group of black West Indians from Colón City would come to Nuevo Emperador every Fourth of July to spend the day at the cantina Casa Blanca. At the day's end they would return to Colón City. This short story struck me when I heard it. Who were the West Indians from Colón who came every Fourth of July? Why did they do so? And why on that day? The person who told me the story did not know. He saw them from afar. He also told me they kept to themselves. It is not too far-fetched to imagine that they were old inhabitants of the original town of Emperador, who came every year to Nuevo Emperador to recreate their lost community for one day. Unable to return to their old town, they went to one close to it that bore its name. This Fourth of July remembrance is a ritual of impossibility and memory: the impossibility of returning but also the importance of remembering.

Dressing the Canal Zone Once Again

In 1865, Harvard professor Louis Agassiz traveled to Brazil to study black, indigenous, and mixed-race Brazilians in their natural environment. Following the science of his time, he believed that the appropriate way to record non-white races was to take pictures of them naked. But nakedness was a complex issue. Like many Europeans and Americans of his time, Agassiz associated clothing with civilization and nakedness with savagery. Where did the Brazilian people of Manaus stand in this division? They wore pants, shirts, and dresses very similar to those of any other rural people of the nineteenth-century Americas and associated public nakedness with shame and indecency. Undeterred by this fact, Agassiz persuaded them to remove their clothes for the camera. With this act, he stripped peasants not only of their clothes but also of their history and identity as members of nineteenth-century Brazilian society, transforming them into timeless, naked tropical savages of the European imagination.[5]

The same thing happened to Panama's isthmian corridor. When canal construction started in 1904, Panama looked nothing like the jungle of the US imagination. Far from being a modern mirage in the unspoiled tropical jungle, the canal was only the latest addition to a place deeply marked with the footprints of nineteenth-century modernity. The Zone was traversed by old mule paths that had served international trade since the sixteenth century and by the railroad that had replaced them in the mid-nineteenth century; it was marked by the incomplete nineteenth-century French Canal and its machinery; and it was filled with towns and farms occupied by the descendants of the multiple waves of workers who had toiled in the centuries-old transportation economy of the isthmian corridor. When the US government depopulated the Canal Zone and allowed the jungle to grow back over its old towns, roads, and fields, it had "undressed" this space, just as Agassiz had undressed the Brazilian peasants, and literally transformed it into the jungle it had once imagined. This transformation was so effective that by 1944, a book aptly titled *Our Jungle Diplomacy* could confidently ignore the old municipal history of the isthmian corridor and state that the three years of Canal Zone municipal life under the US government was a little political experiment of American creation that was bound to disappear. According to the author, William Franklin Sands, the "Canal Zone municipalities in the jungle . . . did not exist and it was never intended that they should exist." They owed their origin entirely to an American idealist named Rufus Lane, who

> took his job very seriously and proceeded to create his municipalities. . . . Jungle Panamanians . . . began to do exactly what Lane told them to do. . . . They cleared the jungle around their huts, they joined their settlements by hard little foot trails, they built tiny electric plants. . . . They held town meetings on the primitive New England plan, they created a small market trade in wild fruits and garden stuff, and in time they put a couple of hundred thousand pesos into the city banks as a cash reserve of their jungle municipalities. Lane's job seemed to me one of the finest things Americans were doing in Panama. It was a lesson in patriarchal self-government by a primitive people. . . . But it was abolished by a visiting Congressional committee.[6]

With these words, the long history of the Panamanian municipalities was erased. The American municipalities of the Zone were not the heirs of an old Panamanian municipal tradition of republican democratic government, but instead the little jungle folly of an enthusiastic American who tried to teach "primitive people" the rules of self-government. To think that such an experiment could survive was to be an "idealist" who did not understand reality.

This book has tried to restore clothes to the Canal Zone. Why is it important to do so and to remember an old geography that is now gone and a place to which you cannot return? Why is it important for the people of Nuevo Chagres and Nuevo Emperador to remember their old towns? Because to recall the landscape of the Canal Zone and its old towns is to remember the multiple ways in which Panamanians, West Indian immigrants, and other immigrants were co-authors of the Zone's history.

To re-dress the Zone is one way to challenge the history that the United States and Europe had been telling about themselves and about others, a history in which Europe and the United States were the sole protagonists of historical changes like constitutional republicanism, representative democracy, industrialization, and global capitalism. In these histories, the inhabitants of the rest of the world had no positive role in these nineteenth-century historical changes. They were only passive recipients who were either the beneficiaries—or victims, depending on the version—of changes introduced by others. They mimicked, copied, and adapted—but never created.

For this historical fantasy to work, the rest of the world had to be represented in a certain way. It had to be depicted as a traditional landscape inhabited by people set in their outdated ways. This view of a world divided between civilized and primitive places was popularized by nineteenth-century travelers who embellished their books with stories that contrasted the modernity of the European—or the US—

traveler with the traditional and odd ways of local natives. The story could be set in the Middle East, China, or Latin America; it did not matter, the structure was the same.[7] This very effective narrative—still popular in Hollywood movies—successfully made anything modern, be it a railroad or a constitutional government, seem out of place outside of the United States or Europe. The people who lived in these often tropical places were never portrayed or imagined as co-authors and coprotagonists of the enormous social, political, and technological changes of the nineteenth century. For this version of history to work, it is imperative to forget the historical commonalities between Europe and the rest of the world and to reinforce differences and degrees of civilization.

In spite of its power and predominance, this version of world history has not gone unchallenged. Already in the nineteenth century, thinkers and writers from regions outside of Europe questioned the idea that Europe had always been "civilized" and that the rest of the world was and remained barbaric. The nineteenth-century Chinese intellectual Wellington Koo reminded Europe that the "penal laws of China, as enforced in the eighteenth and the first part of the nineteenth century, were not severer than those in force in England during the same period."[8] With these words he reminded Europeans that until the legal reforms of the nineteenth century, they had the very same laws they criticized China for having and that China, like England, was in the process of changing. Implicitly, he questioned the idea that China and Europe were at two different historical stages. Was Koo, a nineteenth-century Chinese lawyer who supported legal reforms in China, copying Europe or was he a supporter of nineteenth-century ideas that were novel for everybody, both inside and outside of Europe?

This is the key question. Were nineteenth-century ideas about progress and civilization European ideas or were they new nineteenth-century ideas embraced by many reformers around the world, who together shaped and created the world in which we have lived during the past 200 years? Much is at stake in the answer. As intellectuals from the Caribbean have long known, to be historical agents is a pre-condition to political autonomy and the right to determine one's destiny. They have known that one cannot determine the course of a story that one has not helped to create; whether we have a say in the future of the world in which we live hinges on the question of whether we helped create it. This is why in some of the most powerful historical writing from the Caribbean, authors insert themselves into the two main themes of the history of the current world: capitalism and republicanism.

C. L. R. James (in 1938) and Eric Williams (in 1944) joined words and worlds that until then were not seen as part of the same process. Until James wrote *The Black Jacobins,* the Haitian Revolution and the French Revolution were thought to have had nothing in common. While the French Revolution represented the birth of modern republican ideologies, the Haitian Revolution was seen as a savage slave revolt, a return to base wild instincts. Haiti was the antithesis of anything that was modern or civilized. James masterfully questioned these assumptions. He made it clear that black Haitians were as Jacobin as their French counterparts, and that the French and Haitians both belonged to the same historical and political world; one revolution could not be understood without the other. Together they planted the seeds for a world formed by independent republican nations. A supporter of the independence of African colonies, James knew that for African nations to achieve their independence, they had to know that the history that led to a world of modern independent republics was also their history. Even today, black and Latin American students react with emotion to his book. Their reaction comes from the realization that the history of the political world in which they live is also their history.

Similarly, Eric Williams brought together two systems that were not supposed to belong together. In *Capitalism and Slavery* he convincingly argued that it is impossible to understand the one subject of his title without the other. He insisted that it was the earnings made by English merchants in the Atlantic slave trade that provided the capital needed for industrial investments; furthermore, the famous Manchester mills of the Industrial Revolution could not have existed without the slave-grown cotton of the US South. There was more to this account than setting the record straight. To say that capitalism and slavery are part of the same history is to question the assumption that there are two stages of progress and civilization: one more advanced, in England, the land of the Industrial Revolution, and another, less advanced, in the Caribbean, the land of plantations and slavery. By making these two stages part of the same historical process, Williams questioned the idea that more advanced regions have a natural stewardship over less advanced ones. If every region of the Atlantic contributed to the history of the Industrial Revolution, all its inhabitants were members of the same modern industrial era and had an equal say in its future.

Although they did not express it with the same eloquence, Panamanian politicians and diplomats of the early twentieth century understood how much they could lose if they were deprived of their membership in the modern world. In a world that distinguished between civilized and uncivilized peoples and only granted equality under international law to those deemed civilized, their rights depended on whether they were "natives" or civilized. Just as Koo knew that "extraterritorial judicial privileges enjoyed by aliens" in China were based on the alleged barbarism of Chinese law, which justified taking away from China the full legal control of its own territory, Panamanians also knew that their ability to control their economies and properties depended on whether they were considered equal members of the same historical era as their US counterparts. If they were considered "civilized" property owners, they would be given the rights to economic compensation standard among civilized property owners. Similarly, their right to continue controlling the ports that they had controlled and managed for 400 years depended on whether they were considered civilized enough to control two of the most important global ports of the twentieth century.

The people of Chagres and the people of Nuevo Emperador also claimed their place among civilized people and inverted the history that others told about them. Civilization was not brought to them; quite the opposite, they were civilized people who were sent into the wilderness. As a woman from Nuevo Emperador remembered, "This was wilderness, and who wants to live in the wild?" The people of Nuevo Chagres emphasized their historical and political relevance as members of one of Panama's main historic parties of the nineteenth century. They kept their historical papers because they knew that the right to control their old castle and old town depended on whether they were considered "civilized" enough to control that space—and that depended on the interpretation of their history. Alas, just as in the early twentieth century the US government found it unthinkable that Panama could control the ports of the Panama Canal, it was unthinkable—and remains so—for the Panamanian government of the late twentieth century and early twentieth-first century to imagine Chagreños as the stewards of a historical site as important as the Fort of San Lorenzo de Chagres.

That is why to remember is important and why the fragments of the lost modern landscape of the Canal Zone matter. But that is also the reason these memories can be profoundly uncomfortable. To remind Panama's elites that Panama's black population has always been as modern as they have, and have played an important role in all the

major events of the country's history, is uncomfortable. Just as it is uncomfortable to remind Europeans that capitalism grew as much from
the slave plantations of the Caribbean as from the Manchester mills;
or that the French Revolution was only one event among many in the
creation of modern republicanism; that the first republic was the
United States, not France, and that France's brief republican experiment was kept alive and further developed by the United States and
the Spanish-American republics of the nineteenth century. Or that the
United States, far from leading the world in a path toward liberty, abolished slavery only after all the other American republics had done so.
It is uncomfortable to admit that the entire globe participated in the
eighteenth- and nineteenth-century changes that led to our current
world because doing so destabilizes hierarchies and gives everybody
an equal say in our global future. It takes away the right of stewardship over others that some have arrogated to themselves, whether it
be some regions over others or Latin American elite or middle class—
from the right and the left—over the poor. It is uncomfortable because
it makes it clear that people and regions might be poor but not underdeveloped; that they cannot catch up with the train of modernity
because they have always already been there.[9]

As I write these final pages at Widener Library at Harvard University, I think about how much has changed since men like Theodore
Roosevelt and William Lyman Phillips were Harvard students. I often
wonder what they would have thought about a "native" Panamanian
woman writing a history of their canal in the same space where they
used to study, and giving a public lecture—as a fellow of the W. E. B. Du
Bois Research Institute—while standing next to a portrait of Roosevelt,
the man who "took Panama." Perhaps, as the intelligent and innovative
men they were, they would appreciate the irony. Perhaps they would
understand my desire to write my own history.

Notes

INTRODUCTION

1. According to the 1912 Canal Zone census, the Zone's population was 62,810. According to the 1920 census, quoted in the 1940 census, in 1920 the population was 22,858 (14,350 in Balboa District and 8,508 in Cristobal District). *Census of the Canal Zone* (Mount Hope, Canal Zone: ICC Press, 1912); *Panama Canal Zone Population* (Washington, DC: Government Publishing Office, 1941).

2. Omar Jaén Suárez, *La población del Istmo de Panamá: Estudio de Geohistoria* (Madrid: Ediciones Cultura Hispánica, 1998). According to Suárez, the Zone's population was 90,000 in 1911, but the origin of the figure is not clear.

3. For a literary account, see Gil Blas Tejeira, *Pueblos Perdidos* (Panama: Impresora Panamá, 1962). For the environmental impact of the creation of Lake Gatún and the flooding of Panamanian towns, see Ashely Carse,

Beyond the Big Ditch: Politics, Ecology, and Infrastructure at the Panama Canal (Cambridge, MA: MIT Press, 2014), 93–119.

4. This book builds on a wealth of research and analysis of books about the history of the Panama Canal. Among them are Guillermo Castro, *El agua entre los mares* (Panama: Editorial Ciudad del Saber, 2007); Michael Conniff, *Black Labor on a White Canal: Panama, 1904–1981* (Pittsburgh: University of Pittsburgh Press, 1985); Julie Greene, *The Canal Builders: Making America's Empire at the Panama Canal* (New York: Penguin, 2009); John Lindsay-Poland, *Emperors in the Jungle: The Hidden History of the U.S. in Panama* (Durham, NC: Duke University Press, 2003); John Major, *Prize Possession: The United States and the Panama Canal, 1903–1979* (Cambridge: Cambridge University Press, 1993); Alexander Missal, *Seaway to the Future: American Social Visions and the Construction of the Panama Canal* (Madison: University of Wisconsin Press, 2008).

5. Darcy Grimaldo Grisby, *Colossal: Engineering the Suez Canal, Statue of Liberty, Eiffel Tower, and Panama Canal* (Pittsburgh: Periscope, 2012), 122–151.

6. Greene, *The Canal Builders*, 180–225.

7. Missal, *Seaway to the Future*, 8.

8. Theodore P. Shonts, "The Railroad Men at Panama," *North American Review* 199, no. 699 (1914): 228–231.

9. Here, and throughout the rest of the book, I use the word *modernity* to talk about a historical moment characterized by the advent of industrial technology, capitalist economics, and representative, republican, and constitutional politics.

10. For the enormous task of controlling and organizing the canal's labor force, see Greene, *The Canal Builders*.

11. Daniel Rodgers, *Atlantic Crossings: Social Politics in the Progressive Age* (Cambridge, MA: Harvard University Press, 1998).

12. I build on the historical and theoretical insights of works on Latin American urban history, the relationship between urban change and colo-

nialism in Africa, the historicization of the ideology of development and the idea of the tropics, the use of culture to understand US–Latin American relations, the history of the Progressive Era, and theories about the relationship between space and history. Arturo Escobar, *Encountering Development: The Making and Unmaking of the Third World* (Princeton, NJ: Princeton University Press, 1995); Brodwyn Fischer, *A Poverty of Rights: Citizenship and Inequality in Twentieth-Century Rio de Janeiro* (Redwood City, CA: Stanford University Press, 2010); Greg Grandin, *Fordlandia: The Rise and Fall of Henry Ford's Forgotten Jungle City* (New York: Metropolitan, 2009); Peter Guardino, "Democracy in the Other America: Citizenship in Mexico and the United States in Early Nineteenth-Century Spanish America" (presentation, "Roots and Future of the Democratic Tradition in Latin America," Yale University, New Haven, CT, December 2–3, 2011); Amy Kaplan and Donald Pease, eds., *Cultures of United States Imperialism* (Durham, NC: Duke University Press, 1993); Gilbert M. Joseph, Catherine C. LeGrand, and Richard Salvatore, eds., *Close Encounters of Empire: Writing the Cultural History of U.S.–Latin American Relations* (Durham, NC: Duke University Press, 1999); Jeffrey Needell, *A Tropical Belle Epoque: Elite Culture and Society in Turn-of-the-Century Rio de Janeiro* (Cambridge: Cambridge University Press, 1987); Mark Overmeyer-Velazquez, *Visions of the Emerald City* (Durham, NC: Duke University Press, 2006); Edward Soja, *Postmodern Geographies* (New York: Verso, 1989); Gwendolyn Wright, *The Politics of Design in French Colonial Urbanism* (Chicago: University of Chicago Press, 1991); James Scott, *Seeing Like a State: How Certain Schemes to Improve the Human Condition Have Failed* (New Haven, CT: Yale University Press, 1999).

13. David McCullough, *The Path between the Seas: The Creation of the Panama Canal, 1870–1914* (New York: Simon & Schuster, 1978).

14. Marixa Lasso, "From Citizens to 'Natives': Tropical Politics of Depopulation at the Panama Canal Zone," in Ashley Carse et al., "Panama Canal

Forum: From the Conquest of Nature to the Construction of New Ecologies," *Environmental History* 21 (2016): 206–287.

15. James Sanders, *Vanguard of the Atlantic World: Creating Modernity, Nation, and Democracy* (Durham, NC: Duke University Press, 2014).

16. Cited by Sanders, *Vanguard of the Atlantic World*, 83.

17. Sanders, *Vanguard of the Atlantic World*, 176–224.

18. John Charles Chasteen, *Americanos: Latin America's Struggles for Independence* (Oxford: Oxford University Press, 2008), 185.

19. Meltem Ahiska, "Occidentalism: The Historical Fantasy of the Modern," *South Atlantic Quarterly* 102, nos. 2–3 (Spring / Summer 2003): 354.

20. For the silencing and erasing of Latin American modernity, see M. R. Trouillot, *Silencing the Past: Power and the Production of History* (Boston: Beacon Press, 1995); Fernando Coronil, "Beyond Occidentalism: Toward Nonimperial Geohistorical Categories," *Cultural Anthropology* 11, no. 1 (February 1996): 51–87. For works writing against this history, see Alejandra Osorio, *Inventing Lima: Baroque Modernity in Peru's South Sea Metropolis* (New York: Palgrave, 2008); Sanders, *Vanguard of the Atlantic;* Mauricio Tenorio-Trillo, *I Speak of the City: Mexico City at the Turn of the Twentieth Century* (Chicago: University of Chicago Press, 2012); John Tutino, *Making a New World: Founding Capitalism in the Bajío and Spanish North America* (Durham, NC: Duke University Press, 2011); Mark Thurner, "Historical Theory through a Peruvian Looking Glass," *History and Theory* 53 (2015): 27–45; Jorge Cañizares-Esguerra and Bradley J. Dixon, "The Oversight of King Henry VII," in *The World of Colonial America: An Atlantic Handbook,* ed. Ignacio Gallup-Diaz (New York: Routledge, 2017), 39–58; Lina Del Castillo, *Crafting a Republic for the World: Scientific, Geographic, and Historiographic Inventions of Colombia* (Lincoln: University of Nebraska Press, 2018).

21. David Arnold, *The Tropics and the Traveling Gaze: India, Landscape, and Science* (Seattle: University of Washington Press, 2006); Randall M.

Packard, "The Invention of the 'Tropical Worker,'" *Journal o*
tory 34, no. 2 (1993): 271–292; Nancy Stepan, *Picturing Tro*
(London: Reaktion Books, 2001). For Panama, see Robert *A*
Megan Raby, *American Tropics: The Caribbean Roots of Biodiver*
(Chapel Hill: University of North Carolina Press, 2017); Pau
"Nature's Agents or Agents of Empire? Entomological Worke
vironmental Change during the Construction of the Panama C
98 (2007): 730–732; Paul Sutter, "Tropical Conquest and the R
Environmental Management State: The Case of U.S. Sanitary
Panama," in *Colonial Crucible: Empire in the Making of the Modern*
State, ed. Alfred W. McCoy and Francisco A. Scarano (Madison
sity of Wisconsin Press, 2009), 317–328; Paul S. Sutter, "'The Firs
tain to be Removed': Yellow Fever Control and the Constructio
Panama Canal," in Ashley Carse et al., "Panama Canal Forum: Fi
Conquest of Nature to the Construction of New Ecologies," *E*
mental History 21 (2016): 206–287; Stephen Frankel, "Jungle Stories:
American Representations of Tropical Panama," *Geographic Revi*
no. 3 (July 1996): 317–333; and "Geographic Representations of the 'C
The Landscape of the Panama Canal Zone," *Journal of Historical Cartog*
28, no. 1 (January 2002): 85–99.

22. Robert Aguirre, *Mobility and Modernity: Panama in the Nineteenth-Cei*
   Anglo-American Imagination (Columbus: Ohio State University Press, 2
   Mary Louise Pratt, *Imperial Eyes: Travel, Writing, and Transcultura*
   (New York: Routledge, 1992); Stepan, *Picturing Tropical Nature;* Arn
   The Tropics and the Traveling Gaze.

23. Michael Adas, *Machines as the Measures of Men: Science, Technologies a*
   Ideas of Western Dominance (Ithaca, NY: Cornell University Press, 199
   Héctor Pérez-Brignoli, "El fonógrafo en los trópicos: sobre el concepto d
   Banana republic en la obra de O. Henry," *Iberoamericana* 6, no. 23 (2006
   127–142; Michael Gobat, "The Invention of Latin America: A Transnationa

History of Anti-Imperialism," *American Historical Review* 118, no. 5 (December 2013): 1345–1375; Jason M. Colby, "Race and Tropicality in United Fruit's Central America," in *Making the Empire Work,* ed. Daniel E. Bender and Jana K. Lipman (New York: New York University Press, 2015), 295.

24. Edward Said, *Orientalism* (New York: Vintage, 1979); Ernest Gellner, "Introduction," in *Europe and the Rise of Capitalism,* ed. Jean Beachler, John Hall, and Michael Mann (Oxford: Blackwell Press, 1988), 2; Gregory Blue, "China and Western Social Thought in the Modern Period," and Timothy Brook, "Capitalism and the Writing of Modern History in China," in *China and Historical Capitalism: Genealogies of Sinological Knowledge,* ed. Timothy Brook and Gregory Blue (Cambridge: Cambridge University Press, 1999), 57–109, 110–157.

25. Among the works that have challenged these ideas, see Catherine Le-Grand, "Living in Macondo: Economy and Culture in a United Fruit Company Banana Enclave in Colombia," in Joseph, LeGrand, and Salvatore, *Close Encounters of Empire,* 333–368; John Soluri, *Banana Cultures: Agriculture, Consumption, and Environmental Changes in Honduras and the United States* (Austin: University of Texas Press, 2005), 128–160, 193–215. For an analysis of the pre-1970s scholarship and contemporary debates over whether Latin American societies were feudal or capitalist, see Ernesto Laclau, "Feudalism and Capitalism in Latin America," *New Left Review* 1 / 67 (May–June 1971). For an analysis of new literature on work relations and the overcoming of the feudal category, see Alan Knight, "Mexican Peonage: What Was It and Why Was It?," *Journal of Latin American Studies* 18, no. 1 (May 1986): 41–74.

26. J. Dorsey Forrest, *The Development of Western Civilization: A Study in Ethical, Economic, and Political Evolution* (Chicago: University of Chicago Press, 1907), 2.

27. Gilbert Allardyce, "The Rise and Fall of the Western Civilization Course," *American Historical Review* 3 (1982): 695–725. Chris GoGwilt, "True West:

The Changing Idea of the West from the 1880s to the 1920s," 37–62; Silvia
Federici, "The God That Never Failed: The Origins and Crisis of Western
Civilization," 63–90; and Martin Bernal, "Greece: Aryan or Mediterranean? Two Contending Historiographical Models," 1–12; all in *Enduring Western Civilization: The Construction of the Concept of Western Civilization and Its "Others,"* ed. Silvia Federici (Westport, CT: Praeger Publishers, 1995).

28. For Haitians see C. L. R. James, *The Black Jacobins: Toussaint L'Ouverture and the San Domingo* (New York: Vintage, 1989); David Geggus, *A Turbulent Time: The French Revolution and the Greater Caribbean* (Bloomington: Indiana University Press, 2003); Trouillot, *Silencing the Past;* Malick Ghachem, *The Old Regime and the Haitian Revolution* (New York: Cambridge University Press, 2012); Lauren Dubois, *Avengers of the New World: The Story of the Haitian Revolution* (Cambridge, MA: The Belknap Press of Harvard University Press, 2005). For Spanish-American lawyers see Lilliana Obregón, "Construyendo la región americana: Andrés Bello y el derecho internacional, in *La idea en el pensamiento ius internacionalista del siglo XXI: Estudios a propósito de la conmemoración de los bicentenarios de las independencias de las repúblicas latinoamericanas,* ed. Yolanda Gamarra Chopo (Zaragoza: Institución Fernando el Católico, 2010), 65–86; and "Haiti and the Cosmopolitan Imagination," in *Cosmopolitanism in Enlightenment Europe and Beyond,* ed. Mónica García-Salmones and Pamela Slotte (Brussels: Peter Lang, 2013), 59–179.

29. See, for example, Goerge A. Miller, *Prowling about Panama* (New York: The Abingdon Press, 1919), 15–16; Thomas Graham Grier, *On the Canal Zone* (Chicago: The Wagner and Hanson Co., 1908), 7.

30. Frederick Cooper and Randall Packard, "Introduction," and Frederick Cooper, "Modernizing Bureaucrats, Backward Africans and the Development Concept," in *International Development and the Social Sciences: Essays on the History and Politics of Knowledge,* ed. Frederick Cooper and Randall Packard (Berkeley: University of California Press, 1997), 1–41,

64–92; Escobar, *Encountering Development;* Timothy Mitchell, *Rule of Experts: Egypt, Techno-Politics, Modernity* (Berkeley: University of California Press, 2002).

31. For the importance of Panama in pioneering imperial relationships based on nominal Westphalian sovereignty, see Noel Maurer and Carlos Yu, *The Big Ditch: How America Took, Built, Ran, and Ultimately Gave Away the Canal* (Princeton, NJ: Princeton University Press, 2011), 4–5.

32. For a comparison between Cuba and Panama at the turn of the twentieth century, see Mariola Espinosa, *Epidemic Invasions: Yellow Fever and the Limits of Cuban Independence* (Chicago: University of Chicago Press, 2009), 73–116.

33. Eric Hobsbawm and Terence Ranger, eds., *The Invention of Tradition* (Cambridge: Cambridge University Press, 1983); Trouillot, *Silencing the Past;* Matthew Restall, *Seven Myths of the Spanish Conquest* (Oxford: Oxford University Press, 2003). For nineteenth-century Colombia, see Del Castillo, *Crafting a Republic for the World.*

34. Soja, *Postmodern Geographies;* Henri Lefebvre, *The Production of Space* (Oxford: Blackwell, 1991); Wright, *The Politics of Design in French Colonial Urbanism.*

CHAPTER I • THE PORT AND THE CITY

1. Ramón M. Valdés, *Geografía del Istmo de Panamá,* 2nd ed. (New York: Appleton y Cia., 1905), 10.

2. Valdés, *Geografía del Istmo de Panamá,* 49.

3. Gaspard Théodore Mollien, *Viaggio alla Reppublica di Colombia eseguito nell'anno 1823 dal signor Mollien,* vol. 2, trans. Gaetano Barbieri (Naples: R. Marotta e Vanspondch, 1831), 91–92.

4. Valdés, *Geografía del Istmo de Panamá,* 41.

5. *Notes on Panama* (Washington, DC: Government Publishing Office, November 1903), 145.

6. *Notes on Panama,* 145.

7. John H. Kemble, "Pacific Mail Service between Panama and San Francisco, 1849–1851," *Pacific Historical Review* 2 (1933): 4, 409–410.

8. *Notes on Panama,* 146.

9. *Notes on Panama,* 147.

10. *Memorias dirigida a la asamblea nacional de 1906 por el secretario de Gobierno y Relaciones Exteriores* (Panama: Tip de Torre e Hijos, 1907), 210.

11. *Memorias dirigida a la asamblea nacional de 1906,* 231.

12. Salvador Camacho Roldán, *Notas de Viaje,* vol. 1 (Bogota: Publicaciones del Banco de la República, 1973), 225.

13. Office of the Isthmian Canal Commission, *Circular No. 2* (Washington, DC: Government Printing Office, June 25, 1904).

14. I am taking the argument that mid-nineteenth-century Spanish America was at the vanguard of the Atlantic world from Sanders, *Vanguard of the Atlantic World.*

15. Mauricio Nieto, Paola Castaño, and Diana Ojeda, "El influjo del clima sobre los seres organizados y la retórica ilustrada en el Semanario del Nuevo Reyno de Granada," *Historia Critica* 30 (2005): 91–114; Nancy Appelbaum, *Mapping the Country of Regions: The Chorographic Commission of Nineteenth-Century Colombia* (Chapel Hill: University of North Carolina Press, 2016); Felipe Martínez Pinzón, *Una cultura de invernadero: trópico y civilización en Colombia* (Madrid: Iberoamericana-Vervuert, 2016).

16. Marixa Lasso, "La crisis política post-independentista," in *Historia General de Panamá,* vol. 2, ed. Alfredo Castillero-Calvo (Panama: Comité Nacional del Centenario, 2004), 63–76.

17. Carlos A. Mendoza, *El Pensamiento de Carlos A. Mendoza: Documentos, Escritos, Discursos* (Panama: Biblioteca Cultural Shell, 1995), 78–94.

18. Justo Arosemena, "La Cuestión Americana," *El Neogranadino,* June 15, 1856; Justo Arosemena, *Estudios constitucionales sobre los gobiernos de la América Latina* 1 (1878): 503–504; Aims McGuinness, "Searching for 'Latin

America': Race and Sovereignty in the Americas in the 1850s," in *Race and Nation in Modern Latin America,* ed. Karin Alejandra Rosemblatt et al. (Chapel Hill: University of North Carolina Press, 2003), 87–107.

19. Justo Arosemena, "El Estado Federal de Panamá," in *Estudios Historicos y Jurídicos: Seleccion y Reseña de la Historia Cultural de Panamá,* ed. José de la Cruz Herrera (Buenos Aires: W. M. Jackson, 1945), 51.

20. Alfredo Castillero Calvo, "El Movimiento Anseatista de 1826: la primera tentativa autonomista de los istmeños después de la anexión a Colombia," *Tareas* 4 (1960): 3–25; Alfredo Figueroa Navarro, *Dominio y Sociedad en el Panamá Colombiano (1821–1903)* (Panama: Editorial Universitaria, 1982), 243–244.

21. David Bushnell, *The Making of Modern Colombia: A Nation in Spite of Itself* (Berkeley: University of California Press, 1993), 142–143.

22. Eusebio A. Morales, *Ensayos, Documentos y Discursos,* vol. 2 (Panama: Editorial La Moderna, 1928), 73–75; Ernesto A. Morales, *El Dr. Eusebio A. Morales ante la historia: apuntaciones y comentarios* (Panama: Imp. El Heraldo, 1929).

23. Eusebio A. Morales, "The Political Situation of Colombia," *North American Review* 175 (1902): 347–360, 550.

24. There is much controversy about Panama's separation from Colombia. Some historians see Panama's independence as the sole result of American intervention. Others see it as the result of Bogota's neglect. It is a topic that requires more research. But it is clear that any account of Panama's separation needs to consider all of these factors. For an excellent summary of Panama's independence, see Fernando Aparicio, "La independencia de Panamá de Colombia: entre el nacionalismo y el imperialismo," in *Panamá: Historia Contemporánea,* ed. Alfredo Castillero Calvo (Spain: Mapfre / Taurus, 2014), 146–161.

25. Mendoza, *El Pensamiento,* 138–139; Morales, *Ensayos, Documentos y Discursos,* 1:43–59.

26. Watt Stewart, "The Ratification of the Thomson-Urrutia Treaty," *Southwestern Political and Social Science Quarterly* 10, no. 4 (1930): 416–428.

27. Arnulf Becker Lorca, *Mestizo International Law: A Global Intellectual History, 1842–1933* (Cambridge: Cambridge University Press, 2014), 136.

28. Cited by GoGwilt, "True West," 52.

29. Cited by Greene, *The Canal Builders*, 27.

30. Cited by Greene, *The Canal Builders*, 28.

31. Caitlin Fitz, *Our Sister Republics: The United States in the Age of American Revolutions* (New York: Norton, 2016), 194–239.

32. Gilbert Allardyce, "The Rise and Fall of the Western Civilization Course," *American Historical Review* 3 (1982): 695–725; GoGwilt, "True West," 37–62. Martin Bernal, "Greece: Aryan or Mediterranean? Two Contending Historiographical Models"; Silvia Federici, "The God That Never Failed: The Origins and Crisis of Western Civilization," both in *Enduring Western Civilization: The Construction of the Concept of Western Civilization and Its "Others,"* ed. Silvia Federici (Westport, CT: Praeger Publishers, 1995), 1–12, 63–90.

33. Becker Lorca, *Mestizo International Law*, 39–140.

34. Tomás Arias to John Barret, Panama, July 28, 1904, in *Memorias dirigida a la asamblea nacional de 1906*, 219.

35. Arias to Barret, in *Memorias dirigida a la asamblea nacional de 1906*, 219.

36. Tomás Arias to José Domingo de Obaldía, Panama, July 12, 1904, in *Memorias dirigida a la asamblea nacional de 1906*, 216.

37. J. D. de Obaldía (written by Eusebio A. Morales), "Exposición presentada al Secretario de Estado de los Estados Unidos de América," *Memorias dirigida a la asamblea nacional de 1906*, 234.

38. de Obaldía, "Exposición presentada al Secretario de Estado de los Estados Unidos de América," 231. Emphasis in original.

39. Tomás Arias a José Domingo de Obaldía, Panama, July 12, 1904, in *Memorias dirigida a la asamblea nacional de 1906*, 216.

40. de Obaldía, "Exposición presentada al Secretario de Estado de los Estados Unidos de América," 231.

41. Morales, *Ensayos, Documentos y Discursos*, 1:62.

42. Morales, *Ensayos, Documentos y Discursos*, 1:62–63.

43. Morales, *Ensayos, Documentos y Discursos*, 1:64.

44. Morales, *Ensayos, Documentos y Discursos*, 1:66–68.

45. de Obaldía, "Exposición presentada al Secretario de Estado de los Estados Unidos de América," 234.

46. Héctor Pérez-Brignoli, "El fonógrafo en los trópicos: sobre el concepto de Banana republic en la obra de O. Henry," *Iberoamericana* 6, no. 23 (2006): 127–142.

47. Paul A. Kramer, "Race, Empire, and Transnational History," in *Colonial Crucible: Empire in the Making of the Modern American State*, ed. Alfred W. McCoy and Francisco Scarano (Madison: University of Wisconsin Press, 2009), 204.

48. Kramer, "Race, Empire, and Transnational History," 201–206.

49. Alejandro de La Fuente and Matthew Casey, "Race and Suffrage Controversy in Cuba, 1898–1901," in MacCoy and Scarano, *Colonial Crucible*, 223–224.

50. Governador George W. Davis to Secretario de Estado Tomás Arias, Ancón, July 11, 1904, *Memorias dirigida a la asamblea nacional de 1906*, 212–213.

51. Governador George W. Davis to Secretario de Estado Tomás Arias, Ancón, July 11, 1904.

52. Davis to Arias, Ancón, July 11, 1904.

53. Rogelio E. Alfaro, "El Convenio Taft y el Tratado de 1926," in *La Cuestión Canalera, de 1903 a 1936*, ed. Diógenes A. Arosemena (Panama: [s.n.], 1975), 42–47.

54. Office of the Isthmian Canal Commission, *Circular No. 4* (Washington, DC: Government Printing Office, December 30, 1904).

55. Maurer and Yu, *The Big Ditch*, 4–5.

56. Maurer and Yu, *The Big Ditch*, 2–7.

CHAPTER 2 • THE CANAL ZONE IN 1904

1. "Itinerario que manifiesta las distancias entre los distritos parroquiales expresadas en leguas, con exclusión del territorio del Darién," Archivo General de la Nacion-Colombia, Ministerio de Interior y Relaciones Exteriores, tome 59, folio 163; Ramón M. Valdés, *Geografía del Istmo de Panamá: Texto adoptado oficialmente para la enseñanza en las escuelas de la nación*, 2nd ed. (New York: Appleton y Cia., 1905), 74.

2. Lady Emmeline Stuart Wortley, *Travels in the United States, etc., during 1849 and 1850*, 3 vols. (London: Richard Bentley, 1851), 2:283.

3. Valdés, *Geografía del Istmo*, 74.

4. "Map of Gorgona showing area in which the Commission has authorized the licensing of saloons," NARA, RG 185, General Correspondence 1905–1915, Box 353, File 59-B-1/A; Library of Congress, ICC, December 1908.

5. *Interim Report of the Joint Commission* (Panama: Government Publishing Office, 1914), 31.

6. NARA, RG 185, General Correspondence 1905–1915, Box 353, File 59-B-1/A.

7. Capt. H. C. Hale, *Notes on Panama* (Washington, DC: Government Publishing Office, 1903), 154.

8. Gaspard Théodore Mollien, *Viaggio alla Reppublica di Colombia eseguito nell'anno 1823 dal signor Mollien*, vol. 2, trans. Gaetano Barbieri (Naples: R. Marotta e Vanspondch, 1831), 180.

9. Mollien, *Viaggio alla Reppublica di Colombia*, 2:183.

10. Wortley, *Travels*, 2:251.

11. Wortley, *Travels*, 2:245.

12. Wortley, *Travels*, 2:255.

13. There are numerous examples of this type of narrative. See, for example, J. M. Letts, *California Illustrated: Including a description of the Panama and Nicaragua Routes* (New York: R. T. Young, 1853), 13–27, 38.

14. Cruces had only one slave, while the nearby town of San Juan, in the middle of the mule trail connecting Portobelo and Panama City, had forty slaves. "Cuadro que Manifiesta el número de esclavos que hay en el Cantón de Panamá en 31 de agosto de 1846," Archivo General de la Nacion-Colombia, Ministerio de Interior y Relaciones Exteriores, tome 59, folio 163.

15. Jorge Juan and Antonio de Ulloa, *Relación Histórica del viaje a la América Meridional,* vol. 1 (Madrid: Fundación Universitaria Española, [1748] 1978), 126–131.

16. According to Mollien, in 1811 the province of Panama earned by far the largest amount of rent of any Colombian province (800,000 piastras compared with Cartagena, which earned the second-largest amount, 600,000 piastras. Santa Fe earned only 180,000). Mollien cites Pombo's statistics. Mollien, *Viaggio alla Reppublica di Colombia,* 1:216.

17. Aims McGuinness, *Paths of Empire: Panama and the California Gold Rush* (Ithaca, NY: Cornell University Press, 2008); Alfredo Castillero-Calvo, *La Ruta Interoceánica y el Canal de Panamá* (Panama: Instituto del Canal de Panama, 1999).

18. Mollien, *Viaggio alla Reppublica di Colombia,* 2:183–184. According to Mollien, in 1823 the British from Jamaica monopolized trade in the isthmus where, reputedly, they sent two million piastras worth of merchandise. Ibid., 2:89; Mary Seacole, *Wonderful Adventures of Mrs. Seacole in Many Lands* (Oxford: Oxford University Press, [1867] 1988), 37.

19. Mollien, *Viaggio alla Reppublica di Colombia,* 2:182–183.

20. William Wheelwright, "Report on the Isthmus of Panama," in William Wheelwright, *Report on Steam Navigation in the Pacific with an account of coal mines of Chile and Panama* (1843), 26.

21. Wheelwright, "Report on the Isthmus of Panama," 26.

22. Letts, *California Illustrated*, 13.

23. Wortley, *Travels*, 2:255.

24. For the Gold Rush in Panama, see McGuinness, *Paths of Empire*.

25. Letts, *California Illustrated*, 28; Wortley, *Travels*, 2:283–291.

26. Seacole, *Wonderful Adventures*, 16.

27. Wortley, *Travels*, 2:266.

28. Seacole, *Wonderful Adventures*, 53–54.

29. Valdés, *Geografía del Istmo de Panamá*, 74.

30. *Interim Report of the Joint Commission* (Panama: Government Publishing Office, 1914), 31.

31. Wortley, *Travels*, 2:319.

32. Alfredo Castillero Calvo, "El transporte transístmico y las comunicaciones," in *Historia General de Panama*, ed. Alfredo Castillero Calvo, vol. 1, tome 1 (Panama: Comité Nacional del Centenario de la República, 2004), 374.

33. For colonial upkeep of roads, see Castillero Calvo, "El transporte transístmico y las comunicaciones regionales," 387; for Colombian upkeep, see "Tomás Herran to señor secretario de Relaciones Exteriores y Mejoras Internas," Panama, February 24, 1848, Archivo General de la Nacion-Colombia, Ministerio de Interior y Relaciones Exteriores, tome 59, folio 854.

34. Castillero Calvo, "El transporte transístmico y las comunicaciones," 374.

35. Wortley, *Travels*, 2:272.

36. Castillero Calvo, "El transporte transístmico y las comunicaciones," 377.

37. For colonial upkeep of the Chagres River, see Castillero Calvo, "El transporte transístmico y las comunicaciones regionales," 387; for Colombian upkeep of the Chagres River, see "Tomás Herran to señor secretario de Relaciones Exteriores y Mejoras Internas," Panama, February 24, 1848, AGN-Colombia, Ministerio de Interior y Relaciones Exteriores, tome 59, folio 854.

38. Wheelwright, "Report on the Isthmus of Panama," 25–26; Wortley, *Travels*, 2:257–258.

39. Wheelwright, "Report on the Isthmus of Panama," 25–26; Wortley, *Travels*, 2:257–258.

40. Juan and Ulloa, *Relación Histórica*, 148; Wheelwright, "Report on the Isthmus of Panama," 26.

41. Juan and Ulloa, *Relación Histórica*, 148.

42. Juan and Ulloa, *Relación Histórica*, 148.

43. Juan and Ulloa, *Relación Histórica*, 148.

44. Letts, *California Illustrated*, 13.

45. Wortley, *Travels*, 2:258–259, 269–270.

46. Seacole, *Wonderful Adventures*, 20–21.

47. Seacole, *Wonderful Adventures*, 20.

48. Wortley, *Travels*, 2:246–247.

49. "Acuerdo sobre aplicaciones de terrenos para el ferrocarril del Istmo de Panamá," Gorgona, November 6, 1852, NARA, RG 185, Record of the Joint Land Commission, Land Files of the Panama Railroad Company, Box 2, File 1.

50. "Acuerdo sobre aplicaciones de terrenos para el ferrocarril del Istmo de Panamá," November 6, 1852.

51. No title, April 28, 1851, NARA, RG 185, Record of the Joint Land Commission, Land Files of the Panama Railroad Company, Box 2, File 1.

52. Marixa Lasso, *Myths of Harmony: Race and Republicanism in the Age of Revolution, Colombia 1795–1831* (Pittsburgh: University of Pittsburgh Press, 2007).

53. Alfredo Figueroa Navarro, *Dominio y Sociedad en el Panamá Colombiano (1821–1903)* (Panama: Impresora Panamá, 1978); Lasso, *Myths of Harmony;* McGuinness, *Paths of Empire;* James Sanders, *Contentious Republicans: Popular Politics, Race, and Class in Nineteenth-Century Southwestern Colombia* (Durham, NC: Duke University Press, 2004).

54. Nancy Leys Stepan, *Picturing Tropical Nature* (London: Reaktion Books, 2001).

55. Seacole, *Wonderful Adventures*, 43.

56. Seacole, *Wonderful Adventures*, 45.

57. Seacole, *Wonderful Adventures*, 51–52.

58. Wortley, *Travels*, 2:251.

59. Seacole, *Wonderful Adventures*, 44.

60. Willis J. Abbot, *Panama and the Canal in Picture and Prose* (New York: Syndicate Publishing Company, 1914), 107.

61. Harry A. Frank, *Zone Policeman 88: A Close Study of the Panama Canal and Its Workers* (New York: The Century Co., 1920), 18.

62. *Census of the Canal Zone* (Mount Hope, Canal Zone: I.C.C. Press, 1912), 16.

63. "List of native villages in the Canal Zone which are now being extended or are likely to be extended in the near future," May 20, 1908, NARA, RG 185, General Correspondence ICC, Building Regulations Canal Zone General, Box 88.

64. Valdés, *Geografía del Istmo de Panamá*, 74.

65. Guy L. Edie to Chief of Staff, US Army, December 23, 1903, NARA RG 185, Box 321, File 47-I-53.

66. Frank, *Zone Policeman 88*, 22.

67. Frank, *Zone Policeman 88*, 28.

68. Frank, *Zone Policeman 88*, 32.

69. "Memorandum regarding Isthmian Canal Commission and Panama Railroad Townsites," May 27, 1910, NARA, RG 185, Box 317, File 47-E-1.

70. "International Banking Corporation," *La Estrella de Panamá*, July 13, 1913.

71. G. Johnson to Rufus H. Lane, November 30, 1906, NARA, RG 185, General Correspondence 1905–14, Box 352, File 59-A-3.

72. Greene, *The Canal Builders*, 172–178; Frank, *Zone Policeman 88*, 40–50.

73. Frank, *Zone Policeman 88*, 40.

74. F. N. Otis, *Isthmus of Panama: History of the Panama Railroad and the Pacific Steamship Company* (New York: Harpers Publishers, 1867), 95–96.

75. Valdés, *Geografía del Istmo de Panamá*, 87.

76. John F. Stevens to Jackson Smith, July 16, 1906, NARA, RG 185, General Correspondence, ICC, Box 973, File 47-E-12/45.

77. Jackson Smith to J. F. Stevens, July 14, 1906, NARA, RG 185, General Correspondence, ICC, Box 973, File 47-E-12/45.

78. Ward to Smith, July 12, 1906, NARA, RG 185, General Correspondence, ICC, Box 973, File 47-E-12/45.

79. Division Engineer to Acting Chief Engineer, July 2, 1906, NARA, RG 185, General Correspondence, ICC, Box 973, File 47-E-12/45.

80. J. A. Le Prince, Chief Sanitary Inspector, to Col. W. C. Gorgas, Chief Sanitary Officer, October 12, 1909, NARA, RG 185, General Correspondence, Isthmian Canal Commission, Box 88.

81. J. A. Le Prince to W. C. Gorgas, April 17, 1907, NARA, RG 185, General Correspondence, ICC, Box 88.

82. NARA, RG 185, General Records, 1914–1934, Box 974, File 47-E-12/72 September 1, 1914.

83. NARA, RG 185, General Records, 1914–1934, Box 974, File 47-E-12/72 September 1, 1914.

84. Frank, *Zone Policeman 88*, 70.

85. *The Canal Record*, September 4, 1907, 2–3; *The Canal Record*, January 15, 1908, 157–158; *The Canal Record*, March 18, 1908, 226.

86. *The Canal Record*, July 15, 1908, 362.

87. Grisby, *Colossal*, 122–151.

88. There are numerous publications and pictures that follow these patterns. One example is Willis J. Abbot, *Panama and the Canal in Picture and Prose* (New York: Syndicate Publishing Co., 1913), 57, 60, 68–70, 111–113, 176–177.

89. Tracy Robinson, *Panama: A Personal Record of Forty-Six Years* (Panama: Star and Herald Company, 1907), 179.

90. Robinson, *Panama*, 200.

91. Michael Hardt, "Jefferson and Democracy," *American Quarterly* 59, no. 1 (2007): 41–78.

92. Robinson, *Panama*, 200.

93. Robinson, *Panama*, 244.

94. A. S. Barlett, E. S. Berghoon, and R. Berger, "Fossil Maiz from Panama," *Science* 165 (1969): 389; Dolores Piperno, "Fitolitos, arqueología y cambios prehistóricos de la vegetación de la isla de Barro Colorado," in *Ecologia de un bosque tropical: Ciclos estacionales y cambios a largo plazo* (n.p.: STRI, 1990); Marixa Lasso, "El pasado agrícola de la zona transístmica: Del ferrocarriltransístmico a la creación de la zona del canal," *Revista Universidad* IV, época no. 51 (1994): 167; Francisco Javier Bonilla, "An Environmental History of the Rio Grande in the Panama Canal Zone, 1521–1950" (master's thesis, University of Louisville, 2016), 25, 27.

95. "Informe del Juzgado Politico de Buena Vista al Secretario de Gobierno," Bohío, April 10, 1894, 2, personal collection of Nicolas Liakopulos.

96. In the seventeenth century, this region had more than 6,000 head of cattle. But by the end of the eighteenth century the number had decreased to 2,000. From that moment to the end of the nineteenth century, the number of cattle in the region did not surpass 2,000. Perhaps the land along the isthmian route was too valuable for the extensive forms of cattle ranching typical of Panama and was used instead for agricultural products that found ready markets in the port cities and towns of the route. Alfredo Castillero Calvo, "Niveles de vida y cambios de dieta a finales del periodo colonial en América," *Anuario de Estudios Americanos* 44 (1987): 427–476.

97. Lasso, "El pasado agrícola de la zona transístmica," 173–174.

98. Mollien, *Viaggio alla Reppublica di Colombia*, 2:91, 183.

99. Wheelwright, "Report on the Isthmus of Panama," 26.

100. John Haskell Kemble, "Pacific Mail Service between Panama and San Francisco, 1849–1851," *Pacific Historical Review* 2, no. 4 (1933): 415–416.

101. "Informe del Juzgado Politico de Buena Vista al Secratario de Gobierno," Bohio, April 10, 1894, 2; and "Informe del Juzgado Politico de Gatun," Gatún, December 30, 1893, 1, personal collection of Nicolas Liakopulos.

102. Archivo Nacional de Panamá, Notaria 2, no. 246, 1888.

103. Robinson, *Panama*, 200.

104. Lasso, "El pasado agrícola de la zona transístmica," 175.

105. Alan Krell, *The Devil's Rope: A Cultural History of Barbed Wire* (London: Reaktion Books, 2002).

106. "Cuadro desmostrativo de los alambiques existentes en la Provincia de Panamá, con expresión de su dueño, clases y numero de litros que miden," *Gaceta de Panama*, May 4, 1892.

107. *Annual Report of the Isthmian Canal Commission for the Year Ending December 1, 1905* (Washington, DC: Government Publishing Office, 1905), 46.

108. NARA, RG 185, Records of the Land Commission, Docket Files, 1913–19, Box 1, docket 4.

109. John Soluri, *Banana Cultures: Agriculture, Consumption, and Environmental Change in Honduras and the United States* (Austin: University of Texas Press, 2006), 104–127.

110. *Annual Report of the Isthmian Canal Commission for the Year Ending December 1, 1905* (Washington, DC: Government Publishing Office, 1905), 8.

111. Ibid.

112. Acting Subsistence Officer to Chairman and Chief Engineer, Cristobal, April 16, 1909, NARA, RG 185, General Correspondence of the Isthmian Canal Commission, Box 88.

113. Omar Jaen Suarez, *La Población del Istmo de Panamá del siglo XVI al siglo XX* (Panama: Impresora de la Nación, 1979), 25.

114. *Annual Report of the Isthmian Canal Commission for the Year Ending December 1, 1905*, 7–8.

115. Hugh H. Bennett and William A. Taylor, *The Agricultural Possibilities of the Canal Zone* (Washington, DC: Government Publishing Office, 1912), 47. For the impact of this report on ICC agricultural policies, see Carse, *Beyond the Big Ditch*, 131–142.

116. Bennett and Taylor, *The Agricultural Possibilities*, 5.

117. This is an old idea that acquired new meaning in the nineteenth century. For example, an 1870 report by the Maine Board of Agriculture said that "the plow lies at the foundation of all wealth and of all civilization. So close is its connection with civilization that its mechanical construction has kept even pace with the progress of society. . . . In barbarous countries, where no vestige of civilization or of progress can be traced, no furrows of even the rudest implement which could be considered as bearing a resemblance to the plow, have ever been turned." *Fifteenth Annual Report of the Secretary of the Maine Board of Agriculture for the year 1870* (Augusta, ME: Sprague, Owen & Nach, 1871), 275.

118. Bennett and Taylor, *The Agricultural Possibilities*, 12. For the increasing importance that tools and technology acquire in defining men and society, see Michael Adas, *Machines as the Measure of Men: Science, Technology, and Ideologies of Western Dominance* (Ithaca, NY: Cornell University Press, 1989); and Leo Marx, "Technology: The Emergence of a Hazardous Concept," *Technology and Culture* 51, no. 3 (2010): 561–577.

119. James C. Scott, *Seeing Like a State: How Certain Schemes to Improve the Human Condition Have Failed* (New Haven, CT: Yale University Press, 1998), 262–306.

120. There are countless examples of this narrative. For Panama, two well-known examples are Otis, *Isthmus of Panama*, 107–108; and Robert Tomes, *Panama in 1855: An Account of the Panama Railroad* (New York: Harpers, 1855), 180.

121. Bennett and Taylor, *The Agricultural Possibilities*, 12.

122. Bennett and Taylor, *The Agricultural Possibilities*, 12.

123. Bennett and Taylor, *The Agricultural Possibilities*, 12–15.

124. Bennett and Taylor, *The Agricultural Possibilities*, 42.

125. Bennett and Taylor, *The Agricultural Possibilities*, 14–15.

126. Bennett and Taylor, *The Agricultural Possibilities*, 7, 15.

127. Bennett and Taylor, *The Agricultural Possibilities*, 20.

128. Williams, *Capitalism and Slavery*.

129. Bennett and Taylor, *The Agricultural Possibilities*, 45.

130. Bennett and Taylor, *The Agricultural Possibilities*, 46.

131. Bennett and Taylor, *The Agricultural Possibilities*, 29.

132. Bennett and Taylor, *The Agricultural Possibilities*, 47.

133. *La Estrella de Panamá*, June 22, 1913.

134. Stephen Frankel, "Jungle Stories: North American Representations of Tropical Panama," *Geographic Review* 86, no. 3 (July 1996): 317–333; and "Geographical Representations of the 'Other': The Landscape of the Panama Canal Zone," *Journal of Historical Cartography* 28, no. 1 (January 2002): 85–99; Paul S. Sutter, "Nature's Agents or Agents of Empire? Entomological Workers and Environmental Change during the Construction of the Panama Canal," *ISIS* 98 (2007): 730–732; Héctor Pérez-Brignoli, "El fonógrafo en los trópicos: sobre el concepto de Banana republic en la obra de O. Henry," *Iberoamericana* 6, no. 23 (2006): 127–142; Paul Sutter, "Tropical Conquest and the Rise of the Environmental Management State: The Case of U.S. Sanitary Efforts in Panama," in *Colonial Crucible: Empire in the Making of the Modern American State,* ed. Alfred W. McCoy and Francisco A. Scarano (Madison: University of Wisconsin Press, 2009), 317–328.

135. I am inspired by Eric Wolf's classic *Europe and the People without History* (Berkeley: University of California Press, 1982); Said, *Orientalism;* Michel-Rolph Trouillot, *Silencing the Past: Power and the Production of History* (Boston: Beacon Press, 1997), 70–106; and Fernando Coronil, "Beyond Oc-

cidentalism: Toward Nonimperial Geohistorical Categories," *Cultural Anthropology* 11 (1996): 51–87.

136. A shorter version of this argument was published in Marixa Lasso, "From Citizens to 'Natives': Tropical Politics of Depopulation at the Panama Canal Zone," in Ashley Carse et al., "Panama Canal Forum: From the Conquest of Nature to the Construction of New Ecologies," *Environmental History* 21 (April 2016): 240–249.

CHAPTER 3 • A NEW REGIME FOR OLD ZONE TOWNS

1. Bierd to Gorgas, February 15, 1907, NARA, RG 185, Box 88, General Correspondence, ICC.

2. Bierd to Gorgas, February 15, 1907; Chief Sanitary Officer to J. F. Stevens, February 5, 1907, NARA, RG 185, Box 88, General Correspondence, ICC.

3. George W. Goethals, *Government of the Canal Zone* (Princeton, NJ: Princeton University Press, 1915), 46.

4. Theodore P. Shonts, "The Railroad Men at Panama," *North American Review* 199 (February 1914): 228–231.

5. "Temporary Authority of Alcaldes," Act No. 5, August 22, 1904, in Isthmian Canal Commission, *Laws of the Canal Zone* (Washington, DC: Government Publishing Office, 1906), 21–22.

6. "The Right of Expropriation," Act No. 6, August 27, 1904, *Laws of the Canal Zone,* 22–28.

7. "Municipal Governments," Act No. 7, September 1, 1904, *Laws of the Canal Zone,* 29–52.

8. "Municipal Governments," Act No. 7, *Laws of the Canal Zone,* 29–52.

9. In 1905, the mayor of Ancón was Neira ($100 per month); of Buenavista, Rodolfo Ayarza ($50); of Cristobal, MacNeill ($150); of Emperador, Garzon ($60); and of Gorgona, Paredes ($75). Only one of the mayors of the five

municipalities was not Panamanian. The American mayor of Cristobal had a salary of $150 per month.

10. Rafael Neira to Rufus A. Lane, November 21, 1906, NARA, RG 185, Box 88, General Correspondence, ICC.

11. "Municipal Governments, Act No. 7," *Laws of the Canal Zone*, 29–52; "Ordinance No. 4," NARA, RG 185, General Correspondence, 1905–1914, Box 352, File 59-A-3.

12. "Municipal Governments, Act No. 7," *Laws of the Canal Zone*, 29–52.

13. Tomás Arias to Secretario de Estado en el despacho de Instruccion Publica y Justicia, September 29, 1904, in *Memorias dirigida a la asamblea nacional de 1906 por el secretario de Gobierno y Relaciones Exteriores* (Panama: Tip de Torre e Hijos, 1907), 200–201.

14. Nicolás Victoria Jaén to Secretario de Gobierno y Relaciones exteriores, August 26, 1904; Corte Suprema de Justicia, Panama, January 20, 1905, in *Memorias dirigida a la asamblea nacional de 1906*, 199–200, 203–205; Morales, *Ensayos, Documentos y Discursos*, 1:66–68.

15. Resolución Número 164, República de Panamá—Poder Ejecutivo Nacional—Departamento de Política Interior—Panamá, November 9, 1904, in *Memorias dirigida a la asamblea nacional de 1906*, 60.

16. "Manifiesto de Separación de Panamá y Mensaje dirigido por la Junta de Gobierno provisional a la Convención Constituyente de 1904," in Morales, *Ensayos, Documentos y Discursos*, 1:56.

17. *Memorias dirigida a la asamblea nacional de 1906*, xxxv.

18. Valdés, *Geografía del Istmo de Panamá*, 45.

19. Goethals, *Government of the Canal Zone*, 46.

20. Valdés, *Geografía del Istmo de Panamá*, 45.

21. "Municipal Governments, Act No. 7," *Laws of the Canal Zone*, 29–52.

22. John F. Stevens to W. C. Gorgas, February 9, 1907, NARA, RG 185, Box 88, General Correspondence, ICC.

23. Chief Sanitary Inspector to Chief Sanitary Officer, September 28, 1906, NARA, RG 185, Box 88, General Correspondence, ICC.

24. Chief Sanitary Officer to Stevens, February 5, 1907, NARA, RG 185, Box 88, General Correspondence, ICC.

25. James B. Clow & Sons, "Statement Made to Brigadier General Charles F. Humphreys, USA, with regard to the Sanitary Conditions existing on the Isthmus of Panama," NARA, RG 185, Box 321, File 47-I-53.

26. Guy L. Edie to U.S. Army Chief of Staff, December 23, 1903, NARA, RG 185, Box, 321, File 47-I-53.

27. H. D. Reed to W. C. Gorgas, June 16, 1905, NARA, RG 185, Box 88, General Correspondence, ICC, Building Regulations Canal Zone General.

28. Kalala Ngalamulume, "Keeping the City Totally Clean: Yellow Fever and the Politics of Prevention in Colonial Saint-Louis-du-Sénégal, 1850–1914," *Journal of African History* 45, no. 2 (2004): 183–202; Andrea Patterson, "Germs and Jim Crow: The Impact of Microbiology on Public Health Policies in the Progressive Era American South," *Journal of the History of Biology* 42, no. 3 (2009): 529–559; Stanley K. Shultz and Clay McShane, "To Engineer the Metropolis: Sewers, Sanitation, and City Planning in Late-Nineteenth-Century America," *Journal of American History* 65, no. 2 (September 1978): 389–411; Frank Snowden, *The Conquest of Malaria, Italy 1900–1962* (New Haven, CT: Yale University Press, 2006), 27–52.

29. "Building Regulations for the Canal Zone," NARA, RG 185, General Correspondence, 1905–1914, Box 88; Chief Sanitary Officer to Head of Department of Civil Administration, Canal Zone, October 23, 1908, NARA, RG 185, General Correspondence, 1905–1914, Box 88.

30. G. W. Goethals to Secretary of War, Canal Zone, January 14, 1910, NARA, RG 185, General Correspondence, 1905–1914, Box 88; Chief Sanitary Officer to the Governor of the Canal Zone, January 21, 1905, NARA, RG 185, Box 124.

31. G. W. Goethals to W. C. Gorgas, Canal Zone, September 26, 1907; Sanitary Department to Head of Department of Civil Administration, October 23, 1908, NARA, RG 185, General Correspondence, 1905–1914, Box 88.

32. David Arnold, *Colonizing the Body: State Medicine and Epidemic Disease in Nineteenth-Century India* (Berkeley: University of California Press, 1993); Philip Curtin, "The End of the 'White Man's Grave'? Nineteenth-Century Mortality in West Africa," *Journal of Interdisciplinary History* 21 (1990): 63–88; Philip Curtin, "Medical Knowledge and Urban Planning in Tropical Africa," *American Historical Review* 90 (1985): 594–613; Randall M. Packard, "The Invention of the 'Tropical Worker,'" *Journal of African History* 34 (1993): 271–292.

33. A 1908 ICC map clearly shows the division of Gorgona's houses between "ICC" houses and "Native" houses. "Isthmian Canal Commission Map Gorgona," Assistant Engineers Office Division, Culebra, Canal Zone, July 1908.

34. "Map of Gorgona Showing Area in which the Commission has Authorized the Licensing of Saloons, ICC, Office of Chief Engineer," December 1908, Library of Congress.

35. Le Prince to Gorgas, April 15, 1907, NARA, RG 185, General Correspondence, 1905–1914, Box 88.

36. "Building Regulations for the Canal Zone," NARA, RG 185, Box 88, General Correspondence, 1905–1914.

37. Tomes, *Panama in 1855*, 56–58.

38. Chief Sanitary Inspector to Chief Sanitary Officer, September 29, 1906, NARA, RG 185, Box 88, General Correspondence, 1905–1914.

39. Chief Sanitary Inspector to Chief Sanitary Officer, September 29, 1906.

40. Le Prince to Gorgas, Ancón, April 17, 1907, NARA, RG 185, Box 88, General Correspondence, ICC.

41. "Guideline Regulations for Canal Zone: in Proposed New Towns, Remodeling of Old Towns, Collections of Houses, the following regulations

shall be followed." No date, but next to the 1906 correspondence with mayors, NARA, RG 185, Box 88, General Correspondence, ICC.

42. Mayor of Gorgona to Rufus A. Lane, November 11, 1906, NARA, RG 185, Box 88, General Correspondence, 1905–1914.

43. Mayor of Gorgona to Rufus A. Lane, November 11, 1906.

44. George Johnson to Rufus Lane, Canal Zone, November 13, 1906, NARA, RG 185, Box 88, General Correspondence, ICC.

45. Cited by Shultz and McShane, "To Engineer the Metropolis," 389.

46. Shultz and McShane, "To Engineer the Metropolis," 395.

47. Mayor of Gorgona to Rufus A. Lane, November 11, 1906.

48. Order of the President, Dividing the Canal Zone into Administrative Districts, March 13, 1907, in *General Index: Minutes of the Meeting of the Isthmian Canal Commission* (Washington, DC: Government Publishing Office, 1908), 50; Goethals, *Government of the Canal Zone*, 47–48.

49. Le Prince to Gorgas, December 8, 1906, NARA, RG 185, Box 88, General Correspondence, ICC.

50. Arturo Escobar, *Encountering Development: The Making and Unmaking of the Third World* (Princeton, NJ: Princeton University Press, 1995); Timothy Mitchell, *Rule of Experts;* Scott, *Seeing Like a State.*

51. Order of the President, March 13, 1907, Dividing the Canal Zone into Administrative Districts, in *General Index*, 50.

52. Goethals to Gorgas, August 21, 1908, NARA, RG 185, Box 89, File 13-A-4/v.

53. Hiram J. Slifer to William L. Sibert, Division Engineer, and L. K. Rourke, Acting Division Engineer, June 17, 1909, NARA, RG 185, Box 89, File 13-A-4/v C.S.I.

54. "Circular No 453," February 24, 1910, signed by J. A. Le Prince, Chief Sanitary Inspector, NARA, RG 185, Box 89, File 13-A-4/v C.S.I.

55. Herman Caufrild to Mr. Harry E. Bovay, March 29, 1910, NARA, RG 185, Box 89, File 13-A-4/v.

56. "Memorandum in reference to house of Took Woo Chong, Old Empire," June 29, 1911; Chief Sanitary Inspector to V. A. Holden, June 28, 1911, and District Sanitary Inspector to Chief Sanitary Inspector, August 18, 1911, NARA, RG 185, Box 89, File 13-A-4/v.

57. Sergeant #10 J. N. Shaw to Captain George R. Shanton, May 15, 1908, NARA, RG 185, Box 89, File 13-A-4/v.

58. British Vice-Consul to C. S. Blackburn, Head of Department of Civil Administration, Panama, July 3, 1908, and C. S. Blackburn to Judge Rerdell and Mr. Holocombe, NARA, RG 185, Box 89, File 13-A-4/v.

59. Sergeant #10 J. N. Shaw to Captain George R. Shanton, May 15, 1908.

60. V. B. Miskimon, Inspector, to Acting Chairman, March 23, 1909, NARA, RG 185, Box 89, File 13-A-4/v; Chief Sanitary Officer to Chairman, April 2, 1909, NARA, RG 185, Box 89, File 13-A-4/v.

61. Land Agent to Judge Feuille, April 19, 1910, NARA, RG 185, Box 89, File 13-A-4/v.

62. David Carrillo to Honorable H. D. Reed, July 30, 1907; Herman Caufield, Assistant Chief Sanitary Inspector, to W. C. Gorgas, August 6, 1907; Daniel Quayle, Sanitary Inspector, to Chief Sanitary Inspector, Bohio April 20, 1909; Mcintyre & Rogers to Tom M. Cook, Empire, March 16, 1910; G. W. Goethals to W. C. Gorgas, March 11, 1910, NARA, RG 185, Box 89, File 13-A-4/v.

63. De Phillips to Acting Chief Sanitary Inspector, June 17, 1910; Felicia Armiens to Chief Sanitary Inspector, June 13, 1910; Sanitary Inspector to John L. Phillips, August 23, 1910, NARA, RG 185, Box 89, File 13-A-4/v.

64. Division Engineer to G. W. Goethals, February 26, 1910, NARA, RG 185, Box 89, File 13-A-4/v.

65. Sutter, "Nature's Agents or Agent of Empire," 724–754, and "The First Mountain to Be Removed," 250–259.

66. W. C. Gorgas to Governor of the Canal Zone, Sept. 29, 1909, NARA, RG 185, General Correspondence, ICC, Box 123, File 13-Q-1.

67. Manager to John F. Stevens, September 30, 1905, NARA, RG 185, General Correspondence, ICC, Box 123, File 13-Q-1.

68. J. A. Le Prince to Dr. H. R. Carter, December 6, 1905, Box 89; W. C. Gorgas to Governor of the Canal Zone, March 15, 1906, Box 88; H. D. Reed to John F. Stevens, March 20, 1906, NARA, RG 185, Box 124, General Correspondence, ICC.

69. H. D. Reed to John F. Stevens, March 20, 1906, Box 124; W. M. Belding to C. C. McCulloch, May 14, 1907, NARA, RG 185, Box 89, General Correspondence, ICC.

70. W. C. Gorgas to John F. Stevens, February 11, 1907, NARA, RG 185, Box 89, General Correspondence, ICC.

71. W. C. Gorgas to John F. Stevens, February 11, 1907.

72. H. R. Carter to Chief Sanitary Officer, February 2, 1907, NARA, RG 185, Box 89, General Correspondence, ICC.

73. Unknown to Chief Sanitary Officer, March 21, 1907, NARA, RG 185, Box 89, General Correspondence, ICC.

74. W. M. Belding to Dr. H. R. Carter, June 24, 1907, NARA, RG 185, Box 89, General Correspondence, ICC.

75. W. M. Belding to C. C. McCulloch, May 14, 1907, NARA, RG 185, Box 89, General Correspondence, ICC.

76. R. E. Noble, Acting Chief Sanitary Officer to Chairman ICC, November 30, 1908, NARA, RG 185, Box 89, General Correspondence, ICC.

77. Chief Quartermaster to Colonel Jno. L. Phillips, Culebra, June 28, 1909, NARA, RG 185, Box 89, General Correspondence, ICC.

78. Chief Quartermaster to Colonel Jno. L. Phillips, June 28, 1909; Office of the Chief Sanitary Officer, Circular No. 323, October 22, 1908, NARA, RG 185, Box 89, General Correspondence, ICC.

79. Constructing Quartermaster to Major Devol, July 17, 1909, NARA, RG 185, General Correspondence, ICC.

80. W. C. Gorgas to Chairman and Chief Engineer, July 27, 1909, NARA, RG 185, Box 89, General Correspondence, ICC.

81. G. W. Goethals to Chief Quartermaster, August 9, 1909, NARA, RG 185, Box 89, General Correspondence, ICC.

82. "Memorandum to Chairman," July 17, 1909, NARA, RG 185, Box 89, General Correspondence, ICC.

83. "Memorandum to Chairman," July 17, 1909.

84. "Memorandum to Chairman," July 17, 1909.

85. Chief Sanitary Officer to Chairman and Chief Engineer, April 4, 1911, NARA, RG 185, Box 89, General Correspondence, ICC.

86. August 5, 1911, NARA, RG 185, Box 89, General Correspondence, ICC.

87. My summary of the debate over grass cutting draws on Sutter, *Nature's Agents or Agents of Empire?*, 747–753.

CHAPTER 4 · A ZONE WITHOUT PANAMANIANS

1. McCullough, *The Path between the Seas;* Greene, *The Canal Builders;* Carse, *Beyond the Big Ditch.*

2. Le Prince, Chief Sanitary Inspector, to Colonel Phillips, August 24, 1910; and A. McGown to Colonel D. D. Gaillard, August 25, 1910, NARA, RG 185, General Correspondence, 1905–1915, Box 317, File 47-E12/6.

3. Rafael Neira, November 30, 1906, NARA, RG 185, General Correspondence, 1905–1914, Box 352, File 59-A-3; Chief Sanitary Officer to Governor of the Canal Zone, January 21, 1905, NARA, RG 185, Box 124.

4. Tom M. Cooke to Head of Department of Civil Administration, March 31, 1911, NARA, RG 185, General Correspondence, 1905–1915, Box 317, File 47-E12/6.

5. A. McGown, August 25, 1910, NARA, RG 185, General Correspondence, 1905–1915, Box 317, File 47-E12/6.

6. George W. Goethals to D. D. Gaillard and S. B. Williamson, January 28, 1911, NARA, RG 185, General Correspondence, 1905–1915, Box 317, File 47-E12/6.

7. "Memorandum Regarding Isthmian Canal Commission and Panama Railroad Townsites in the Canal Zone," NARA, RG 185, Box 317, File 47-E-1; *Canal Record,* no. 32, April 8, 1908, 249.

8. George W. Goethals to Mr. M. H. Thatcher, November 11, 1910, NARA, RG 185, General Correspondence, 1905–1915, Box 317, File 47-E12/6.

9. Tom M. Cooke to Head of Department of Administration Colonel W. C. Gorgas, Lieutenant Colonel D. D. Gaillard, Mr. S. B. Williamson, Mr. H. H. Rousseau, Mr. Frank Feuille, Major T. C. Dickson, January 14, 1911, NARA, RG 185, General Correspondence, 1905–1915, Box 317, File 47-E12/6.

10. Tom M. Cooke to Head of Department of Administration Colonel W. C. Gorgas, Lieutenant Colonel D. D. Gaillard, Mr. S. B. Williamson, Mr. H. H. Rousseau, Mr. Frank Feuille, Major T. C. Dickson, January 14, 1911.

11. Head of Department of Civil Administration to Tom M. Cooke, January 24, 1911, NARA, RG 185, General Correspondence, 1905–1915, Box 317, File 47-E12/6.

12. H. O. Cole to S. B. Williamson, January 25, 1911, NARA, RG 185, General Correspondence, 1905–1915, Box 317, File 47-E12/6.

13. W. C. Gorgas to George W. Goethals, November 1, 1910, NARA, RG 185, General Correspondence, 1905–1915, Box 317, File 47-E12/6.

14. Richard Rogers to George W. Goethals, April 27, 1907, NARA, RG 185, General Correspondence, 1905–1914, File 59-A-3, Box 352.

15. D. D. Gaillard to Tom M. Cooke, January 24, 1911, NARA, RG 185, General Correspondence, 1905–1915, Box 317, File 47-E12/6; emphasis added.

16. Committee on Interoceanic Canals, NARA, RG 46, 63A-F12, Box 95; Panama Canal Memorial and Statues, NARA, RG 66, Box 140.

17. D. D. Gaillard to Tom M. Cooke, January 24, 1911, NARA, RG 185, General Correspondence, 1905–1915, Box 317, File 47-E12/6.

18. D. D. Gaillard to Tom M. Cooke, January 24, 1911.

19. D. D. Gaillard to Tom M. Cooke, January 24, 1911.

20. D. D. Gaillard to H. H. Rousseau, January 31, 1911, NARA, RG 185, General Correspondence, 1905–1915, Box 317, File 47-E12/6.

21. S. B. Williamson to Mr. Tom M. Cooke, January 26, 1911, NARA, RG 185, General Correspondence, 1905–1915, Box 317, File 47-E12/6.

22. S. B. Williamson to Mr. Tom M. Cooke, January 26, 1911.

23. Tom M. Cooke to George W. Goethals, January 31, 1911, NARA, RG 185, General Correspondence, 1905–1915, Box 317, File 47-E12/6.

24. H. F. Hodges to M. H. Thatcher, February 23, 1911, NARA, RG 185, General Correspondence, 1905–1915, Box 317, File 47-E12/6.

25. Townsite Committee to Chairman and Chief Engineer, March 1, 1911, NARA, RG 185, General Correspondence, 1905–1915, Box 317, File 47-E12/6; Tom M. Cooke to Head of Civil Administration, March 6, 1911, NARA, RG 185, General Correspondence, 1905–1915, Box 317, File 47-E12/6.

26. D. D. Gaillard to G. W. Goethals, March 15, 1911, NARA, RG 185, General Correspondence, 1905–1915, Box 317, File 47-E12/6.

27. George W. Goethals to M. H. Thatcher, March 9, 1911, NARA, RG 185, General Correspondence, 1905–1915, Box 317, File 47-E12/6.

28. Tom M. Cooke to Head of Department of Civil Administration, March 31, 1911, NARA, RG 185, General Correspondence, 1905–1915, Box 317, File 47-E12/6.

29. Tom M. Cooke to Head of Department of Civil Administration, March 31, 1911.

30. George W. Goethals to M. H. Thatcher, April 6, 1911, NARA, RG 185, General Correspondence, 1905–1915, Box 317, File 47-E12/6.

31. S. B. Williamson to George W. Gorgas, November 29, 1910, NARA, RG 185, General Correspondence, 1905–1915, Box 317, File 47-E12/6.

32. Cooper and Packard, "Introduction," and Cooper, "Modernizing Bureaucrats, Backward Africans and the Development Concept," in Cooper and Packard, *International Development and the Social Sciences*, 1–41, 64–92; Escobar, *Encountering Development;* Mitchell, *Rule of Experts.*

33. For an examination of Progressive ideas about the social problems brought by the "world of iron" to Europe and the United States, see Rodgers, *Atlantic Crossings*, 8–75.

34. Goethals, *Government of the Canal Zone;* NARA, *The Panama Hearings before the Committee on Interstate and Foreign Commerce*, 62nd Congress, 2nd Session, House of Representatives, document no. 680 (Washington, DC: Government Publishing Office, 1912).

35. NARA, *The Panama Hearings*, 274; emphasis added.

36. NARA, *The Panama Hearings*, 250.

37. William F. Sands, *Our Jungle Diplomacy* (Chapel Hill: University of North Carolina Press, 1944), 31.

38. NARA, *The Panama Hearings*, 241–243.

39. NARA, *The Panama Hearings*, 259–275.

40. Goethals, *Government of the Canal Zone*, 57–69.

41. Goethals, *Government of the Canal Zone*, 57.

42. Goethals, *Government of the Canal Zone*, 58–62.

43. Goethals, *Government of the Canal Zone*, 66.

44. Goethals, *Government of the Canal Zone*, 69.

45. Goethals, *Government of the Canal Zone*, 67.

46. Goethals, *Government of the Canal Zone*, 65.

47. Carolyn Merchant, "Shades of Darkness: Race and Environmental History," *Environmental History* 8 (2003): 380–394; Monica Quijada, "La Ciudadanización del 'Indio Bárbaro': Políticas Oficiales y Oficiosas hacia la Población Indígena de la Pampa y la Patagonia, 1870–1920," *Revista de Indias* 59 (1999): 217, 675–704; Louis S. Warren, *The Hunter's Games: Poachers and Conservationists in Twentieth-Century America* (New Haven, CT: Yale

University Press, 1997); Richard White, *"It's Your Misfortune and None of My Own": A New History of the American West* (Norman: University of Oklahoma Press, 1991).

CHAPTER 5 • AFTER THE FLOODS

1. "Rush of Tourists to Panama Canal All Eager to Inspect the Big Ditch before the Water Is Turned into It," *New York Times*, February 14, 1912, 12.

2. Frederic J. Haskin, *The Panama Canal* (New York: Doubleday, 1913), 34; McCullough, *The Path between the Seas*, 489.

3. "Petition," Jose I. Vega et al. to The Honorable Deputies to the National Assembly, *La Prensa*, October 19, 1912, translation in NARA, RG 185, May 29, 1913, Alpha Files, Box 132, Folder 47-E / New Gorgona, Part 1.

4. "A Resolution of the Executive," *La Estrella de Panamá*, May 29, 1913; "Petition," Jose I. Vega et al. to The Honorable Deputies to the National Assembly.

5. "A Resolution of the Executive"; "Petition," Jose I. Vega et al. to The Honorable Deputies to the National Assembly.

6. "Tax List," NARA, RG 185, Alpha Files, Box 132, Folder 47-E / New Gorgona, Part 1.

7. McCullough, *The Path between the Seas*, 489.

8. "Hamlets and Towns Whose Sites Will Be Covered by Gatún Lake," *Canal Record*, December 6, 1911, cited by Carse, *Beyond the Big Ditch*, 113.

9. "Hamlets and Towns Whose Sites Will Be Covered by Gatún Lake," cited by Carse, *Beyond the Big Ditch*, 113.

10. Cited by Carse, *Beyond the Big Ditch*, 111.

11. Law 37 of December 9, 1912, *Official Gazette*, Panama, December 18, 1912, in NARA, RG 185, Alpha Files, Box 132, Folder 47-E / New Gorgona, Part 1.

12. Law 37 of December 9, 1912, *Official Gazette*.

13. *La Prensa,* June 14, 1913.

14. "A Resolution of the Executive"; "Petition," Jose I. Vega et al. to The Honorable Deputies to the National Assembly.

15. NARA, RG 185, Alpha Files, Box 132, Folder 47-E / New Gorgona, Part 1.

16. E. T. Lefevre to Richard L. Metcalfe, August 26, 1913, and Frank Feuille to G. W. Goethals, Ancón, August 30, 1913, NARA, RG 185, Alpha Files, Box 132, Folder 47-E / New Gorgona, Part 1.

17. Frank Feuille to George W. Goethals, August 28, 1913, NARA, RG 185, Alpha Files, Box 132, Folder 47-E / New Gorgona, Part 1.

18. Frank Feuille to George W. Goethals, August 5, 1913, NARA, RG 185, Alpha Files, Box 132, Folder 47-E / New Gorgona, Part 1.

19. W. J. Showalter, "The Panama Canal," *National Geographic Magazine* 23, no. 2 (1912): 195.

20. George W. Goethals to John D. Patterson, August 8, 1913; R. & F. A. & P. C. to John D. Patterson, August 16, 1913, NARA, RG 185, Alpha Files, Box 132, Folder 47-E / New Gorgona, Part 1.

21. Frank Feuille to Captain Barber, Chief of Police, July 30, 1913, NARA, RG 185, Alpha Files, Box 132, Folder 47-E / New Gorgona, Part 1.

22. Letter of July 22, 1913, NARA, RG 185, Alpha Files, Box 132, Folder 47-E / New Gorgona, Part 1.

23. General Superintendent to C. H. Mann, July 22, 1913; George W. Goethals to John D. Patterson, July 22, 1913, NARA, RG 185, Alpha Files, Box 132, Folder 47-E / New Gorgona, Part 1.

24. Frank Feuille to John D. Patterson, July 18, 1913, NARA, RG 185, Alpha Files, Box 132, Folder 47-E / New Gorgona, Part 1.

25. R. & F. A. & P. C. to John D. Patterson, August 16, 1913, NARA, RG 185, Alpha Files, Box 132, Folder 47-E / New Gorgona, Part 1. R. & F. A. & P. C. to John D. Patterson, August 16, 1913.

26. George W. Goethals to J. D. Patterson, August 8, 1913, NARA, RG 185, Alpha Files, Box 132, Folder 47-E / New Gorgona, Part 1.

27. "Information desired by D. W. Ogilvie," June, 21, 1913, NARA, RG 185, Alpha Files, Box 132, Folder 47-E / New Gorgona, Part 1.

28. "Panamanian Commission of Claims before the Canal Zone Government," no. 90, September 8, 1913, NARA, RG 185, Alpha Files, Box 132, Folder 47-E / New Gorgona, Part 1.

29. "Memorandum for the Chief of Division," August 13, 1913, NARA, RG 185, Alpha Files, Box 132, Folder 47-E / New Gorgona, Part 1.

30. "Memorandum for the Files," September 4, 1913, NARA, RG 185, Alpha Files, Box 132, Folder 47-E / New Gorgona, Part 1.

31. George W. Goethals to R. L. Metcalfe, September 3, 1913, NARA, RG 185, Alpha Files, Box 132, Folder 47-E / New Gorgona, Part 1.

32. "Memorandum to Chairman," September 16, 1913, NARA, RG 185, Alpha Files, Box 132, Folder 47-E / New Gorgona, Part 1.

33. Frank Feuille to George W. Goethals, Ancón, September 20, 1913, NARA, RG 185, Alpha Files, Box 132, Folder 47-E / New Gorgona, Part 1.

34. George W. Goethals to B. Porras, July 12, 1913, NARA, RG 185, Alpha Files, Box 132, Folder 47-E / New Gorgona, Part 1.

35. George W. Goethals to B. Porras, July 12, 1913.

36. "Memorandum for Chief of Division," August 17, 1913, NARA, RG 185, Alpha Files, Box 132, Folder 47-E / New Gorgona, Part 1.

37. "Memorandum for Chief of Division," August 17, 1913.

38. *La Estrella de Panama,* June 17, 1913.

39. Frank Feuille to J. D. Patterson, July 18, 1913, NARA, RG 185, Alpha Files, Box 132, Folder 47-E / New Gorgona, Part 1.

40. Virginia Arango, "La inmigración prohibida en Panamá," *Anuario de Derecho,* Año XX 20 (1992): 45–84.

41. "Ley 20 del 31 de Enero de 1913 sobre tierras baldias e indultadas y en el decreto 33 del 1ro de Julio de 1913 en desarrollo de la Ley 37 de 1912 sobre la poblacion de Nueva Gorgona," *La Prensa,* August 1, 1913.

42. "Law 37 of December 9, 1912," *Official Gazette,* Panama, December 18, 1912, NARA, RG 185, Alpha Files, Box 132, Folder 47-E / New Gorgona, Part 1.

43. Various Victims to George W. Goethals, September 30, 1914, NARA, RG 185, Alpha Files, Box 132, Folder 47-E / New Gorgona, Part 2.

44. "Memorandum to Governor," October 16, 1914, NARA, RG 185, Alpha Files, Box 132, Folder 47-E / New Gorgona, Part 2.

45. "Memorandum to Governor," October 16, 1914.

46. "Notice to Persons Having Title or Claim to Canal Zone Lands," Joint Land Commission, March 8, 1913, NAE, Colonial Office Records, 318 / 331, 46E, 3W1574, 9056381, courtesy Julie Greene.

47. The members of the Joint Land Commission representing Panama in 1905 were the Honorable Federico Boyd and Dr. Carlos A. Cooke. In 1907 they were the Honorable Ramon Arias and Dr. Samuel Lewis. Arias was later replaced by the Honorable Constantino Arosemena. In 1908 the members were Dr. Gil Ponce and Dr. Julio J. Fabrega. In 1913 they were the Honorable Federico Boyd and Dr. Samuel Lewis. *Final Report of the Joint Commission* (Canal Zone: Panama Canal Press, 1920), 3–10.

48. *Final Report of the Joint Commission,* 3–10.

49. *Final Report of the Joint Commission,* 5–7.

50. See, for example, their advertisement in *La Prensa,* Panama, June 2, 1913.

51. *Final Report of the Joint Commission,* 3–10.

52. Sanders, *Vanguard of the Atlantic World;* Constanza Castro, "'As a Citizen of This City': The Urban Reform of Radical Liberalism: Bogotá 1848–1880" (PhD diss., Columbia University, 2015).

53. Frank Safford, *The Ideal of the Practical: Colombia's Struggle to Form a Technical Elite* (Austin: University of Texas Press, 1976).

54. *Interim Report of the Joint Commission* (Panama: Government Printing Office, 1914), 30.

55. NAE, Colonial Office Records, 318 / 331, 46E, 3W1574, 9056383.

56. Frank Feuille to Umberto Vaglio, August 15, 1913; E. T. Lefevre to Richard L. Metcalfe, August 26, 1913, NARA, RG 185, Alpha Files, Box 132, Folder 47-E / New Gorgona, Part 1.

57. *Interim Report of the Joint Commission*, 34.

58. *Interim Report of the Joint Commission*, 38; emphasis in original.

59. *Interim Report of the Joint Commission*, 38.

60. *Daily Star and Herald*, June 5, 1913.

61. *Interim Report of the Joint Commission*, 36–38.

62. For the recognition of these rights, see Frank Feuille to G. W. Goethals, October 20, 1913, NARA, RG 185, Alpha Files, Box 132, Folder 47-E / New Gorgona, Part 2.

63. NAE, Colonial Office Records, 318 / 331, 46E, 3W1574, 9056381.

64. NAE, Colonial Office Records, 318 / 331, 46E, 3W1574, 9056381.

65. NAE, Colonial Office Records, 318 / 331, 46E, 3W1574, 9056381.

66. NAE, Colonial Office Records, 318 / 331, 46E, 3W1574, 9056381.

67. NAE, Colonial Office Records, 318 / 331, 46E, 3W1574, 9056381.

68. *Final Report of the Joint Commission*.

69. Frank Feuille to G. W. Goethals, October 20, 1913, NARA, RG 185, Alpha Files, Box 132, Folder 47-E / New Gorgona, Part 2.

70. NAE, FO 288 / 161, 36E, 4E131, 90530.

71. *Final Report of the Joint Commission*.

72. Various Victims to George W. Goethals, September 30, 1914, NARA, RG 185, Alpha Files, Box 132, Folder 47-E / New Gorgona, Part 2.

73. Various Victims to George W. Goethals, September 30, 1914.

74. E. T. Lefevre to R. Metcalfe, August 26, 1913, NARA, RG 185, Alpha Files, Box 132, Folder 47-E / New Gorgona, Part 1.

75. Various Victims to George W. Goethals, September 30, 1914, NARA, RG 185, Alpha Files, Box 132, Folder 47-E / New Gorgona, Part 2.

76. I first developed these arguments in Marixa Lasso, "A Canal without a Zone: Conflicting Representations of the Panama Canal," *Journal of Latin American Geography* 14, no. 3 (October 2015): 157–174.

77. Various Victims to George W. Goethals, September 30, 1914.

78. I found the recording at the Biblioteca Ernesto Castillero in Panama City. *Discography of American Historical Recordings*, s.v. "Victor matrix XVE-58784. Coge el pandero que se te va / Grupo Istmeno," http://adp.library.ucsb.edu/index.php/matrix/detail/800029508/XVE-58784-Coge_el_pandero_que_se_te_va, accessed April 13, 2017.

79. My translation.

80. *Daily Star and Herald,* June 26, 1913.

CHAPTER 6 • LOST TOWNS

Epigraphs: Vecinos de Nuevo Gatún a Presidente de la República, February 20, 1915; E. T. Lefevre to George W. Goethals, March 6, 1915, AMRE, Zona del Canal, Expedientes 4–7, 1936; "Buildings—Nonemployees, at New Gatún," June 15, 1916, NARA, RG 185, General Records 1914–1934, Box 974, File 47-E-12/72.

1. Frank Feuille to Colonel Chester Harding, January 26, 1915, NARA, RG 185, General Records 1914–1934, Box 974, File 47-E-12/72.

2. A. Preciado to the General Superintendent of the PRR, May 28, 1914, NARA, RG 185, General Records 1914–1934, Box 974, File 47-E-12/72.

3. George W. Goethals to A. Preciado, Culebra, June 8, 1914, NARA, RG 185, General Records 1914–1934, Box 974, File 47-E-12/72.

4. G. Wells to E. H. Chandler, December 19, 1914, NARA, RG 185, General Records 1914–1934, Box 974, File 47-E-12/72.

5. "Private Water Connections in Canal Zone," March 1, 1915, NARA, RG 185, General Records 1914–1934, Box 974, File 47-E-12/72.

6. Frank Feuille to Chester Harding, March 10, 1915, NARA, RG 185, General Records 1914–1934, Box 974, File 47-E-12/72.

7. George W. Goethals to Reverend S. Witt, April 17, 1915, NARA, RG 185, General Records 1914–1934, Box 974, File 47-E-12/72.

8. Frank Feuille to George W. Goethals, April 16, 1915, NARA, RG 185, General Records 1914–1934, Box 974, File 47-E-12/72.

9. Memorandum for Major Grove, July 31, 1915; D. Ewright to E. H. Chandler, Balboa Heights, August 4, 1915, NARA, RG 185, General Records 1914–1934, Box 974, File 47-E-12/72.

10. W. W. Wilson to Colonel Chester Harding, September 18, 1915; District Quartermaster to Chief Quartermaster, October 5, 1915, NARA, RG 185, General Records 1914–1934, Box 974, File 47-E-12/72.

11. District Sanitary Inspector to Acting Chief Health Officer, May 12, 1916; E. E. Persons to Land Agent, May 16, 1916, NARA, RG 185, General Records 1914–1934, Box 974, File 47-E-12/72.

12. Frank Feuille to Colonel Chester Harding, January 26, 1915.

13. Frank Feuille to Captain H. D. Mitchell, October 1, 1915; Frank Feuille to H. D. Mitchell, April 7, 1916, NARA, RG 185, General Records 1914–1934, Box 974, File 47-E-12/72.

14. "Circular no. 256," December 31, 1915, NARA, RG 185, General Records 1914–1934, Box 974, File 47-E-12/72.

15. H. H. Morehead to All Concerned, June 16, 1916, NARA, RG 185, General Records 1914–1934, Box 974, File 47-E-12/72.

16. "Buildings—Nonemployees, at New Gatún," June 15, 1916, NARA, RG 185, General Records 1914–1934, Box 974, File 47-E-12/72.

17. Yee Ranling, Tai Woo, Lois Solis, and Yee Wo to Chester Herding, June 23, 1916, NARA, RG 185, General Records 1914–1934, Box 974, File 47-E-12/72.

18. Frank Feuille to Colonel Chester Harding, June 30, 1916, NARA, RG 185, General Records 1914–1934, Box 974, File 47-E-12/72.

19. H. H. Morehead to All Concerned, June 16, 1916, NARA, RG 185, General Records 1914–1934, Box 974, File 47-E-12/72.

20. "Memorandum for the Acting Governor," August 8, 1916, NARA, RG 185, General Records 1914–1934, Box 974, File 47-E-12/72.

21. H. O. Chalkley to Colonel Chester Harding, May 31, 1915, NARA, RG 185, General Records 1914–1934, Box 974, File 47-E-12/72.

22. Frank Feuille to Colonel Chester Harding, May 26, 1915, NARA, RG 185, General Records 1914–1934, Box 974, File 47-E-12/72; Chester Harding to H. O. Chalkley, British Consul, May 26, 1915, NARA, RG 185, General Records 1914–1934, Box 974, File 47-E-12/72.

23. Frank Feuille to Colonel Chester Harding, May 26, 1915; Chester Harding to H. O. Chalkley, British Consul, May 26, 1915.

24. Frank Feuille to Colonel Chester Harding, June 9, 1915, NARA, RG 185, General Records 1914–1934, Box 974, File 47-E-12/72.

25. Frank Feuille to Colonel Chester Harding, June 9, 1915.

26. Murray to Morrow, February 11, 1916; Frank Feuille to J. J. Morrow, February 18, 1916; Frank Feuille to George W. Goethals, April 7, 1916, NARA, RG 185, General Records 1914–1934, Box 974, File 47-E-12/72.

27. Frank Feuille to C. F. Mason, July 28, 1915, NARA, RG 185, General Records 1914–1934, Box 974, File 47-E-12/72.

28. Carse, *Beyond the Big Ditch,* 133–144.

29. For a wonderful account of contemporary memories about Limón's displacement, see Carse, *Beyond the Big Ditch,* 122–130.

30. "Canal Zone Boundaries," September 12, 1914, Law Library of U.S. Congress, 38 Stat. 1893; Treaty Series 610.

31. M. H. Thatcher to Federico Boyd, March 20, 1911, AMRE, OTRP, vol. 3, Zona Del Canal-1936.

32. Agrimensor Oficial de Colón, October 15, 1914, AMRE, OTRP, vol. 3, 1908–1936, expedientes 8–14.

33. Vecinos del Pueblo de Limón to Presidente de la Honorable Asamblea Nacional, October 15, 1914, AMRE, OTRP, vol. 3, 1908–1936, expedientes 8–14.

34. Gobernador de la Provincia de Colón to Secretario de Estado en el despacho de Gobierno y Justicia Colón, October 20, 1914, AMRE, OTRP, vol. 3, 1908–1936, expedientes 8–14.

35. Vecinos del Pueblo de Limón to Presidente de la Honorable Asamblea Nacional, October 15, 1914.

36. E. T. Lefevre to C. H. McIlvaine, October 15, 1914, AMRE, OTRP, vol. 3, 1908–1936, expedientes 8–14.

37. Vecinos del Pueblo de Limón to Presidente de la Honorable Asamblea Nacional, October 15, 1914.

38. Roberto Iglesias et al. to Secretario de Relaciones Exteriores, Colón, October 13, 1914, AMRE, OTRP, vol. 3, 1908–1936, expedientes 8–14.

39. Roberto Iglesias et al. to Secretario de Relaciones Exteriores, Colón, October 13, 1914.

40. Gobernador de la Provincia de Colón to Secretario de Estado en el despacho de Gobierno y Justicia, October 20, 1914.

41. Vecinos del Pueblo de Limón to Presidente de la Honorable Asamblea Nacional, October 15, 1914.

42. Roberto Iglesias et al. to Secretario de Relaciones Exteriores, October 19, 1914, AMRE, OTRP, vol. 3, 1908–1936, expedientes 8–14.

43. Ernesto T. Lefevre to Richard Metcalfe, December 11, 1913; Richard Metcalfe to Ernesto T. Lefevre, December 31, 1913; and Ernesto T. Lefevre to Richard Metcalfe, February 16, 1914, AMRE, OTRP, Correspondencia Zona del Canal, Octubre-Diciembre 1913.

44. Carlos A. Mendoza, E. Verlad, and N. Delgado to Sres. Diputados Panama, November 23, 1914, AMRE, OTRP, vol. 3, 1908–1936, expedientes 8–14.

45. Hamilton to E. T. Lefevre, March 8, 1915, and McIlvaine to E. T. Lefevre, April 14, 1915, AMRE, OTRP, vol. 3, 1908–1936, expedientes 8–14.

46. Alfredo Castillero-Calvo, *La Ruta Interoceánica y el Canal de Panamá* (Panamá: Imprenta de la Universidad de Panamá, 1999), 36–37; Alfredo Castillero-Calvo, *Portobelo y San Lorenzo del Chagres: Perspectivas Imperiales, Siglos XVI–XIX* (Panama: Editora Novo Art SA, 2016); Bonifacio Pereira, *Biografía del Río Chagres* (Panama: Imprenta Nacional, 1964).

47. Mollien, *Viaggio alla Reppublica di Colombia*, 2:182–183.

48. McGuinness, *Path of Empire*.

49. "Conferencia efectuada el día 23 de mayo de 1916, en la Secretaría de Relaciones Exteriores, entre los comisionados de Chagres y el señor Secretario del Ramo," AMRE, Zona del Canal 1936, expedientes 1–3.

50. Executive Secretary to Secretary of Foreign Relations, January 28, 1916, AMRE, Zona del Canal 1936, expedientes 1–3.

51. "Al Señor presidente de la República," April 5, 1915, AMRE, Zona del Canal 1936, 1909–1935, no. 4, correspondencia relacionada con la ocupación y traslado del pueblo de Chagres.

52. "Al Señor presidente de la República," April 5, 1915.

53. "Al Señor presidente de la República," April 5, 1915.

54. President Porras to Don Alejandro Galván, Panama, April 24, 1915, AMRE, Zona del Canal 1936, 1909–1935, no. 4, correspondencia relacionada con la ocupación y traslado del pueblo de Chagres.

55. E. T. Lefevre to W. P. Copeland, May 18, 1915, AMRE, Zona del Canal 1936, 1909–1935, no. 4, correspondencia relacionada con la ocupación y traslado del pueblo de Chagres.

56. Alejandro Galván, al Secretario de Relaciones Exteriores, Mayo 31, 1915. AMRE, Zona del Canal 1936, 1909–1935, no. 4, correspondencia relacionada con la ocupación y traslado del pueblo de Chagres.

57. George W. Goethals to President Belisario Porras, December 8, 1915, AMRE, Zona del Canal 1936, no. 3a.

58. Colonel Chester Harding to E. T. Levefre, May 27, 1915, AMRE, Zona del Canal 1936, 1909–1935, no. 4, correspondencia relacionada con la ocupación y traslado del pueblo de Chagres.

59. George W. Goethals to President Belisario Porras, December 8, 1915.

60. Colonel Chester Harding to E. T. Levefre, May 27, 1915.

61. E. T. Lefevre to Eusebio A. Morales, December 28, 1915, AMRE, Zona del Canal 1936, 1909–1935, no. 4, correspondencia relacionada con la ocupación y traslado del pueblo de Chagres.

62. "Acta," Chagres, January 31, 1916, AMRE, Zona del Canal 1936, expedientes 1–3.

63. José B. Calvo to E. T. Lefevre, Panama, February 2, 1916, AMRE, Zona del Canal 1936, fol. 4, expedientes 1–3.

64. E. T. Lefevre to Eusabio A. Morales, December 28, 1915, AMRE, Zona del Canal 1936, 1909–1935, no. 4, correspondencia relacionada con la ocupación y traslado del pueblo de Chagres.

65. George W. Goethals to E. T. Lefevre, December 28, 1915, AMRE, Zona del Canal 1936, expedientes 1–3.

66. To Ernesto T. Lefevre, June 25, 1915, AMRE, Zona del Canal 1936, no. 3a; Belisario Porras to Ernesto T. Lefevre, December 11, 1915, AMRE, Zona del Canal 1936, no. 3a.

67. Belisario Porras to Ernesto T. Lefevre, July 3, 1915, AMRE, Zona del Canal 1936, no. 3a.

68. Porras to Lefevre, July 3, 1915, and Juan Blanco to Secretario de Relaciones Exteriores, July 26, 1915, AMRE, Zona del Canal 1936, no. 3a.

69. Eusebio A. Morales to Ernesto T. Lefevre, February 29, 1916, AMRE, Zona del Canal 1936, expedientes 1–3.

70. To President Belisario Porras, January 26, 1916, AMRE, Zona del Canal 1936, expedientes 1–3TK.

71. No title, signed by "dueños de propiedades urbanas y rurales, naturales y residentes del distrito de Chagres," January 3, 1915, AMRE, Zona del Canal 1936, expedientes 1–3.

72. José B. Calvo to E. T. Lefevre, February 2, 1916, AMRE, Zona del Canal 1936, fol. 2, expedientes 1–3.

73. "Acta," Chagres, January 31, 1916.

74. José B. Calvo to E. T. Lefevre, February 2, 1916.

75. "Acta," Chagres, January 31, 1916.

76. "Lo de Chagres," AMRE, Zona del Canal 1936, expedientes 1–3.

77. Enrique Lefevre, *Mas Alla del Olvido: Ernesto Lefevre y el Imperialismo Yanqui* (San José: Editorial Texto, 1972), 102–123.

78. "Conferencia efectuada el día 23 de mayo de 1916, en la Secretaría de Relaciones Exteriores, entre los comisionados de Chagres y el señor Secretario del Ramo," AMRE, Zona del Canal 1936, expedientes 1–3.

79. "Conferencia efectuada el día 23 de mayo de 1916."

80. Alcadía Municipal del distrito de Colón to Ernesto Lefevre, Colón, May 22, 1916, AMRE, Zona del Canal 1936, expedientes 1–3.

81. "Conferencia efectuada el día 23 de mayo de 1916."

82. Leopoldo Arosemena to Secretario de Relaciones Exteriores, June 19, 1916, AMRE, Zona del Canal 1936, expedientes 1–3.

83. "Acta," Chagres, January 31, 1916.

84. Simon Quintana to Secretario de Relaciones Exteriores, May 20, 1916, AMRE, Zona del Canal 1936, expedientes 1–3.

CHAPTER 7 • THE ZONE'S NEW GEOGRAPHY

1. Gil Blas Tejeiria, *Pueblos Perdidos* (Panama: Impresora Panamá, 1962).

2. McCullough, *The Path between the Seas*, 488–489, 586–588; Carse, *Beyond the Big Ditch*, 122–130.

3. Tomás Enrique Mendizábal, "Informe de Monitoreo arqueológico en Gorgona," Evaluación Técnica, no. 32, 2015, unpublished document submitted to the Panama Canal Authority.

4. McCullough, *The Path between the Seas*, 489.

5. McCullough, *The Path between the Seas*, 489.

6. William L. Sibert and John F. Stevens, *The Construction of the Panama Canal* (New York: Appleton and Company, 1915), 52–53; Tomás Mendizábal, Juan Guillermo Martín, and John Griggs, "Informe de Inspección Arqueológica a dos drenajes en el antiguo cerro Paraíso Canal de Aproximación del Pacífico 3, (CAP3) del Canal de Panamá," Evaluación Técnica, no. 16, 2010, unpublished document submitted to the Panama Canal Authority.

7. "Panama Canal Memorial and Statues," NARA, RG 66, Box 140.

8. Ruth Schwartz Cowan, *More Work for Mother: The Ironies of Household Technology from the Open Hearth to the Microwave* (New York: Basic Books, 1985); Carroll Purcell, *The Machine in America: A Social History of Technology*, 2nd ed. (Baltimore: Johns Hopkins University Press, 2007); Shawn William Miller, *An Environmental History of Latin America* (Cambridge: Cambridge University Press, 2007). There is a large literature on the impact of race on the selection of the location for projects with negative environmental impact. For an appraisal of this literature, see Merchant, "Shades of Darkness: Race and Environmental History," 380–394.

9. Sibert and Stevens, *The Construction*, 53.

10. *Canal Record* 4, no. 39 (May 21, 1913).

11. Katherine A. Zien, *Sovereign Acts: Performing Race, Space, and Belonging in Panama and the Canal Zone* (New Brunswick, NJ: Rutgers University Press, 2017), 41–53.

12. Ashley Carse, "'Like a Work of Nature': Revisiting the Panama Canal's Environmental History of Gatun Lake," in Ashley Carse et al., "Panama Canal Forum: From the Conquest of Nature to the Construction of New Ecologies," *Environmental History* 21 (2016): 231–239.

13. This section builds heavily on Missal, *Seaway to the Future,* 55–163, and Green, *The Canal Builders,* 180–266.

14. Gail Bederman, *Manliness and Civilization: A Cultural History of Gender and Race in the United States, 1880–1917* (Chicago: University of Chicago Press, 1996).

15. Owen Wister, *The Virginian* (New York: Macmillan, 1902).

16. Cited by Missal, *Seaway to the Future,* 49.

17. Cited by Missal, *Seaway to the Future,* 41.

18. Carol McMichael Reese and Thomas F. Reese, *The Panama Canal and Its Architectural Legacy* (Panama: Fundación Ciudad del Saber, 2012), 192.

19. "Panama Canal Memorial and Statues," NARA, RG 66, Box 140.

20. Amelia Denis De Icaza, *Hojas Secas* (León: Talleres Gráficos Robelo, 1927), 2.

21. Reese and Reese, *The Panama Canal,* 175–176.

22. Richard Guy Wilson, "Imperial Identity at the Panama Canal," *Modulus: The University of Virginia School of Architecture Review* (1980 / 1981): 28.

23. Wilson, "Imperial Identity at the Panama Canal," 23.

24. Robert H. Kargon and Arthur P. Molella, *Invented Edens: Techno-Cities of the Twentieth Century* (Cambridge, MA: MIT Press, 2008); Oliver Dinius and Angela Vergara, eds., *Company Towns in the Americas: Landscape, Power, and Working-Class Communities* (Athens: University of Georgia Press, 2011); Margaret Crawford, *Building the Workingman's Paradise: The Design of American Company Towns* (London: Verso, 1995); Herbert and Mary Knapp, *Red, White, and Blue: The American Canal Zone in Panama* (San Diego: Harcourt Brace Jovanovich, 1984).

25. "Professional Experience," William Lyman Phillips Papers, Frances Loeb Library, Harvard University, Box 1, Folder B1.

26. "Notes," Phillips Papers, Box 1, Folder B8.

27. "Notes on Tropical Landscape," Phillips Papers, Box 1, Folder B4.

28. "Notes on Tropical Landscape."

29. Reese and Reese, *The Panama Canal,* 190.

30. William Lyman Phillips to Frederick Law Olmstead, March 29, 1914, cited in Reese and Reese, *The Panama Canal,* 199.

31. "Notes on Tropical Landscape."

32. George W. Goethals to George Catlin, April 15, 1913, NARA, RG 185, General Records, 1914–1934, Box 973, File 47-E-12/42.

33. Resident Chaplain Loveridge to George W. Goethals, August 11, 1913, NARA, RG 185, General Records, 1914–1934, Box 973, File 47-E-12/42.

34. *Annual Report of the Governor of the Panama Canal for the Fiscal Year Ended June 30, 1920* (Washington, DC: Government Publishing Office, 1920), 300.

35. William Lyman Phillips to R. E. Wood, January 16, 1914, NARA, RG 185, General Records, 1914–1934, Box 973, File 47-E-12/42.

36. Goethals to Mr. Wells, December 11, 1913; Acting General Inspector to Acting Chief Sanitary Officer, January 14, 1914, NARA, RG 185, General Records, 1914–1934, Box 973, File 47-E-12/42.

37. William Lyman Phillips to R. E. Wood, January 29, 1914; La Boca Townsite Committee to H. F. Hodges, February 16, 1914, NARA, RG 185, General Records, 1914–1934, Box 973, File 47-E-12/42.

38. Rodgers, *Atlantic Crossings;* Greene, *The Canal Builders,* 180–225.

39. Escobar, *Encountering Development,* 52.

40. Engineer of Terminal Construction to George W. Goethals, October 16, 1914, NARA, RG 185, General Records, 1914–1934, Box 973, File 47-E-12/42.

41. George W. Goethals to Charles F. Mason, W. R. Grove, and G. M. Wells, October 17, 1914, NARA, RG 185, General Records, 1914–1934, Box 973, File 47-E-12/42.

42. "Report of Committee on Appearance of Town and Interests of the Residents of La Boca," October 24, 1914, NARA, RG 185, General Records, 1914–1934, Box 973, File 47-E-12/42.

43. "Report of Committee on Appearance of Town and Interests of the Residents of La Boca."

44. George W. Goethals to P. M. Ashburn, November 2, 1914, NARA, RG 185, General Records, 1914–1934, Box 973, File 47-E-12/42.

45. Greene, *The Canal Builders,* 267–302.

46. "Placards to be posted at La Boca," November 16, 1914, NARA, RG 185, General Records, 1914–1934, Box 973, File 47-E-12/42.

47. District Quartermaster to Acting Chief Quartermaster, June 2, 1916; Chief Quartermaster to District Quartermaster, September 27, 1916, NARA, RG 185, General Records, 1914–1934, Box 973, File 47-E-12/42.

48. "Policing around Panama Canal Quarters at La Boca," October 10, 1914, NARA, RG 185, General Records, 1914–1934, Box 973, File 47-E-12/42.

49. Petition to George W. Goethals, April 20, 1915, NARA, RG 185, General Records, 1914–1934, Box 973, File 47-E-12/52.

50. "Sanitary Conditions at La Boca," August 14, 1916, NARA, RG 185, General Records, 1914–1934, Box 973, File 47-E-12/52.

51. District Quartermaster to Major Grove, January 25, 1916, NARA, RG 185, General Records, 1914–1934, Box 973, File 47-E-12/52.

52. "Sanitary Conditions at La Boca."

53. "Building of New Negro Town, Paraiso," June 1, 1915, NARA, RG 185, General Records 1914–34, Box 974, File 47-E-12/76.

54. "Building of New Negro Town, Paraiso."

55. Paraiso Committee to Panama Canal Governor, July 2, 1915, NARA, RG 185, General Records 1914–34, Box 974, File 47-E-12/76.

56. Conniff, *Black Labor on a White Canal,* 24–74; Herbert and Mary Knapp, *Red, White, and Blue Paradise.*

57. Greene, *The Canal Builders,* 180–225.

58. Eduardo Tejeira Davis, "El Chorrillo: Su Historia y su Arquitectura"; Raul Gonzalez Guzman, "Escrutinio Histórico sobre el desarrollo urbano del arrabal santanero con especial referencia al sector del El Chorrillo"; and Alvaro Uribe, "Cuál Chorrillo?," *Cuadernos Nacionales* 5 (1990): 23–49.

59. Cited by Missal, *Seaway to the Future,* 43.

60. Eduardo Tejeira Davis, *La Arquitectura del Canal de Panamá, Colonialismo, Sincretismo y Adaptación al Tropico* (San Jose: Instituto de Arquitectura Tropical, n.d.); Peter A. Szok, *"La Ultima Gaviota": Liberalism and Nostalgia in Early Twentieth-Century Panamá* (Westport, CT: Greenwood Press, 2001), 65–90; Adrienne Samos, ed., *Panamá Cosmopolita: La Exposición de 1916 y su legado* (Panama: Biblioteca 500, 2017).

61. Michael Donaghue, *Borderland on the Isthmus: Race, Culture, and the Struggle for the Canal Zone* (Durham, NC: Duke University Press, 2014).

EPILOGUE

Epigraph: Danilo Pérez Urriola's father was born around 1900 and was twelve years old when he had to leave Pedro Miguel.

1. This section draws inspiration from *Imperial Debris: On Ruins and Ruination,* ed. Ann Stoler (Durham, NC: Duke University Press, 2013).

2. Rodolfo Sanmaniego, "Estudio Regional del Corregimiento de Nuevo Emperador" (BA thesis, Universidad de Panamá, 1994), 54; Edilia Camargo, "De Maquenque a Carabalí por Emperador," *Lotería* (1999): 107–120; Carlos E. Rodriguez, "Modern Urban Infrastructure in Panama City during the Panama Canal Zone Era: The Bridge of the Americas" (unpublished paper written for an MA in Urban Planning at CCNY-CUNY, March 2013).

3. "Memorandum to Governor," October 16, 1914, NARA, RG 185, Alpha Files, Box 132, Folder 47-E / New Gorgona, Part 2.

4. Michael Donoghue, *Borderland on the Isthmus: Race, Culture, and the Struggle for the Canal Zone* (Durham, NC: Duke University Press, 2014).

5. I take this story from Stepan, *Picturing Tropical Nature,* 85–119.

6. Miller, *Our Jungle Diplomacy,* 29–31.

7. Arnold, *The Tropics and the Traveling Gaze;* Timothy Brook and Gregory Blue, eds., *China and Historical Capitalism: Genealogies of Sinological Knowl-*

edge (Cambridge: Cambridge University Press, 1999); Mary Louise Pratt, *Imperial Eyes: Travel Writing and Transculturation* (New York: Routledge, 1992); Said, *Orientalism;* Sanders, *Vanguard of the Atlantic World.*

8. Arnulf Becker Lorca, *Mestizo International Law: A Global Intellectual History, 1842–1933* (Cambridge: Cambridge University Press, 2014), 25.

9. Ahiska, "Occidentalism," 354.

Acknowledgments

THE RESEARCH AND WRITING of this book began in summer 2011 and ended in summer 2018. During that time I incurred many personal and institutional debts. I began working on the book as a professor at Case Western Reserve University, where my colleagues John Broich, Dan Cohen, Ken Ledford, Miriam Levin, Alan Rocke, Jonathan Sadowsky, Peter Shulman, Ted Steinberg, Gillian Weiss, and Rhonda Williams generously offered crucial feedback on the early stages of the project. I am particularly grateful to Jia-Chen Fu, with whom I twice taught a class on the history of comparative development between China and Latin America, an experience that forced me to think about global history in fundamentally different ways.

I am especially grateful to the American Council of Learned Societies and the National Humanities Center for their support, which allowed me to spend the 2013–2014 academic year at the National Humanities Center, where I benefited greatly from an environment exclusively dedicated to thinking, reading, and writing in the humanities. Special thanks go to Luis Carcamo-Huechante, Julie Greene, Cindy Hahamovitch, Jean Hebrard, Martha Jones, Betsy Krause, Anna Krylova, Timothy Marr, Charles McGovern, Jocelyn Olcott, Norah Fisher

Onar, Anna Christina Soy, and Martin Summers for their friendship and insights.

I am also greatly indebted to the W. E. B. Du Bois Research Institute at the Hutchins Center of Harvard University, where I wrote the last part of the book during a fellowship in fall 2016. Sharing my research with a group of first-rate scholars from different disciplines and various parts of the world took the book in new, richer directions. My special thanks go to Vincent Brown, Christian Crouch, Dawn-Elissa Fischer, Márcia Lima, Ingrid Monson, Lorena Rizzo, and, of course, Alejandro de La Fuente and Henry Louis Gates Jr., for creating such a wonderfully warm and stimulating research environment. While in Cambridge I was also able to participate in the Harvard Institute for Global Law and Policy's workshop "Author(is)ing the South," and I thank Lilina Obregón for the invitation. The impact of this workshop is evident in the book. In Boston I had the good fortune to meet the Panamanian jazz musician Danilo Pérez and his wife and fellow musician, Patricia Pérez. They introduced me to Danilo's father, Danilo Pérez Urriola, who kindly shared some family memories about the Zone's depopulation. I am also grateful to Jeffrey Blossom of Harvard's Center for Geographic Analysis for graciously and patiently examining many historical maps of the Zone with me to create the map of the lost Zone landscape included in the book.

In Panama, special thanks go to the people of Nuevo Emperador and Nuevo Chagres, who generously opened their doors and shared their stories with me. Thanks also to Guillermo Castro, Daniel Holness, Lourdes Lozano, and Tomás Mendizábal for sharing their knowledge about the Zone's geography and environment; to fellow Panama Canal historians Ashley Carse, Christine Keiner, Noel Maurer, Aims McGuinness, Megan Raby, Blake Scott, and Paul Sutter, who commented on earlier versions of this project; to Nicolas Liakopulos, who generously opened his historical collection for this research; and to Ana Sánchez and Ricardo López-Arias for kindly allowing me to use some of the images in their wonderful collection of historical photos.

In Colombia, where I now teach, my colleagues Constanza Castro, Alexis De Greiff, Max Hering, Claudia Leal, Catalina Muñoz, Francisco Ortega, Ana María Otero, Amada Pérez, Stefan Pohl, Carlo Tognato, and Paolo Vignolo read chapter drafts and provided invaluable comments, as did my fellow Colombianists Nancy Appelbaum and James Sanders.

My warmest thanks go to my cousins in the Washington, DC, metropolitan area, who kindly opened their homes during my many research trips to the archives and libraries there; to my sister Lucia, who also hosted me during my research periods in Panama; and to the friends and family who accompanied me throughout this process and provided much-needed love, food, drinks, conversation, and laughter. Named or unnamed, they are the most important part of my life.

The work of a historian relies on the indispensable work of librarians and archivists. This project took me to libraries and archives in the United States, Panama, and Colombia. I am grateful to all of them, but I am particularly grateful to Patrice Brown of the National Archives in College Park for guiding me through the Panama Canal documentation, and to Mario Hudson of the Biblioteca Ernesto Castillero for teaching me about the music of early twentieth-century Panama.

My final thanks go to my editor, Thomas LeBien, for believing in the book and providing the best advice during the various stages of writing it, and also to the anonymous peer reviewers for their intelligent, insightful, and detailed comments. This book is better because of them.

Index

administration building: design, 230–232; murals, 231–232. *See also* Van Ingen, William B.

administrative districts, 95, 105, 119, 120–125

aesthetic / s, 126–128, 140–141, 231–241; principles, 237

agreement / s: on behalf of the US government, 213; direct, 161; Gorgona railroad, 65; with the ICC, 161, 179; with the local *cabildo* / individuals, 64; over monetary compensation, 214; Taft, 47

agricultural: endeavors, 191; experts, 85–87; geography, 147; history, 2, 80; practices, 88; workers, 85

agricultural productivity, language about, 89

agriculture: civilized / non-primitive, 85; effortless, 86; European-style, 79; local, 86, 235; primitive, 85–86; tropical, 87–90; in the tropics, 78–91

aid, 17, 18; to Limón relocation, 205; technological, 245

American: citizenship, 240; clientele, 195; democracy, 11, 228; engineering, 6, 91; farming, 150; government, 96, 102, 105, 203, 219; imperialism, 44; model towns, 245; modernity, 6, 12, 13, 25, 145; municipalities, 96, 100, 120, 261; side, 51, 53, 70, 112, 226, 228; travelers, 66, 67; urban modernity, 139, 141; women, 63

Ancón, municipality of, 98, 100, 104–106, 137. *See also* municipalities

Ancón, port of, 24, 26, 48–49, 98, 105–106, 230; governor chosen for, 99; naming of, 40–41; new district of, 105. *See also* Balboa

Ancón Hill, 127, 141, 230, 246

anguish, 120, 156, 192

slaves, 7, 21, 56, 67, 255

slums, 8, 141, 143, 146, 245

social engineering process, 147

social priorities, 223

soil, 12, 86–88, 117, 150

squatters, 123, 172, 178, 224

status, 19, 34, 43, 60, 67, 138, 150, 168, 173, 253

steamers, 7, 14, 21, 24, 58–59, 81, 84, 154

stereotypes, 51, 55, 58, 234

Stilton Addition ("Sodom Hill") case, 195

story / stories, 55, 87, 244; civilization or barbarism, 153; depopulation, 3, 11; erased, 224; expelled people, 180–182; expulsion, 221; Fourth of July, 259; Lake Gatún flooding, 220–225; Limoneros fighting, 205; lost towns, 8, 20; murals, 231–232; the Progressive Era, 9, 244; significant changes, 58; Tejeira's, 220

strategic: asset, Lake as, 201; importance, 31, 46, 144, 208; location / areas, 193; world areas, 226

struggle, 49, 76, 96, 172, 202, 246

suburbs, 93, 135, 144

supervision, 108, 122, 237

symbol / ism, 6, 145, 128, 199, 230, 234, 235, 246, 254, 255, 257–258

symbolic: function, 143; gestures, 212; importance, 3, 33, 141, 236; role, 229; space, 11; value, 230

Taft, William H., 2, 26; agreement, 47; depopulation/Executive Order, 221, 224; 1912 executive order, 2, 224; as president, 146; as secretary of war, 48

Taylor, William M., US Department of Agriculture, 85

technical: administration, 231; challenges, 155; experts, 120; intervention, 97; language, 218; problems, 101

technological: decisions, 223; influences, 53; triumph, 9, 156, 232

tenement / s: El Chorillo, 245; houses, 95, 133; La Boca, 137; of la Línea, 68–74; private, 145–146, 243

Tivoli's hotel, symbolism and aesthetics, 127–129, 131

town council, 23, 64, 214

towns: historical importance of, 211; reasons for relocation, 222

Town Site Committee, 137, 139, 143–144

tradition / s: *bogas,* 62; farming, 80, 150, 287; of house construction, 54; municipal, 10, 119; political, 33, 115; republican / democratic, 33, 49

tragedy, 158, 167, 183, 224